Nicolas Stebbing CR

BEARERS OF THE SPIRIT:
Spiritual Fatherhood in Romanian Orthodoxy

CISTERCIAN STUDIES SERIES: NUMBER TWO HUNDRED ONE

BEARERS OF THE SPIRIT:
Spiritual Fatherhood in Romanian Orthodoxy

Nicolas Stebbing CR

BEARERS

Spiritual Fatherhood

CISTERCIAN STUDIES SERIES: NUMBER TWO HUNDRED ONE

OF THE SPIRIT:
in Romanian Orthodoxy

by

NICOLAS STEBBING CR

cistercian publications
KALAMAZOO, MICHIGAN

The work of
cistercian publications
is made possible in part
by support from
WESTERN MICHIGAN UNIVERSITY
to The Institute of Cistercian Studies

ISBN 0 87907 701 8

Cover design by Elizabeth King

Typography by Gale Akins at
Humble Hills Press, Kalamazoo, Michigan

Text type is *FF Scala* by Martin Majoor of The Netherlands,
issued by FontShop International, Berlin, Germany, 1999

Table of Contents

A SHORT GUIDE TO ROMANIAN PRONUNCIATION

â and î	'i' in 'till'.
ă	'u' in 'hurt'
c	'c' in 'cat' unless followed by 'i' or 'e' when it becomes as 'ch' in 'cheese'.
ch	k
g	'g' in 'get', unless followed by 'i' or 'e', when it becomes as 'j' in 'jam'.
gh	'g' in 'get'
i	When ending a word and preceded by a consonant, it is not pronounced. Otherwise , like 'i' in 'machine' or when beginning diphthongs, as 'y' in 'yes'.
j	zh
oa	wa
ş	sh
ţ	ts
u	'oo' in 'root'; when beginning a diphthong, as 'w'.

✠ *Foreword*

I N EVERY MAN AND WOMAN living on earth there must be something monastic. When Jesus said, 'He who loves father or mother more than me is not worthy of me. And he who loves son or daughter more than me is not worthy of me' (Mt 10:37), or '. . . deny yourself, take up your cross and follow me' (Mt 16:24), or '. . . you shall be perfect, as your Father in heaven is perfect' (Mt 5:48), these words were not addressed to monks, for at that time Christian monasticism did not exist. They were commandments to everyone, including married persons. The goal of man's creation and calling is deification (Gen 1:27). Monastic virtues like humility, obedience, patience, chastity and even not worrying about materials things, are also spiritual qualities of every good family. They were cultivated by the members of the Church from the beginning. Christ commands us to give ourselves totally to him. Saint John Chrysostom says that we greatly delude ourselves and err in thinking that one thing is demanded from the layperson and another from the monk. Surely the monk and the married have different ways of life, but this does not alter their common responsibility towards God's commandments. The inner monk belongs to both. They differ only in their ways of attaining perfection.

With this in mind, I think the Romanian people have a special monastic vocation that goes back to their pre-christian religion. It is similar to the Celtic roots of monasticism.

The Dacians' religion was monotheistic. They believed in one single God who was spiritual. Zamolxix, of whom Herodotus speaks in Book Four on the *Persian War,* was only a high priest. In vain todays' archaeologits try to discover remnants of idolatry in Romania. The Dacians worshipped God as pure spirit, without material representation. They believed strongly in the immortality of the soul and looked upon death as a blessed return home. Dacian priests were unmarried, vegetarians, and lived in abstinence. The High Priests dwelt somewhere on top of the holy mount Cogaionon, which is a fictitious name and 'will remain unknown unto the end of time'.[1] I believe that Cogaionon was a cave where all the monastic congregations of *capnobotii, ctistii,* and *Polisteii* were initiated. These High Priests were consulted by the kings regarding political matters.

The temples of the Dacians were built on top of the mountains. While worshiping, they looked into the clear sky. Herodotus relates that, 'When there is thunder and lightning, these Thracians tribes shoot arrows skyward to kill the demons, believing in no other god but their own god who is in heaven.' Iordanes speaks of some Thracian anchorites called *skistai.* The ancients used to say about the Dacians that they are the only people who are born and grow up, but never die.

Only this way can we explain the Romanian monastic miracles. In a country no larger than the state of Michigan and having twenty million Orthodox, there are today four hundred active monasteries, in addition to little *schituri* and hermitages. And another miracle: nobody knows the year when the Romanian people were converted to Christianity. No historian is able to explain this enigma. The transition to Christianity from their pre-christian religion and spirituality was so smooth and unremarkable that from the beginning they felt at home in the Christian Church, being

1. Dinu Cruga, 'Al Doilea Athos,' *Lumină Lină* 2 (1992) 39.

already inclined by nature towards abstinence and asceticism.[2]

Romanian monks are not cloistered. Monks are present everywhere—in the monasteries, in parish churches, on the streets of the large cities, in the market place—because the rules are not as strict as they are in western monasticism. Christians in the West call us 'basilians', but this is incorrect. What gives structure to Orthodox monasticism is not the rule, but the spiritual father with his disciples around him. And his spiritual sons and daughters include both monks and lay persons.

It is true that Saint Basil wrote some important principles of salvation which inspired Saint Benedict to establish strict disciplinary rules. And later quasi-military monastic orders appeared in the West as a continuation of 'what remained among Romans of their pristine sternness and legalism'.[3] The fact that we in Orthodoxy do not have monastic 'orders' once caused one Western historian to call our type of monasticism 'Eastern disorders'.[4] This is only an outward impression. Monastic rules exist in Orthodoxy, but they are local and often depend on the will of the abbot, of the diocesan bishop, and of the spiritual environment in which the monks live.

Three things are obligatory for monks in all Orthodox monasteries: participation in the liturgical cycle of worship; hospitality; and work to provide a means of existence for the community. There are risks and benefits in both the Eastern and the Western systems. In the West, monasticism is viable because of the rule, even in the absence of spiritual personalities. But strict rules and discipline may hold back the spiritual growth of a monk. In Orthodoxy, on the other hand, the risk is even greater. As long as we

2. See Hieromonk Ioanichie Bălan, *Vetre de Sihăstrie Românească* (Bucharest 1982) 10.
3. *Dictionnaire d'archéologie et de Liturgie* 2:221.
4. Herbert Workman, *The Evolution of the Monastic Ideal* (Boston: Beacon Press, 1913, 1962) 120.

have holy spiritual fathers, monasteries thrive. In the absence of great elders, however, Orthodox monasticism is in great trouble and great danger. Orthodox parish priests in Romania are married, with large families. Often they invite monks to administer the sacrament of confession to the faithful. Today many priests in Romania encourage the building of monasteries close to their villages, knowing very well that the goal of monasteries today is not flight from the world, but the transfiguration of society.

Some great monks in Romanian history were even involved in politics. This is not unusual in a country where, from the beginning, Orthodoxy was the dominant religion. In Romania there was never a total separation of the Church and state, not even during the communist regime, when the Synod of Bishops found a *modus vivendi* with the communist government by which the salaries of priests were paid and the sacramental life of the Church secured. Once again, for clarification, we appeal to national history.

In the Middle Ages, the Metropolitan of the country, besides being the first counselor of the Prince, also had the function of Chief Justice, who judged the Boyars and the privileged aristocracy. The Chancellor and tutor of the Crown Prince was a monk. The last will and testament of Prince Neagoe Basarab (1512-1521) to his son Theodosios, extant in Slavonic at the Romanian Academy Library, is about the Prayer of the Heart. The influence of his monastic education is obvious. Romania is the only Orthodox country, I think, whose patriarch was nominated (in 1938) by the king as Prime Minister. And until 1938 Romanian bishops, who are elected from among the monks, were senators *de iure* in the Romanian parliament. All this is not strange for the historian who reads in Herodotus, Strabo, and Jordanes about the role taken by the high priests Deceneu and Comosogicus in the life of the Dacian king Burebista. If we believe Jordanes, who was a Goth and a christian bihsop in the fourth century, the High Priest Deceneu succeeded Burebista as the king of the country.

All this belongs to the past, of course. But as Fr Nicolas Stebbing points out in this book in speaking about the liturgy in the vernacular: 'This must give the Romanian Orthodox a greater sense of national identity'. And not only Romanians, but all Orthodox Christians sanctify the national ethos and incorporate national history and culture into their church life, considering their identity as a condition for the salvation of their souls. Scripture testifies to this. In the Book of Daniel (10:13), it is clear that each nation has a guardian angel. The Lord himself said: 'Go and teach all the nations' (Mt 28:19), and promised that at the Last Judgement, 'all the nations will be gathered before him' (Mt 25:32)—not isolated individuals. If there is one thing that scares the Orthodox people, it is the contemporary idea of 'globalism'. The frontiers between nations may disappear under economic and political pressure, but the distinctive characteristics of individuals, nations, and culture should remain.

It is a great joy for me to write a Foreword to this book on spiritual fatherhood in Romanian Orthodoxy. To the English-speaking reader Fr Nicolas Stebbing presents Orthodox spirituality in the context of Romanian history and culture. And he does it very well.

ARCHIMANDRITE ROMAN BRAGA

Holy Dormition Monastery
Rives Junction, Michigan
The Feast of Saint Sebastian the Martyr
18 December 2002

✠ Preface

OUR FATHER.' Few phrases can be more frequently on the lips of worshippers than these, which begin the prayer which Jesus taught his disciples. The phrase speaks of both the unity and intimacy between Jesus and his Father, and also of the invitation to his people to participate in that unity of love. The relationships within the Godhead and within the Church are referred to in terms of fatherhood. So a book which introduces us to a new way of thinking about fatherhood, as this book will do, can open up new ways of understanding the Christian faith. The concept and, more importantly, the practice of spiritual fatherhood may be seen as a commentary on the opening phrase of the Lord's Prayer.

The word Father, since it is used throughout the Gospels by Jesus Christ of his Father, must refer first and most properly to the Creator, rather than to anything created. This point is made firmly by such Fathers of the Church as Athanasius, Basil, and John of Damascus.¹ The word Father, they remind us, refers primarily and most properly to God, and any human fatherhood can only be derived from that perfect fatherhood and reflect it partially. Spiritual fatherhood, as it is exercised in the Church, can only be

---

1. See, for example, Athanasius, *Against the Arians* 1.23; Basil, *Against Eunomius* 2.23.41-9; John of Damascus, *On the Orthodox Faith* 8.120.

understood within this all-embracing fatherhood of God, as part of God's reaching out in love.

A second verse of the Bible gives further insights into the role of a spiritual father. In Saint John's Gospel there is a short parable:

> Jesus said, 'Very truly, I tell you, the Son can do nothing on his own but only what he sees the Father doing, for whatever the Father does, the Son does likewise. The Father loves the Son and shows him all that he himself is doing and he will show him greater works than these so that you will be astonished'.[2]

Here Christ uses the example of a father teaching a son, or a craftsman teaching an apprentice, to point to the relationship He has with the Father. Not only is this a direct, open, and trusting relationship in which the one gives of himself to the other, and the other opens himself in his turn, but also it is shown that this openness has an educational or rather a transforming and creative power. In this relationship, our action, potentiality, and personality are shaped and directed. Its richness is shown by the flexible use of the example of father and son in this passage: it can be applied first to the unknowable and mysterious relationship of the Father and the Son within the Trinity, and then to the relationship of Jesus Christ with the Father, and also to the relationship of the disciple with the teacher.

These two quotations can give us a glimpse of what spiritual fatherhood is. It is that open and intimate relationship between two persons in which the father's being is open and available to the son who in turn listens and receives, his person and action shaped by the father who loves and gives. The spiritual fatherhood which is the subject of this book belongs within the saving work of God, making God's

2. John 5:19-20.

people into sons and daughters in an ever more real and experienced way. Spiritual fathers are called and empowered by the Spirit of God and provide their care within the working of God's Spirit.

This point may go some way towards explaining the embarrassing—at least embarrassing to us nowadays—absence of reference to spiritual motherhood and spiritual mothers. If God is described as Father then it follows that this work of the personal mediation of this relationship will be called spiritual fatherhood. Women can, and do, exercise this care, but they appear relatively infrequently in the literature.

Spiritual fathering happens whenever we learn from the personal example or direction of another Christian. Alongside the word of God in Scripture and the presence of God in sacrament and liturgy goes the personal leading of each disciple to God through the teaching and example, the discernment and wisdom, of those who truly love us. If this is a real action of God, then we should expect it to be given widely. If we can point to persons who have influenced us in our life of faith—friends, priests, teachers—and whom we remember with love and respect, then we should acknowledge them as our fathers in the faith, 'fathers' who have shown us by their example how much God loves us and how we can also love one another.

As well as recognising that fatherhood is a normal part of Christian life, we can also identify a more formalised level of spiritual fatherhood in the great spiritual movements within all parts of the church. Ignatius Loyola, wounded in battle at Pamplona in 1521, passed his recuperation period in reading, especially the Life of Christ and lives of the saints. This process of reflection culminated in a year spent alone at Manresa in northern Spain, a time of intense spiritual struggle during which he grasped and formulated a way of approach to God which he set out in the *Spiritual Exercises*. This he taught to others in Paris and elsewhere and also wrote down in a clear and structured text. This hugely influential spiritual method had its origin in a set of relationships: first, between God and the teacher; and then between the teacher and his disciples. This process can be understood as a form of spiritual fatherhood. The importance of fatherhood is retained within Ignatian spirituality in the role the director has in the giving of the *Exercises* and as he or she applies them carefully to the personality, needs, and circumstances of each individual.

It is easy to make the exercise of spiritual fatherhood seem specialised and restricted by emphasising the role of such great saints of the eastern church as Seraphim of Sarov or the *startsy* of Optino—a tradition made familiar by Dostoevsky in the figure of the elder Zossima in *The Brothers Karamazov*. And it is certainly within this tradition that the spiritual fathers of Romania belong. But in order to understand the nature of this tradition, we need to recognise its biblical roots and its place within the dealings of God with all his people, in each part of the church. So again, we must recognise that all spiritual fatherhood derives from the relationship of Jesus the Son with his Father, from which comes the relationship of the disciples as sons by adoption and grace, and which is re-created and renewed through the work of the Holy Spirit and passed on in the tradition of the Church. Spiritual fatherhood is universal and available.

Yet the spiritual fatherhood described in this book also has a more specific reference and belongs within an historical tradition which can be seen as having a starting point in the early fourth century of the Christian era, when the Emperor Constantine accepted the Christian faith and society became progressively christianised. This political triumph was seen by some as a spiritual defeat by which institutionalisation and compromise infiltrated the Church, and as a result a huge movement of withdrawal—perhaps of protest—began. What we call monasticism was in essence a return to the gospel. The monks wanted to live the Christian life in its simplicity and purity. Saint Benedict was being frank and accurate when he described his way as 'a little rule for beginners'[3], since what he aimed to do was enable his monks to live according to the gospel. There was nothing specialised or esoteric in the monks' way of life. It is the way of the gospel.

Within this communal enterprise in living the gospel, personal direction and personal teaching constituted the central method of growth in Christ. The monk would seek out somebody more experienced and ask guidance. 'Abba, give me a word' was the request which would be answered, the questioner hoped, with a piece of instruction which would give the guidance needed to live rightly. Often the monk would attach himself to the teacher and live as an apprentice, learning from the example of the father. In this relationship the father, or *abba*, gave personal direction in all aspects of life in order to help the disciple to overcome the passions of sin and become conformed to the life of God.

The literature of the desert is full of examples of how this spiritual fatherhood worked. They are shown in the life of one of the first monks, Antony of Egypt (c 250-356). Antony spent twenty years living in a deserted fort and only at the age of fifty-five did he come out of his seclusion. He then began to receive the many visitors who came to him. The Elder Cleopa also—as the reader of this book will discover—spent several years in solitude and obscurity before entering into his final stage of ministry as a spiritual leader and father in the Romanian Church. In both cases we can discern a double authorisation for this work of fatherhood which comes first from God who calls the father into a period of solitude or other form of intense and transforming encounter, and second from the people who recognise the gifts given to the father and come to him in ever growing numbers.

3. Rule of Benedict 73.8: *minimam inchoationis regulam.*

The grace of the spirit thus offered and received makes the person of the father—and not only his words—creative and healing. 'Father', said a man who had regularly visited Antony without asking him any questions, 'it is enough for me just to look at you'.[4] To such a spirit-bearing person the disciple must be open and transparent, revealing everything. Again Antony advised the disciple to 'Ask your father and he will tell you. If possible for every step a monk takes, for every drop of water that he drinks in his cell, he should entrust the decision to the old men, to avoid making some mistake in what he does'.[5]

Above all, it is his thoughts which the disciple sets out to his father. Between confession of sins and confession of thoughts there is an important distinction to be recognised. Disclosure of thoughts is based on the careful and sensitive psychological understanding of sin which the fathers had. They knew that a sinful action is not a simple act of will by which the offender chooses to commit the sin, but rather the result of a process by which the personality loses its freedom and capacity for good. This process was meticulously analysed by the monks, who were acute and sensitive psychologists of the spirit. The first step on the road to sin is the suggestion (*prosbole*), which is a small and possibly innocent stimulus from outside. Then comes the coupling (*sundiasmos*), when we recognise the suggestion. Then follows a struggle (*pale*) which can result in either victory over the temptation or consent to it (*sunkatathesis*). Action may result which, if repeated, develops into a passion (*pathos*), the end result of which is captivity of the soul (*aichmalosia*). Since we are caught up in this death-dealing process, we need restoration on more than one level. First we do, of course, have to seek forgiveness for our sinful acts, from each other and from God, so that we can be restored into the fellowship of the Church. But the

4. *The Sayings of the Desert Fathers (Apophthegmata Patrum)* Antony 27.
5. *Ibid.*, Antony 38.

spiritual father is more concerned with how this destructive process can be halted and overcome; and so how the person can be freed from sin and enabled to live as the child of God. For him, sin is overcome at the beginning of the process—when it is still a suggestion and has not been admitted. So the father encourages the confession of thoughts.

John of the Ladder (c 579-649) describes a visit to a monastery in which he observed the confession of thoughts being practised. He noticed that the brother looking after the guests had a small book attached to his belt and he would regularly stop and write something in it. He was noting the thoughts which came to him, and at the end of the day he would go and reveal these to the father. The fact that John, an experienced monk, was struck by this exercise suggests that such a meticulous practice of the confession of thoughts may have been unusual, but he clearly admired and commends the practice. Monasteries in the Byzantine period were based on this kind of fatherhood. The foundation documents of many of them restricted the number of monks to be admitted to the monastery, presumably in order to make this fatherhood possible and not to overwhelm the abbot. Even with numbers restricted at forty or so, it remained a demanding discipline for father and disciple alike.

After the Turkish capture of Constantinople in 1453, the practice of spiritual fatherhood fell into decline. Its revival is attributed in large part to Paisius Velichkovsky (1722-1794). Educated in Kiev, in what is now the Ukraine, Paisius travelled to Mount Athos to look for a spiritual father to guide him. When he did not find one, he had to teach himself, eventually gathering a group of disciples around him. The use of the Jesus Prayer and practice of spiritual fatherhood were practised in his community. When their number grew they moved to Moldavia. It was perhaps fortunate that Catherine II of Russia was on the throne at this time and was acting to restrict the freedom of the Russian Church, limiting both the number and size of the monasteries. Large numbers of monks fled from Russia and the obvious destination was Moldavia, just over the border. So Russians came to Paisius' monastery at Neamţ and later took his methods with them when they returned home. So, from Moldavia, the practice of spiritual fatherhood spread through Russia, influencing, among other places, the important monastery of Optino with its succession of spiritual fathers in the nineteenth and early twentieth centuries.

The monasteries of Moldavia in north-eastern Romania have been a centre of silent prayer—or hesychasm, to give this form of discipline its correct title—and of spiritual fatherhood. Their continuing witness to this practice is described here by Fr Stebbing. As it has developed and as it is described in this book, spiritual fatherhood has a varied application. Communist persecution during the second half of the twentieth century has ensured that many monks and laypeople were forced into a deeper dependence on the spirit of God either through imprisonment or through an enforced or voluntary withdrawal, as in the case of Cleopa. They emerged with a richness and depth of spiritual experience which has enabled them to fulfil the role of spiritual fatherhood in a variety of contexts. We are shown how they are teachers for the younger monks, giving them a spiritual formation in the classic tradition of spiritual fatherhood. They are guides and directors to the many people who come to the monastery seeking advice and encouragement. The numbers both of those who join the monasteries and of those who visit them are huge, with the result that the spiritual fathers of modern Romania are not only teachers in the church but also healers in the fragmented and confused society of a Romania emerging from the years of communism and encountering modern secularism.

It is this movement which is presented here. Like many before him, Fr Stebbing has travelled and listened. He has included his travel companions, friends, and teachers as

co-authors, allowing them to speak through him with openness and frankness about how they regard and learn from
their spiritual fathers. The result is a fascinating insight
into how the traditional practice of spiritual fatherhood is
maintained in a contemporary society, how it continues to
shape new sons and daughters of God, and how it gives
renewal to society. In an age when spiritual direction is
enjoying something of a revival in popularity elsewhere
the experience of the Romanian Church provides an important example for the modern church in all places.

Here then is a challenging presentation of an old art in a
modern context. The words of Athanasius, writing about
the greatest father of them all, Antony of Egypt, apply in a
sharply appropriate manner to the Elder Cleopa and other
described in this book.

> Antony was like a physician God had given
> to Egypt. For who came to him in grief and
> did not return rejoicing? Or who drew near
> him mourning his dead and did not at once
> put off his sorrow? Who arrived angry and
> did not turn his aggravation into friendship?
> What discouraged monk did not become
> stronger after speaking with him? Who
> when tempted by the demon came to him
> and did not find rest? Who arrived harassed
> by evil thoughts and did not find peace of
> mind?[6]

In the search for God, personal teaching and example
will always speak more eloquently than words. As Saint
Francis is reputed to have told his disciples, 'Preach the
Gospel at all times—use words if necessary', The Romanian spiritual fathers, like the countless fathers who have
gone before them, give a rigorous attention and complete

6. Athanasius, The Life of Antony, 88.

offering of self to this ancient practice of spiritual fatherhood, an art and a science and still more besides.

JOHN BINNS

Cambridge
January 2003

✦ Introduction

Romania is often described by those who have been there as a fairy tale country. Strange things happen there. So it has been for me. In 1987 I was reading Patrick Leigh-Fermor's *Between the Woods and The Water* which includes an enchanting account of his visit to Transylvania in 1934. 'How I would love to go there', I thought, 'but I never will, not with communism there.' Three years later communism had collapsed. In June 1990, four of us from the Community of the Resurrection arrived in Bucharest.[1] The centre of city was still shattered both by the revolution which had toppled Nicolae Ceausescu six months earlier and by a miners' rampage against picketing students just the previous fortnight.

We had come to visit the monasteries and form links between the Romanian Church and our own Church of England. The links in fact had been forged more than sixty years earlier. In 1923, Bishop Charles Gore, founder of our Community,[2] paid a visit to Romania[3] and met various bishops and theologians. In the 1930s Fr Victor Shearburn began to visit. He learned Romanian[4] and es-

1. Bucureşti in Romanian.
2. The Community of the Resurrection is an Anglican religious community founded in Oxford in 1892, and now has its mother house at Mirfield in Yorkshire.
3. See G. L. Prestige, *Life of Charles Gore* (London: Heinemann, 1935) 470-471.
4. See *Mirfield Gazette* (Christmas 1936) pp. 12-13.

tablished a link between theological colleges in Romania and our College of the Resurrection at Mirfield, in Yorkshire, and in 1937 took a party of students to Romania, leaving two of them at Cernauți and two at Sibiu for most of that year. It was a tough time for them. At the same time some Romanian students came to the College at Mirfield.[5] The next year only two students were sent. They spent a few weeks at Arad in the west, then some months at Sibiu in central Transylvania (where Fr Dumitru Stăniloae, one of the finest theologians of the twentieth Century, was then Principal), and finally arrived at Cernauți in what is now the Ukraine, where the first signs of the Second World War sent them fleeing homeward early. What had seemed like a fruitful link disappeared under the darkness of war and its aftermath, Communism.

Yet links between Romanians and Anglicans remained. In 1935 a high level meeting had taken place in Bucharest between Anglican and Romanian theologians in which agreement on fundamental ideas of sacrament and church was reached,[6] and the Romanian Orthodox Church formally accepted the validity of Anglican orders.[7] The Archbishop of Canterbury, Arthur Michael Ramsey, visited Romania in 1965, a visit remembered with awe over twenty years later. Chaplains at the British Embassy made friends

---

5. Stefan Badescu,'Romania, The Land of Old Traditions', *Mirfield Gazette* (Christmas 1937), and a letter from Martin Pierce from Sibiu. The very full, though unpublished, diaries of Martin Pierce and Patrick Baron (1937-38) and George Vince (1938-39) have also been used as background to this study. Patrick Baron's diaries are held by the Witwatersrand University in Johannesburg, South Africa. Martin Pierce's are still with his widow in Durham. Since the recent death of George Vince, I am uncertain of the location of his diaries.

6. *Report of the Conference at Bucharest, 1-8 June 1935* (Bucharest, n.d.). The Conference statement is available in E. R. Hardy, ed., *Orthodox Statements on Anglican Orders* (New York: Morehouse-Gorham, 1946 1966).

7. Anglicans have had a long and often fruitful history of conversations with the Orthodox as some other statements, less substantial than the

and one of them, the (present) Archbishop of York, may well be the only Anglican prelate in Britain who speaks Romanian. Fr A. M. (Donald) Allchin formed a warm friendship with Dr Stăniloae and acquired an honorary Bucharest doctorate. Bishop Mervyn Stockwood of Southwark (south London) diocese made characteristically enthusiastic relationships with Romanians and managed to get several to England and America to study.[8] It was men like these who kept alive a hope for a brighter future and maintained in the Romanian church a spirit of openness to other Christians.[9] English people have a particular advantage in Romania as England has always been seen as a friend. She never colonised Romania and so Anglicanism has never been seen as a threat to Orthodoxy. Roman Catholicism, on the other hand, is viewed as an enemy because it was the religion of Austria and Hungary, who for several centuries occupied Transylvania and parts of the Bucovina, often oppressing the Orthodox, whom they tended to regard as centres of nationalist opposition to this rule. This is also true of Calvinism, which is almost entirely Hungarian in Transylvania. The Romanian Church is, however, part of the Eastern Orthodox family of churches. Anglicans have often found the Orthodox attractive because they are an ancient Christian Church which does not submit to the jurisdiction of the Pope, and they share many of the reservations Anglicans have about the papal ministry. Like Anglicans they have married priests as well as monks and an understanding of episcopacy which

---

Romanian, yet still significant, testify. cp. *Orthodox Statements on Anglican Orders*, ed. E. R. Hardy. (London 1946), and *The Moscow Resolution on Anglican Orders 1948, Church Quarterly Review* (April 1949).

8. Dr Aurel Jivi, Professor of Universal Church History in Sibiu, has been a wonderful inspiration to all of us who have visited that lovely city.

9. The aim of creating links between Romanian Orthodoxy and our own church has been particularly fruitful in respect of the Theological College at Mirfield, and every year visits are made in both directions.

is similar to our own. The Romanian Church is open to the West since their language and culture tend to be Western while their religion is Eastern. They like to see themselves as a bridge between Eastern and Western Christianity, just as the Anglican Church often sees itself as a bridge between Protestantism and Rome.

Romania is a small country, not well known in the West, and a book about the spiritual fathers in Romania may seem to have little of interest to Western Christians. In fact, all of us who have visited Romania have found the opposite to be true. Romania provides a gateway into Eastern Christianity. The Eastern Christian tradition is deeply rooted in the early Church Fathers—the great theologians, monks, preachers, and writers who formed the theology and created the spirituality out of which the Christian Church grew. These early patristic writers have in recent years come to be better known in the West, and Western Christians in considerable numbers have begun to read them. Yet in Romania John Chrysostom, Maximus the Confessor, and Gregory of Palamas are not just the long-dead writers of works read only by a few scholars. They are living personalities whose writings and teachings are felt to be contemporary with the modern Christian experience. Getting to know Romanian Orthodox is rather like taking a leap through fifteen hundred years to share the early excitement of living out the new Christian faith.

When the four of us from Mirfield arrived the flood of westerners visiting Romania was just beginning. We hoped to help Romanians find their way into the western theological world. Far more than that, we came to learn, to find out what it was that had enabled their monasteries to flourish at a time when our religious orders in the West were so often struggling both for recruits and for a clear sense of purpose. This book is an attempt to describe something of what we found.

While I try to meet solid academic criteria, this book is not merely an academic exercise. I have tried to lay before

Western Christians a strong, living form of the christian faith with characteristics which were once ours as well, and which, I believe, can be recovered by or re-imported into the Western tradition, to our great advantage. God has been with his Romanian Orthodox people—as with Russians, Bulgarians, and other Christians—through many centuries of persecution, and has given them gifts which we can all enjoy. It is my great hope that this book will bring some of these gifts to other Christians trying to find a way forward in this postmodern secular world.

Writing on a Romanian theological subject has its problems. During the years of communism very little could be published except liturgical or text books. Some areas of theological study were reasonably well served—Church History, Dogmatics, Biblical Studies. Yet anything to do with mystical theology or, of course, politics was not allowed and works on moral theology could not dwell on the sinfulness of a humankind which was being transformed into the new communist man. The main Theological Institutes at Bucharest and Sibiu published a regular theological journal,[10] as did the Metropolitanate of Iaşi. These helped to feed an interest in theology which has been a characteristic of the Romanian Church. Publishing anything under their own names was extremely difficult for Romanians. A few articles appeared in English[11] and other European languages,[12] but only since

10. The April 1958 issue of the journal *Ortodoxia* is devoted entirely to relationships between Orthodoxy and Anglicanism and includes full accounts of the talks which led up to the agreements between Orthodox and Anglicans at the 1930 Lambeth Conference of Anglican bishops from around the world and also a full account of the conversations in Bucharest in 1935, referred to above, n. 6.

11. See the Bibliography for details of articles by Dumitru Stăniloae and Antonie Plămădeală in *Sobornost* and two Staniloae booklets published by Fairacres Press and available in the United States through Cistercian Publications.

12. An excellent article by Andrei Scrima, published anonymously in *Istina* 1958 no 3 and 4, 'L'Avènement Philocalique dans L'Orthodoxie Roumanie', tells far more fully some of the story given in the first Chapter of this book concerning this crucially important part of Romanian church history.

1990 have people been able to write freely. Since then much
has been done to produce basic texts in Romanian and the
transcripts of talks by various spiritual fathers. Little yet exists
in English.

For this reason the research for this study has depended
very heavily on quite a small number of books and on interviews with spiritual fathers and with the clergy and lay
persons who go to them. Most of the interviews I conducted
orally. On the whole, the standard of the answers given to
my questions was very high. Respondents talked fluently
and confidently and were willing to think for themselves.
One did not often get the feeling that they were parroting
learned responses. Most of those interviewed had some
theological education. Those without theological education
were often reluctant to talk about theological matters, and,
sadly, nuns were reluctant to let themselves be interviewed
at all. Almost all the interviews were conducted in Romanian. Some were translated by my assistants during the
interview. Many more were recorded and translated afterwards. Written responses I translated myself, as I did the
various quotations I have included from written Romanian
works.[13] To all those who let me interview them I am immensely grateful, but I owe a particularly great debt of
thanks to Anişoara Carol, Constantine Jinga, Călin
Sămărghiţan and Andrei Vlădăreanu, who acted as translators, found me informants, shared with me their generous Romanian friendship and gave me wonderful hospitality. I owe great thanks also to my Community, who made
it possible for me to visit Romania several times, and to my
two supervisors at Leeds University: John McGuckin, who
enthusiastically started me off, and Alistair Mason, who
patiently corrected my many errors and challenged every
occasion of sloppy thinking. More recently, as this book
was prepared for publication, I discovered the delights of

---

13. In footnotes these interviews are referred to only by their date and the
name of the informant.

working with Rozanne Elder of Cistercian Publications who has made rigorous standards and a more imaginative presentation acceptable through her sense of humour. It is my hope that through this work some wisdom from the East, sadly lost in the West, may be recovered and the witness of the courageous church of a little known but heroic people may lead us back onto some long abandoned and nearly forgotten paths of holiness.

Nicolas Stebbing CR

BEARERS OF THE SPIRIT:
Spiritual Fatherhood in Romanian Orthodoxy

CHAPTER I

Romanian Orthodoxy

I N THE NORTH OF ROMANIA in the region of Maramureş lies the village of Bârsana. It is not untypical of the region, set in good agricultural land surrounded by hills, with a good river running past it. In summer it is beautiful; in winter it is bleak and covered in snow.

It is, by our standards, a large village of nearly five thousand inhabitants and is strung along the main road from Baia Mare. A few muddy tracks lead back from this road to houses placed without much order on the side of a hill. The houses exhibit considerable variety. Many are built entirely of wood in the traditional style, others are in brick or concrete blocks. Some are tumbled down dwellings, others quite large, ascending to two or even three stories and indicating some degree of prosperity. The houses are a disordered jumble, set at various angles to each other, and the road has its share of chickens, ducks, horses, and carts.

The people often dress in traditional style even today— women in short black skirts with woollen aprons and leggings, with a scarf, sometimes coloured, wrapped tightly round their heads; men less often in traditional clothes though the thick woollen trousers and jackets must be much used in the biting winters. It is easy to be sentimental about this life. The village is beautiful and the houses look charming. Sanitation tends to be primitive. By the end of winter food, even if plentiful, has become very boring: a diet of maize meal, potatoes, cabbage, beans, and preserves—not lightened by milk or eggs if one is observing the lenten fast.

The religious profile of the village is more complex than the visitor might expect, seeing that the people of Maramures are well known amongst the rest of the Romanian Orthodox for their piety and their preservation of traditional values. The present population of the village was given by the parish priest (in 1997) as 4,860 people, of whom 3,970 are Orthodox—about 3,000 of those receive communion at Easter— four hundred Greek Catholics, two hundred Jehovah's Witnesses, forty-five Pentecostalists, and fifty Adventists. Until 1948 the village was largely Greek Catholic with a thriving Jewish population. Most of the Jews perished in Auschwitz. One old Jewish survivor remains. In 1948 the Greek Catholics were compelled by the state to become Orthodox. After 1990 most elected to remain Orthodox but about sixty families returned to the Greek Catholic, often called Uniate, tradition and, with the co-operation of the Orthodox priest, they built a beautiful wooden church. Despite their continued allegiance to Orthodoxy rather than 'Uniatism' the devotional life of the people of Bârsana is much influenced by their Greek Catholic past, as is generally true in this district of Baia Mare. Religious art tends to be more Western than Eastern and to include many pictures of the Sacred Heart of Jesus and pious representations of Mary and other saints. There are more pews in the Churches than one would normally find in Orthodox churches. Baptisms are often performed by pouring water rather than by immersion.[1]

The Orthodox priest in Bârsana, Fr Gheorghe Urda, is a remarkable man, having great enthusiasm, intelligence,

1. There is a considerable ambiguity about Romanian Orthodox identity in relation to the Greek Catholic which it is not the function of this book to explore, but needs noting. In many places in Romania whole villages and congregations have reverted to Uniatism after fifty years in which one might have thought that identity had been lost. In Bârsana this has not happened. One wonders whether the crucial factor in this instance may

humour, piety, and a delightful family of six children. In the centre of the village stands the Orthodox church. On another hill stands an exquisite ancient wooden church with charming, though greatly damaged, wall paintings. At the other end of the village is a monastery, built in five years, a lovely wooden church having the highest wooden spire in Europe (Fr Urda deliberately overtopped its nearest Romanian rival by a metre), a large, picturesque wooden convent and twenty-two nuns, almost all of whom are young sisters who have arrived here since 1993. The *staretsa* (abbess), Maica Filoteia, is a very energetic, practical person determined to restore a community (as opposed to idiorrhythmic) form of monasticism in a village which had a monastery before the great Austro-Hungarian destruction of the Transylvanian monastic life in the eighteenth century.

There is a tough cohesion in these Maramuresean peasants. They are not immediately outgoing and look rather suspiciously on the stranger. Yet, as with most peasant people whose life has been a constant battle for survival as much against a demanding environment as against the wars and empires that have swept over them, they have learned to hold firmly to tradition and to keep the outsider at bay. They resisted communist collectivism more successfully than most rural communities in Romania and their Orthodoxy was untouched by communist propaganda. One can see why the former dictator Nicolae Ceauşescu set out to destroy such villages. Only their destruction could break the bonds of centuries.

It is from villages such as these that most of the monks and great spiritual fathers of Romania come.[2] This earthy,

have been the many years of devoted pastoring by a really first rate and dedicated priest. Other parishes were not so fortunate and poor quality priests are undoubtedly one factor (but only one) in the switching of traditions.

2. Romanian Orthodox tend, like people throughout the Western world, to idealise village Christian life. Their idealisation needs to be set against a remark by a sensitive young woman in Timisoara: 'Priests around Romania

enduring life is the soil in which a rich spirituality has grown. Monastic life in Romania is rooted in the peasant life from which it draws most of its members. Much of the spiritual life of Romanian Orthodox shares this background, which can pose difficulties for the urban and intellectual. In this study we will see this village background emerging constantly. The spiritual father who forms the centre of this study, Fr Cleopa Ilie,[3] preached to the peasant people with a directness that a westerner often finds shocking.[4] Even the Patriarch of Romania, when talking about the spiritual life of the people, reverted to his own village background for illustrations.[5] At the same time, Fr Urda, a well educated and intelligent man, must keep cows and pigs and farm some land to feed his large family on an inadequate stipend. His education and priesthood in no way separates him from his people. Fr Urda's teenage children work hard in the fields. This provides part of an explanation for another feature we shall observe. Monasteries in Romania, especially in the devout north, are overflowing with young monks and nuns. One cannot for a moment question their devotion and enthusiastic embracing of the monastic life but it is easy to discern an unbroken continuum between the hard-working, devout life of the village and the equally hard-working and devout life of a monastery. In a climate of unemployment and limited horizons, the choice of monastic life is a natural alternative to village life. The culture shock Romanians experience is far less than a westerner would feel on entering a western monastery.

in many places are not very good. The Church is better in the cities than in the villages.' The classic image of the devoted (or slovenly) village priest needs to be balanced by the many hard working and passionately committed city priests with equally determined Christian congregations who can be found all over Romania.

3.   Fr Cleopa died on 2 December 1998. See below, pages 45-86.

4.   A description he gives of heaven, for instance, as of each person relaxing in lovely weather under a fruit-laden tree seems hopelessly naive, until one remembers it is for peasant people who must work hard all their lives, and for whom rest and good food is the dreamed-of reward.

5.   See below, Chapter 6, pages 177f.

Bârsana was the birth place of this study. Staying there in August 1995, I began to see the relationship between a village like this and the monastic life I had already met. I had heard of Fr Cleopa of Sihăstria. I began to read his works and to hear from the people how much he meant to them. I became fascinated by the relationship between village and monastery, between Christians 'in the world' and the monastic spiritual fathers. Orthodox Christian life in the villages is strong and rich in its devotion. Did it draw its strength from the monasteries and from the great pillars of the Church whose heroic lives have preserved the Church through decades of great suffering?

The study began with Fr Cleopa, who is thought to have been the greatest of recent Romanian spiritual fathers and quite a lot of whose preaching has now been published. It quickly became clear that Fr Cleopa could not be studied in isolation. For one thing, his teaching, powerful as it is, is not original, nor would he have claimed it to be. He teaches what the spiritual fathers have always taught, from the time of John Climacus (a favourite writer of his) to the present day. Fr Cleopa must be seen within the tradition of spiritual fatherhood in the Orthodox Church. His significance lies partly in the fact that he is a twentieth-century example of this ancient tradition which continues, though unchanging, to have enormous relevance to a modern age very different from life in past centuries. Nor can spiritual fathers be understood without reference to the Orthodox faithful who take them as their guides. This book is as much a study of the way people understand and value their spiritual fathers as it is a study of the spiritual fathers themselves. Both people and spiritual fathers find their identity in the Romanian Orthodox Church. It therefore becomes necessary to see how the Romanian identity is in part derived from the Church, and how the Church is essential to the history of the country and its life. Fr Cleopa must be placed in context, both present and past, if one is to understand his impact on Romania today and to see how he and the other spiritual fathers of Romania may continue to be of critical importance as the people struggle to adapt to the very different demands of a post-communist society.

TRADITION

We have used the term 'tradition'. This is a crucial word in Orthodox Christianity and needs to be carefully understood if we are to appreciate how Fr Cleopa and the other spiritual fathers of Romania find within it an integral role which is both contemporary and ageless. We may begin with a western definition. Tradition, says the *Little Oxford Dictionary* is an 'opinion or belief or custom handed on from one generation to another'. That may do for the western world, but it is inadequate to describe the Orthodox concept of tradition. Amongst the Orthodox you cannot long discuss spirituality or the monastic life, or indeed the Church itself, without mentioning tradition— usually Holy Tradition or the Tradition of the Holy Fathers. What then is this tradition and what role does it play within Orthodox spiritual life, particularly in Romania?

In Romania Orthodox tradition is indissolubly bound up with Romanian tradition. Romania is a Christian country with a Christian people, we are told, because Christianity reached Romania in the first or second century AD, just at the time when the Dacian people were merging with their Roman conquerors to form the Romanian people. So Romanians were born a Christian people. Later, in the fourteenth century, when Moldavia and Wallachia began to be identifiable as modern states, they had at their head Ștefan the Great and Michael the Brave, Christian princes since canonised. In Romania's long Christian history, bishops and monasteries have played a crucial role in developing the culture and preserving the character of the nation. Even under communism Romanian Christianity was so identified with the people that Romanian communists, being themselves nationalistically Romanian, could not easily attack it.

Historically, the Romanians appear to be a predominantly western european people. Their language is clearly Latin; they look west for their culture and political inspiration, and have done so for at least four centuries. But Orthodox tradition is Eastern. In spirituality the Romanians are closely linked with the Russians to the north—with whom they share the same *Philokalia* and often the same teachers—and with Mount Athos in the south. They are an autocephalous church with their own patriarch, but look to the Patriarchate of Constantinople for their historical continuity in the Orthodox family; and their links with the Greek (and Serbian) Orthodox are strong since a partially independent Romania gave great material help to these countries during the centuries of Ottoman rule. Spirituality and theology have reached the Romanians through these sources, and habits of thinking very foreign to the West dominate their ecclesiastical minds. It often happens that a perfectly simple and intelligible discussion between a Englishman and a Romanian, whether in English or Romanian, suddenly undergoes a shift which reveals another world—a world of meaning, a history, a set of prejudices and historical norms so different from the ones familiar to the westerner that he is not even aware of them. So it happens that a discussion of the importance of retaining the Holy Liturgy unchanged in the present, as it is believed to have been since the time of the Apostles, can suddenly shift to the iniquity of the Yalta Agreement which gave Romania into the hands of Russian communism. Such an explosion of feeling reveals a deep anger lurking beneath the friendly exterior, an anger at the way Romanians have been treated by other nations, even Christian nations. Trying to understand that anger is a part of understanding what tradition means to a modern Romanian. To betray Christian tradition is to betray the Romanian people, and to betray Romanian tradition is to betray one's Christian faith.

In trying to understand this one must see a kind of two-way movement, backwards and forwards, along the line of tradition. In the first place tradition is—as the word itself connotes—a handing down. The first eight Christian centuries were crucial centuries for Christianity, the crucible in which the great trinitarian doctrines were hammered out, in which the traditions of prayer, monasticism, and Christian living were formed. It was also the time when the liturgy was developed—a liturgy begun by Saint James in the first century and completed by Basil and John Chrysostom in the fourth. Salvation is contained within the teaching and practice of these centuries. Therefore it is of utmost importance that this tradition should be handed down in its purest form. It is of equal importance that the present generation should accept this tradition as it has come down to them, changing nothing and allowing only such translation as is necessary for its continued communication and understanding. A spiritual father would not reckon himself to teach anything new; nor would a theologian. If something is new, it is false, because it departs from the tradition. In theory, it is as simple as that.

Through the holy tradition a believer is taken back to the earliest Christian centuries. Here salvation is assured because it is here that the truth closest to that taught by Jesus and the apostles is to be found. In the Holy Tradition we do not merely receive valuable information. We become part of the same world to which John Chrysostom and John Climacus and the apostles themselves belonged. This is most clearly demonstrated by the liturgy, which has a timeless quality, but it is equally true of the theology and the moral teaching of the Church. In Romanian Orthodox worship and theological discussion the centuries disappear and one becomes a fourth-century Christian participating in that great outpouring of grace which took place in those first centuries when the Holy Spirit was most active.

Tradition can, of course, become traditionalism. It can become ossified, and has often become so in both west and

east. 'Tradition' can be a code word. In modern western
Europe it can mean simply nostalgia. Unreal memories and
fantasies of the past are sometimes dressed up as tradition,
usually to sell some product—material, political, or ideo-
logical. 'Tradition' can denote a fierce conservatism which
clings to past patterns of belief and behaviour regardless of
their relevance or appropriateness. People can be imprisoned by 'tradition' in a way which makes it impossible for
them to live in the modern age. Or they can be liberated
from 'tradition' in a way which leaves them with no values
by which to live in the modern age.

By contrast, Metropolitan Antonie Plămădeală of Sibiu
entitles one of his books *Tradition and Liberty in the Romanian Orthodox Church*. He perceives not ossification, but
rather a freedom which tradition gives Christians to live
their lives without the straitjackets of religious behaviour
which he perceives (not always fairly) in the West. Only in
freedom, he tells us, can a person choose his own way.
'Tradition without freedom and openness in the way it is
carried out would be a death, a prison, an end. . . . Tradition is a yesterday which is always becoming today.'[6]

Tradition needs a people to keep it alive. Orthodox Christians accept as a responsibility of the whole people of God,
not just of the hierarchy, the preservation and passing on
the tradition. A particular responsibility, however, is laid
on the spiritual fathers. Tradition is passed on not just by
the teaching or repetition of sacred texts. It is passed on by
the holiness of people's lives. To hand on tradition faithfully one needs to be holy; one needs to be sharing the
spiritual life of the people who first formed the tradition. It
is perhaps for this reason that Orthodox tradition, at least
in Romania, does not appear to have become ossified. It is
a lived tradition, not a yearning for a long-dead world. Insofar as it has always been lived by holy men, tradition has
actually participated in changes that have brought it into

6. Plămădeală, p. 146.

the twentieth century not identical in form, but authentic
in the spirit of its earlier formation.

George Florovsky expresses in a quite radical way this
understanding of a living independent tradition. Tradition,
in his view, is the catholicity of the Church which exists in
its smallest part, perhaps in a single member. Tradition is
not a body of material to be learned but a life to be lived. In
this it may be seen as the presence of the Holy Spirit within
the Church. So, Florovsky writes:

> Tradition is not only a protective, conserva-
> tive principle; it is primarily the principle
> of growth and regeneration. Tradition is
> not a principle striving to restore the past,
> using the past as a criterion for the
> present. Such a concept of tradition is re-
> jected by history itself and by the con-
> sciousness of the Church. Tradition is
> authority to teach, authority to bear wit-
> ness to the truth. The Church bears wit-
> ness to the truth not by reminiscence or
> from the words of others, but from its own
> living, unceasing experience, from its
> catholic fullness. . . . Tradition is a charis-
> matic, not a historical principle. [7]

This is important to keep in mind as we begin to look at the
monastic life which provides one of the keys to understanding Romanian Orthodoxy today. For though monastic life
appears to be very institutionalised and is deeply rooted in
history, it is in essence a charism and its charismatic character makes it live.

---

7. G. Florovsky, *Bible, Church, Tradition* (Belmont Mass, 1972) 47.

ROMANIAN HISTORY

Romania is a land filled with monasteries. It is a land with a long and tragic history and a people who have stubbornly held on to a common national identity in the face of almost constant oppression either by foreign governments or by their own rulers. Wars have swept back and forth over Romania down the centuries, so that little remains in the way of historical records or buildings from before the seventeenth century. Monasteries are among the few enduring institutions which have survived the destructions and kept some history intact. Firm historical landmarks have been difficult to come by in Romania until quite recent centuries and the interpretation of historical data is even more doubtful, influenced as it is by partisan sentiments. Uncertain though it is, Romanian history is of immense importance to Romanian spirituality. Any conversation with Romanians about their spirituality will immediately take one down the centuries to the birth of the Romanian people.

This birth, it would seem, took place in Roman times. The Dacian people north of the Danube were invaded and defeated by the Romans under the Emperor Trajan, who himself led his armies across the Danube in 105 AD and defeated the great Dacian leader Decebal. Roman veterans were settled in the Dacian territories and a Roman province established which endured until 271 AD. In that year the emperor withdrew his armies but left behind a people so thoroughly romanised that their language remains one of the most latin languages of Europe and contains within it only a small number of Dacian words (eighty, say some scholars; one hundred sixty, say others).

Where the Romans went Christianity was not slow to follow. Legend has it that the apostle Andrew preached in Dobrogea (the territory south of the Danube of disputed Romanian and Bulgarian ownership). Already in the first century this part of the Black Sea coastland was Roman, and the poet Ovid lived out his unhappy exile in Tomis

near modern-day Romanian Constanța. In fact, Christianity appears to have entered the new territory in the second
century. By the end of the third century there seem to have
been bishops in the Dobrogea. Certainly by the time of
Diocletian (285-305) there were Christians from this region
who suffered martyrdom in his persecution.[8] John Cassian
(*c.* 360-435) is claimed, though not very securely, as a native of this area. If he did indeed come from this part of
modern Romania there must have been an early Christian
presence there, for he certainly knew monks during his
childhood. Archaeological discoveries suggest a Christian
presence in Transylvania by the fourth century.[9] Relying
partly on archaeology and partly on scattered references,
Joantă is able to give, if not a history, then at least considerable evidence of a fairly widespread monastic life during
the centuries after this in the area of modern day Romania.[10] Christianity came into Romania 'not by the preaching of a great missionary, . . . nor by the conversion of a
political leader. . . but through a slow and quiet penetration
of the new religion into the Daco-Roman community'.[11] It
is doubtless of some significance that the new faith thus
found its place among anonymous ordinary people and so
made its home in their hearts, forming their identity and
laying the foundation of their culture.

After the Romans left, Romania was invaded by other
tribes, or nations, as they moved about or passed into Europe. Goths and Visigoths were followed by Slavs and Huns
and finally by the Magyars. The Romanians survived probably by seeking refuge in the forests and valleys of the
Carpathian mountains and it is now part of their self perception that their Dacian and Roman roots gave them a
stubborn ability to survive the centuries of oppression. Village life appears to have been well established at an early

8. Constantinu, p. 45.
9. Constantinu, p. 46.
10. Joantă, pp. 13-22.
11. Constantinu, p. 47

stage[12] and has remained the fundamental Romanian social unit ever afterwards. The tenacity of village life is remarkable since Romania has few natural boundaries. The
people spread south of the Danube (into Dobrogea), across
the Prut into modern Bassarabia, north into the Bucovina
(now partly absorbed into the Ukraine), and through
Transylvania into the Banat which borders on Serbia. The
natural boundaries—the Danube and the Carpathians—in
fact have Romanians living on both sides of them. The
Carpathians sweep in a great crescent through the centre
of the country, forming both a hindrance to Romanians
trying to form themselves into one country and a help in
preventing waves of invaders—Turks from one side and
Hungarians from the other—from ever completely possessing the land. Romanians on both sides of the
Carpathians have always helped their neighbours to resist
the current invaders. Surrounded as they are by Bulgarians, Russians, Ukrainians, Poles, Slovaks, Hungarians,
and Serbs, Romanians proudly describe themselves as 'a
Latin people surrounded by a Slavic sea'. Although firmly
Orthodox in religion they cling equally firmly to their latin
culture and their western links. We shall see that their Orthodox religion contains numerous western influences
learned mostly from the Hungarian Catholic overlords of
Transylvania. Their identity, deprived of a single national
political unit, is derived from their language, culture, and
Church, and from their attachment to the land where Romanians have lived from time out of mind and to the historical pressures of being continually squeezed by Turks to
the South, Russians to the North, and Hungarians to the
West.

Romanian history begins to emerge from the shadows
in the eleventh century, when the Magyars established a
suzerainty over Transylvania, Wallachia (the south eastern
part of modern Romania), and Moldavia. In the fourteenth

12. Constantinu, p. 40

century, Wallachia and Moldavia managed to throw off Hungarian control and establish their own political identity. It was about this time that, ecclesiastically, they identified themselves firmly with the Eastern Church rather than with the Latin Church of their former Hungarian overlords[13]. Wallachia was created as a state under the reign of Basarab I (1310-1352) who in 1330 defeated King Charles I of Hungary at Posada. Moldavia seems to have come into existence a few decades later under Prince Bogdan. Its most famous ruler was Ştefan the Great (1457-1504). Canonised by the Orthodox in 1992, he is particularly famous for the forty-four monasteries he founded (one apparently after each successful battle with the Turks!), ten of which still exist. The independence established by these great rulers was not maintained. Threatened always by Russians and Poles in the North, Hungarians in the West, and Bulgarians in the South, Wallachia and Moldavia increasingly fell under Ottoman influence. Although never taken fully into the Ottoman Empire these two provinces were compelled to pay a heavy tribute and their princes were obliged to pay huge sums of money for their offices. Although from time to time a few greatly venerated leaders (Neagoe Basarab, Michael the Brave, Constantin Brâncoveanu are renowned among these) managed to fight off the Turks, the respite they gained was short and Turkish suzerainty was effectively acknowledged even by the West until the mid nineteenth century, when these two principalities finally gained their independence.

When Moldavia and Wallachia achieved recognition as independent states they sought internationally recognised bishops. These were supplied by Constantinople. In return for considerable financial support from the Romanian provinces, the Church in these states received bishops who had been formed in Constantinople, Athens, and Jerusalem. It is not surprising then that the hesychast spirituality

13. Georgescu, p. 33

which had recently been greatly reinvigorated by the teaching of Gregory Palamas[14] should have found its way into Romania. Thus the *voivode* Neagoe Basarab (1512-1521), founder of Curtea de Argeş monastery, had as his spiritual father in his youth the future Patriarch of Constantinople, Niphon. When Neagoe came to write his *Teachings to his Son Theodosius* he gave his people a document heavily laced with a monastic spirituality. It did not demand that people become monks but its author believed 'in the possibility for each person, from the *voivode* to the most humble of his subjects, to attain to Christian perfection while exercising his proper duties without leaving the world or retiring into solitude'.[15] Thus the *Teachings* insist on an active phase of perfection through 'the traditional means of asceticism—personal prayer and communion, fasting, continence, and chastity, charity towards the poor, justice and mercy and confession'.[16] Its hesychast influence is clearly seen in the importance which the author gives to the activity of the mind and the heart. The mind commands everything, and everything depends on it. That is why it must be cleansed of all impurity by prayer, sobriety, and recollection. The heart in its turn is the place of God. It also is purified by prayer and tears. By this means the mind and the heart become united in prayer.[17]

Despite these high points political factors in the sixteenth century prevented the Romanians from coming together as a nation and monastic life seems to have gone into a certain decline, mirroring perhaps the decline experienced throughout the Eastern Church in the wake of the Turkish domination. The next great Romanian figure is Constantine

14. Although hesychasm is particularly linked with the name of Gregory of Palamas, for reasons we shall see, he did not invent it. On the contrary he learned it from Theoleptus of Philadelphia and the Patriarch Athanasius. (cp. Meyendorff [1964] pp. 17-18).
15. Joantă, p. 90
16. Joantă, p. 93
17. Joantă, pp. 13-22

Brâncoveanu, who ruled Wallachia at the beginning of the seventeenth century and died with his sons and son-in-law as a martyr in Istanbul. His importance, though, is largely national and cultural. During his time life in Moldavia and Wallachia, despite their semi-independent state, was dominated by heavy taxation both through the greed of rapacious *voivodes* and the demands of their Turkish overlords.[18] This heavy taxation crushed national life. The great monasteries came under a like oppression; they were in fact often owned by the Church in Greece and Constantinople and most of their income went to maintaining the Church in these countries.

During the two hundred years between the time of Neagoe Basarab and the eighteenth century there appears to have been a well maintained tradition of monks living both in Moldavia and in the Carpathian mountains, usually in very small communities. Yet the two monks on whom the revival of Romanian monastic and spiritual life in the 18th century can be seen to depend were both Ukrainians who made their home in Romania and whose immense contribution to the spiritual life of their adoptive country gives proof of the fruitfulness of Romanian hospitality, a tradition of which they are proud.[19]

Basil and Paisius

Basil of Poiana Mărului was the first of these Ukrainians. Born about 1692 he was compelled to leave Russia on account of the Russian government's hostility to a prayer centred form of monastic life and settled in Poiana Mărului

---

18. Seton-Watson, pp.50, 26ff.
19. This hospitality characterises Romanian spirituality as it does the people. A people with a latin language and mixed slavonic and latin ethnic background influenced by Russians to the north and Greeks to the south, they present an extraordinary synthesis of different European and Christian traditions.

(near modern day Braşov) in about 1733. Here he built up a good library and introduced his Romanian brethren to the spirituality of Russia as well as that of the Greek fathers. He himself wrote a great deal and his teaching centred on the Jesus Prayer. He makes a distinction in this, describing an 'active' stage when the prayer is an 'activity of the mind' and a 'contemplative' stage when prayer becomes the gift of the Holy Spirit and is transformed into a 'prayer of the heart'.[20] He insists, somewhat unusually for his time, that the Jesus Prayer is not only for monks, but is for all Christians who have a duty to practise it in order to purify the soul from the passions and to keep the mind sheltered from temptations.

In vigorously defending the practice of the Jesus Prayer, Basil was entering into a contemporary controversy amongst eastern writers as to whether it is better to use psalmody or the Jesus Prayer as the basis of monastic life. A monk living in community has, of course, an obligation to join in the liturgical prayer of his brethren. For Abbot Basil, and for the whole hesychastic tradition,[21] however, psalmody is considered chiefly an ascetic practice which prepares the soul for contemplative prayer. Basil goes so far as to see the continual praying of the psalms as a potential danger if pursued for too long, as it 'hinders the mind from being attentive to God and from concentrating itself in the heart, where all the powers of the soul are reunited and where are born all thoughts, good or evil'.[22] To pray only the psalms means 'one marches endlessly in place like a donkey turning a mill-wheel'.[23] In the somewhat polemical atmosphere of the day Basil clearly thought too much attention was being given to psalmody and he contrasted the two:

20. Joantă, p. 114.
21. Joantă, p. 116.
22. *Introduction to Nil Sorsky*, p. 121–cited by Joantă, p. 118.
23. *Introduction to Hesychius*, p. 111–cited by Joantă, p. 118.

> I would like to add something more pre-
> cise, to make the difference between the
> two ways of understanding progress in the
> spiritual life more clear. The one submits
> himself to the rule and accomplishes only
> the work of chanting. The other, on the
> contrary, abandons himself to the interior
> practice and has the name of Jesus Christ
> always with him, so as to destroy the en-
> emy and the evil thoughts of the passions.
> The one rejoices when he has completed
> his chanting; the other gives thanks to God
> when he practises the prayer in calm and
> far from evil thoughts. For the first, quan-
> tity is important; for the other quality. As
> the first one increases the quantity of his
> chant, he tends to have a proportionately
> higher opinion of himself; . . . the other,
> on the contrary, who tries to assure the
> quality of his prayer, has experience of his
> own feebleness and of the help of God.[24]

Starets Basil was clearly a great teacher in his own right
and brought the tradition of study and of praying the Jesus
Prayer into a far greater prominence than it had been previously. He spoke both to exiled Russian and to Romanian
monks and greatly influenced the lives of the lay people by
making clear to them (as Neagoe Basarab had done two
centuries earlier) that the spiritual life is as available to lay
persons as it is to the monks, and that fostering it is indeed
incumbent on them as earnest followers of Christ. In most
of what he taught Basil of Poiana Mărului was followed by

---

22. *Introduction to Nil Sorsky*, p.121–cited by Joantă, p. 118.
23. *Introduction to Hesychius*, p. 111–cited by Joantă, p. 118.
24. *Introduction to Hesychius*, p. 103–cited by Joantă, p. 119.

his younger contemporary and sometime disciple, Paisius Velichkovsky.

Like Basil, Paisius was born in the Ukraine. Finding it impossible to live the monastic life in his native land on account of the hostility of Catherine the Great, he moved south to Wallachia, where for a time he found a home in the Trăisteni Skete, in the region of Buzău, and came under the influence of Starets Basil. After four years, seeking greater quiet and the opportunity to grow in 'the peace of the soul and the prayer accomplished by the heart' he moved south to Athos. The Holy Mountain, unfortunately was at this time going through a period of stagnation and Paisius was unable to find the spiritual father he sought, and so he chose to live as a hermit, finding his own way with God. In 1750 Starets Basil visited him, advised him to seek some brothers to share in his monastic life, and tonsured him as a monk. Several Romanians and Russians gathered around him, amongst them some (notably Macarius and George) who were good scholars of Greek. By 1763 the community had grown too large for Athos and so Paisius, with sixty-four monks, set off for Moldavia, where the Metropolitan, Gabriel of Iaşi, settled them in the monastery of Dragomirna. Paisius remained here until 1775, when the Austrians took over the Bukovina and Paisius moved with his monks to Secu and then to Neamţ.

Paisius formed his monasteries on the classic monastic pattern with a strong emphasis on the liturgy celebrated according to the Athonite typikon.[25] As well as the traditional practices of eastern monasticism Paisius founded his community on the two virtues of absolute personal poverty and unconditional obedience to an elder. These two virtues exemplify an ideal. We shall see a bit later how spiritual fathers go about the task of making them realities in the lives of their disciples. Poverty is measured not so much by

25. That is in the style and liturgical order of the major monasteries on Mount Athos.

the number of goods one has in one's cell but in the freedom one has from a need to possess them. Unconditional obedience towards a revered spiritual father may come easily to a young novice (or to any earnest young Christian). Yet the actual process of opening up the dark corners of one's soul to the light of the Holy Spirit, which this obedience to a spiritual father enables, requires a whole lifetime's growth in the Christian life. Father Paisius made these two virtues extremely attractive, and it is evident from his success that they were not just ideals, but realities. One indication of his effectiveness as a monastic leader may be seen in the sheer size of the monasteries he governed. By the time he had been a few years at Neamţ the monastery had grown to number seven hundred monks. Paisius is somewhat unique in having established a monastic life which was both coenobitic (that is, community based) in its organisation and hesychastic in its spirit. Until his time there had been a considerable division between those who lived in monastic communities and devoted all their devotional activity to the chanting of the liturgy and the recitation of the psalms, and those who preferred hesychastic prayer and withdrew to live either on their own, or with two or three companions in a small skete. Paisius was devoted to hesychastic prayer, as we have seen, but he brought this devotion into the monastic common life and so united the two great traditions, as they have remained united, at least in principle, in Romania ever since.[26]

We must see Paisius not just as a remarkable individual but as a great leader of men. It was not by performing miracles that he inspired so many hundreds of men to join his monasteries, but simply by his teaching. He inspired even the laziest of men to seek after the heights of the spiritual life. At the same time, he established his monas-

---

26. In uniting these two traditions of hesychasm and the common monastic life Paisius was doing what Simeon the New Theologian had done in tenth-century Constantinople. For it was he who first integrated the earlier desert tradition of hesychasm with the city tradition of community life.

tery on carefully worked out practice of the community life. His ideal of community was that each supported the others, each encouraged the other. Discipline was strict, but humane and regulated to the ideal of serving God and the world around.[27]

What then was his teaching? Partly it was the hesychastic teaching which he had learned first from Basil of Poiana and then from his years on Athos. Partly it was the monastic life, the duties, responsibilities and asceticism of simply living in community. In this he believed that

> the essence of monastic life is not the ascetic virtues since they can be practised just as well by the laity. The particular purpose of monasticism is its social relationship, the creation of a new world, in this world and at the same time apart from it. Monks are lights and the source of salvation for the whole world, models of virtue which indicate the path of spiritual progress.[28]

One major expression of all this was the work of translating the Greek fathers and making available to the people both of Russia and Romania the treasures of the *Philokalia*. We remember that when Paisius first arrived on Athos he could find no spiritual father and had to teach himself. At this time Athos was in decline and although liturgical celebrations may have been well observed, study had been seriously neglected. However, while Paisius was on Athos, and perhaps partly through his inspiration, Nicodemus the Hagiorite and Macarius of Corinth began to put together the Greek Philokalia which was published in 1782. But already by 1767 Paisius had begun to publish much of this material in Romania at Dragomirna. It was at Dragomirna that the first Philokalia in a vernacular language was born.[29]

27. Zamfirescu, pp. 73-76.
28. Zamfirescu, p. 71.
29. Joantă, p. 147.

Paisius took this work of translation extremely seriously. He sent monks off to Bucharest Academy to learn Greek and other relevant languages. He himself translated mostly into Russian which enabled the monks in his homeland also to receive the Philokalia in their own language.

We must see the importance of this great work of translation and publication in the life of the Romanian Church. In the first place it made available to monks and, indirectly, to lay people the teaching of the richest periods of the Eastern Church's spiritual tradition. Secondly, it inspired a remarkable intellectual ferment in the monasteries of Neamţ, Secu, Cernica and elsewhere. Monastic life, to be healthy, must always be intellectually alive, though the intellect must be harnessed to the spiritual goal of the life. Romanian monastic life, drawing almost completely on the peasant population for its monks, always has within it the possibility of slipping into a manner of life not much different from those of devout peasants. The intellectual tradition which Paisius established helped to prevent this happening and turned the peasant monks into some of the great educators of Romania. Moreover, this work of translation focussed people's attention on the tradition of the Church. Tradition, as we have seen, is not, in an Orthodox context, merely the handing on of old stories and beliefs. It is the living presence of the Spirit, preserving and guarding the Church from heresy and giving it life. In Romania's rather precarious position, invaded often by surrounding nations and forced to defend its Orthodox religion against Islam from the south and Roman Catholicism or Protestantism from the West, a love for tradition has been an all-important factor in their successful defence of their faith. And finally, this work of translation must be seen to have had a great cultural impact on the Romanian nation. It helped to bring a larger awareness of Greek sources into the life of the nation, and contributed towards the growth and development of the Romanian language itself. Though Paisius was a Ukrainian, he was a neighbour of the Romanian people and was taken by them to be very much one of their own. His contribution to the cultural life of Romania, itself strongly influenced by and often a product of the Romanian church, cannot be underestimated. Paisius taught nothing new. His knowledge and appreciation of the ancient tradition meant that he was concerned to 'bring new treasures out of his storehouse'. The new feature for his time was the synthesis he achieved between coenobitic monastic life and hesychasm, and also between scholarship and the demands of sustaining a monastic life in a rural situation. He established a pattern of monastic life which has continued in Romania to the present day, with of course the usual ups and downs that characterise monastic history. We must see these three factors—cenobitic life, hesychasm, and biblical and patristic study—as the three external characteristics of Paisianism. His spiritual teaching is more difficult to sum up. He insisted that all Christians should pray the Jesus Prayer and seek God through the ascetical life. This life was not the preserve of monastics. Yet he believed that prayer of the heart was only suitable for monks because

> the principal and unshakable foundation of the activity of the mind is 'true obedience' from which is born 'true humility'. Humility in its turn protects against all illusions which mislead those who make themselves their own masters.[30]

He insisted, too, that every monk must have an experienced spiritual father. This was partly because of the importance he gave to the virtue of obedience and also because of his own experience of the dangers to be found in trying to lead a spiritual life without competent direction and support. The importance he gave to this relationship may be guessed from one of his best known disciples, Starets George of

30. Joantă, p. 156.

Cernica, who used to insist on frequent confession (three times a week)— a practice he likely learned from Fr Paisius. Its purpose was partly to enable the monk continually to be absolved from his sins, without allowing them time to do damage to the soul and also to make possible the intimate relationship between spiritual father and son which is essential in the practice of hesychastic prayer.

After Paisius

Politically, life in the principalities of Wallachia and Moldavia began to improve in the nineteenth century. A weakening Ottoman empire found it more and more difficult to impose its will, though it was not until 1859 that the two principalities were able to elect Alexandru Cuza as prince of both states. In 1866 he was replaced by the first Romanian King, Carol I. This was a time of enormous change politically and socially as a well-educated intelligentsia began to develop and a vibrant literary and cultural life, typical perhaps of revolutionary eras, grew up. Life at the time, however, was less happy in Transylvania. Here an unhappy conflict raged between Austro-Hungarian rulers and Romanian people which led to the establishment of the Greek Catholic, or 'Uniate', Church which dominated Transylvania until after the Second World War. Although a time of conflict and savage oppression, this was also a time of increasing education and growing cohesion. The work of Andrei Şaguna, the most famous Transylvanian prelate of the nineteenth century, laid the foundations for the modern Romanian Church in that territory.

Monastic life in Romania appears to have maintained a great fervour for some decades after Paisius, especially through the monasteries of Neamţ and Secu, and at Cernica, where disciples of Father Paisius inspired a similar synthesis between coenobitic life, hesychasm, and patristic study. In Moldavia Metropolitan Benjamin Costachi of Iasi played an important role, building up a system of church education, printing, and scholarship from which the whole principality benefited. In Wallachia at about the same time the great Bishop Calinic of Cernica (1787 -1867) was doing a similar work, first as abbot of his monastery at Cernica outside Bucharest and then from his diocese of Râmnic.[31] In the mid nineteenth century the liturgy was translated from Slavonic into Romanian and came to be generally celebrated in that language. This must have given Romanian Orthodox a greater sense of national identity and deepened their active participation in the liturgy. In the middle of the century, however, monastic life suffered a decline which was brought about at least in part by the secularisation of much monastic property after 1859. The background to this requires some explanation. At this time about twenty-five percent of the land belonged to the Church. Much of the income of the monasteries, however, went to support the monasteries on Athos and the Church in Greece and Constantinople.[32] Some interpret this secularisation of Church land as a typical anti-Church measure of the Masonic Prince Alexander Cuza. Others see it as a just redistribution of Romanian land, a reform constantly raised but never properly attended to before the disaster of communist rule swept all questions of land ownership away. It is likely, too, that the enthusiasms and confusions of life in Wallachia and Moldavia as they came together to form the Romanian Kingdom also contributed to a loss of zeal for monastic life. In the words of one monk:

> The Paisian current dried up, the spiritual radiance of the monasteries was dimmed, patristic literature fell into forgetfulness and the secular spirit strove to conquer the 'droit de cité'[33] even in the enclosure of theology.[34]

31. Joantă, pp. 186f.
32. Cf. 'Cândea', 'L'Athos et les Roumains' in A. Bryer and M. Cunningham, edd., *Mount Athos and Byzantine Monasticism* (Brookfield: Ashgate, 1996) 249-256.
33. 'influence of the place'.
34. 'L'avènement philocalique dans l'Orthodoxie Roumaine', in *Istina* (n. 3:

The First World War proved a further watershed in Romanian political life. Although largely occupied by the German forces quite early in the War, Romania reaped the rewards of having joined in on the Allied side. In 1918 the greatly enlarged country of Romania—including now Transylvania, Bessarabia, the Bukovina, and Dubrogea—was proclaimed at Alba Iulia. This led in 1925 to the Romanian Church being raised to autocephalous status and the election of its first Patriarch, Miron Cristea.

MONASTIC REVIVAL

Monastic life was slow in catching up with this revival. In Transylvania it had been brutally and utterly destroyed by the Austrians in the eighteenth century. Monasteries began to be refounded in Transylvania; Sâmbătă de Sus near Sibiu and Rohia near Baia Mare were two of the best known. The great revival of monastic life in Romania, however, came after 1945 and, under God, may be attributed to three factors.

The first might be communism itself and the spirit of resistance it engendered amongst the Romanian people. Church life was limited to the liturgy and social involvement was forbidden to Christians, so the monastic life became one of the few areas in which a committed Christian could express his faith, and feel the conviction that he or she was playing a crucial role in the struggle for the nation's soul.

The second factor, according to Joantă[35] and others in Moldavia, was the life and example of Starets Ioanichie Moroi, who came from Athos to the monastery of Sihăstria before the Second World War and established Sihăstria on so firm a foundations that after the war most of the abbots

---

September 1958) p. 314.
35. Joantă, p. 209.

and spiritual fathers in Romania were drawn from this monastery. It was from him that the much loved Father Paisie Olaru and the great Father Cleopa Ilie received the monastic life.

A third reason for the post war revival could be the Romanian alliance of scholarship with a genuine spirituality; this found particular expression in the work of Fr Dumitru Stăniloae. His contribution, in addition to his own very original work on dogmatic theology, has been his translation of and commentary on the entire *Philokalia,* the first four volumes of which were published immediately after the Second World War, and the remaining seven during the 1960s. This has placed before the Romanian Orthodox a selection of the most important texts on the spiritual life, in its hesychastic expression, and one is constantly reminded of this in conversation with Romanians who quote the philokalic fathers liberally. The importance of this work cannot be underestimated. The translation enables Romanian Orthodox intellectuals to read within the most important tradition of Orthodox spiritual life and Staniloae's commentary allows them to maintain a well informed and modern dialogue with this tradition.

This is the tradition out of which Fr Cleopa appears and it is tempting to see him as a Paisian figure. He was certainly the most venerated modern exponent of the spiritual tradition that Paisius represented. Unlike Paisius he did not have great formal scholarship, though he was himself extremely well read in the fathers. He did, however, pass all his life (apart from his early years as a shepherd and some years in hiding from the Communists) in two coenobitic monasteries where the Athonite tradition is lived. Like Father Paisius he had about him a magnetic quality which drew people of all ages and social conditions to listen to him preach and to seek his counsel. His own term as abbot of Sihastria showed him to be a good leader, and his experience after 1962 as the spiritual father of the monastery demonstrated his grasp of monastic spirituality. At the same time he never lost the common touch. His ability to speak to the peasant people accounts for the numbers who came to his cell each day. Fr Cleopa does not stand alone; Fr Ioanichie Bălan and Fr Teofil Părăian are academically better trained and also much sought after for spiritual counsel. And there are others.

How far this tradition can be maintained in the stresses and dislocations of life after communism is a question which causes great anxiety both to the bishops and to those who love the Romanian Orthodox Church. Since the Second World War Romania has changed greatly. Communism relocated large numbers of peasants into the cities and the traditional (and certainly much idealised) village life is far less a feature of Romania than it once was, though monks still tend to speak as if village life was the only authentic pattern for Romanian Orthodox to follow. In fact, Orthodox Christian life is strong in the cities and some very dedicated and holy parish priests exercise the ministry of spiritual fatherhood among their people. Later we shall consider what young, educated, urban Romanian Christians think of the spiritual life of their Church. We must remember that the Second World War was a traumatising experience for Romania. The pre-War years had been dominated by an extremely right wing Iron Guard in conflict with a not much less right wing intelligentsia often closely allied to the Church[36]. Romania's natural political links were with France and England. As war came upon Europe, however, Romania could see herself being devoured by Russia and to protect herself from Russia she turned to an alliance with Germany. This decision led to much of Transylvania being reabsorbed into Hungary, and to the German invasion of Romania as the two countries moved to attack Russia, quite successfully at first. With the coming of the Red

---

36. Though right wing, the intellectuals were impressive. Mircea Eliade is perhaps the best known. Nichifor Crainic (who spent twenty years in prison) is now being rediscovered (see the unpublished thesis by Christine Hall, *Jesus in my Country*).

Army in 1944, however, Romania changed sides again, hoping desperately that the Western allies would protect her against the Russians. It was a vain hope. It is very unlikely the Western allies could have protected Romania if they had tried, and they did not try. Romania was left feeling abandoned by her friends, and bitterness over this betrayal extends into conversations on the spiritual life today. Meanwhile, although they represented only a small part of the population, Romanian communists backed by the occupying Red Army took over the country. It is true to say, however, that Romanian communists tended to be Romanians first and communists second. Never very friendly towards Russia, they managed to keep a certain distance from Russia after they had got the Red Army out of their country. Many Romanian communists also had more sympathy with the Church than did their Russian counterparts, at least as an inherent part of Romanian identity. The Church was sporadically but not systematically persecuted. The main attacks were launched against the monasteries, many of which were closed in the late 1950s and many, probably hundreds, of the monks disappeared into prison and labour camps. The project of building the Danube Canal (never completed) was one such labour area which accounted for the lives of thousands of priests, monks, and Romanian intellectuals.

It was not only monks who were imprisoned. Hundreds of parish priests were confined for spells of five or ten years. Usually they were described simply as 'enemies of the people'. Some of them were certainly identified with right wing movements or personalities.[37] Many, however, were arrested simply because they were very good priests. Perse-

37. Fr Negruțiu, for instance, was a member of the Iron Guard before the War (see below, Chapter 6). Fr Sămărghițan (the father of Mihai Sămărghițan, interviewed below) gave shelter to the right-wing poet and writer Nichifor Crainic and so was imprisoned for five years. The priest who baptised Bishop Streza was shot for criticizing a local boy's red (communist) scarf.

cution eased off in the later 1950s, but in 1958 the Russian premier, Nikita Krushchev, visited the country and complained about the number of monasteries still thriving. This led the Dictator Nicolae Ceauşescu to attempt to close all of them down. The Patriarch Justinian and his bishops seem to have fought a skilful battle. Many thousands of monks and nuns were compelled to leave their monasteries but most continued to live devout lives amongst the people until they were able to return, either before or after 1989. Yet monasteries were kept open, either as cultural centres, social centres, or theological schools. The liturgy continued to be celebrated and monastic life endured. Under communism the church lost many of its buildings, most of its institutions, and much of its farm land. But the communist government itself, being Romanian first and communist second, often allowed surprising freedom. Many churches (two thousand, said one bishop) were built or restored under communism, at the same time as many churches and monasteries were being destroyed. For a host of reasons Romanian Christianity proved to be very resilient towards the atheistic, materialistic regime. Perhaps it was the long established tradition of prayer throughout ages of domination which made Romanian Orthodoxy survive this latest testing so well. To understand the importance of this tradition and to expand on some of the assertions made above we must turn now to a closer look at the Romanian monasteries.

CHAPTER 2

Monasteries in Romania Today

WHEN ROMANIA EMERGED FROM ITS NIGHTMARE of rule by Nicolae Ceauşescu and a repressive communist regime in 1990, one of the astonishing things that struck all of its visitors was the spiritual strength of the Romanian Orthodox Church. There was much wrong with the Church. Some of its leaders had compromised to an unacceptable degree with the old regime. Some had profited from this. In some respects the teaching, theology, and pastoral practice was obscurantist and out of touch with a modern world, as was inevitable after forty-five years of communist domination following a disastrous six years of war. Yet all over the country the Orthodox Church was flourishing. Churches were full, the liturgy was conducted with manifest devotion. Priests were devout, some were even holy. Monasteries were full, and the welcome visitors received in these monasteries testified to a Christian spirit of hospitality. Whence came all this? How had such a vigorous Christian faith have survived the darkness? One part of the answer to that question was to be found in Moldavia.

Moldavia is one of the ancient centres of Romanian culture and life, and its monastic life provides the spiritual centre of the Romanian Orthodox Church. The reign of the great Moldavian ruler Stefan cel Mare really marks the beginning of modern Romanian history. And it is from his time (1457-1504) that the great monasteries of Romania—

among many others in Moldavia and throughout the country, Putna, Voroneţ, Suceviţa, Moldoviţa, Agapia, Văratec, Secu, Neamţ, and Sihăstria—can be firmly dated. Each monastery has its own varied history of success, devotion, decay, suppression, and often resurrection. Visiting these monasteries one finds hundreds of Romanians also visiting—some to pray, some to seek spiritual advice, some to look round the museums and to see the articles of Romanian history and culture which these monasteries have been able to preserve. Visitors come from all over Romania, from Bassarabia, the Ukraine, and, of course, the West. Historical and cultural riches exist here along with the living presence of spiritual life. What has kept this alive?

Ask the monks and they will answer, it is the liturgy, it is the strong Orthodox ascetical tradition, and it is a handful of spiritual fathers whose holiness, wisdom, prayers, advice, and sheer spiritual toughness have been the inspiration and the strength of Romanian Orthodox through the many long and turbulent years of war and occupation. And today the name you hear most often is that of Fr Cleopa of Sihăstria. Throughout Romania people ask, 'Do you know of Father Cleopa?' They tell stories about him. They quote his sayings. Bus loads of seminarians used to go to see him before their ordination.

Who was this Father Cleopa? He was not an isolated figure. He was a product of the monastic life and his teaching is typical of it. Before we can meet Fr Cleopa, then, we need to see something of the monastic life which formed him and of which he was a part. During the Communist era monastic life was more savagely attacked than any other part of Church life. For us, then, who visited the country shortly after the fall of Communism, the vigor of the monastic life which had survived Communist depredations was astonishing.

Setting off from Bucharest on a Sunday morning in June 1990, we drove north for our first taste of Romanian monasticism. Just outside Bucharest we turned off towards a lake. Alongside it we could see the onion topped towers of the monastery of Cernica. Although we were still more than a mile from the monastery we saw people walking along the road, obviously going for their Sunday worship to the same church as we were. Cernica is a famous monastery, its reputation enhanced by Saint Gheorghe, who followed in the tradition of Paisius Velichkovsky, and by Saint Calinic, abbot of the monastery and bishop of Râmnicu Vâlcea.

We arrived to find what we later recognised as the classic pattern for a Romanian monastery: a large walled rectangular construction in which are set the main cells, refectory, library, abbot's quarters, and reception rooms. Freestanding in the middle of this is the church. We were met by Fr Jerome, a nephew of the previous abbot, now an assistant bishop in Bucharest, and we were taken to stand in the liturgy which was already under way and would continue for another two hours. The crowds of faithful people continued to grow. Some moved around the church kissing icons. Some queued by a door on the left hand side to hand in requests for prayer to one of the monks. As the liturgy proceeded with its (to us) unfamiliar chants, clergy appeared from time to time at the doors of the iconostasis and the monks on either side of the church sang the major part of the service. At the Great Entrance, when the Bishop and priests came out of the sanctuary bearing the eucharistic gifts, the faithful crowded round, touching their vestments. Two women laid their babies on the floor in front of the priests so that they would have to step over them.[1] After the service a queue of people, some very obviously sick, made their way forward for prayers and anointing. Although the congregation participated little in the vocal offering of the liturgy, it was clear they were very much present in spirit and the anxiety of the sick persons to be touched, to come close to the sacred, was a moving witness

1. It seems likely that this practice dates back to byzantine times, when people gathered in the streets to touch the Patriarch and his attendants on their way to the Liturgy.

to their conviction that here God's power was present and could be felt.

After the liturgy Fr Jerome took us to lunch in the monastic refectory. Here the monks sat at long tables, with us at the head. The abbot sat alone. The meal began in silence but soon conversation broke out. At the far end of the refectory many lay people, worshippers and friends, joined the meal. Monastic hospitality in Romania is generous and open. Two years later eight of us arrived without warning at Cernica at 2:30 in the afternoon, after the monks' lunch was over, and were still served a good meal. The English members of the party were very embarrassed by this, but the Romanians, including a monk, insisted it was quite normal.

From lunch we were taken to our rooms for a siesta and warned that another service, *vecernie* (evening prayer), would begin at 5:00. Being good Anglicans, we arrived back at the church just before five and found it almost empty. A few minutes after five two monks came in, arranged some books and in a desultory fashion began to sing. As time went by they were joined by more, some of whom joined in the singing, others of whom simply sat around the edges. By six the church was quite full and the service was in full swing. It continued until seven when we were taken out, this time to Abbot Doroftei's dining room, where we had an excellent supper, followed by wine on the balcony which overlooked the beautiful lake in which, the abbot assured us, seventy kilogram carp could be caught. Although the monks were generous with food and wine they did not eat a great deal themselves. A combination of monastic fasting and Romanian food shortages seems to have taught them not to eat as abundantly as westerners do when given the chance.

The next evening, after several more services and meals we set off by train to Moldavia on the next stage of our monastic journey. This took us to the monastery of Neamț, outside the town of Tirgu Neamț, which we reached at five in the morning. A monk met us at the station and drove us to the monastery where we were sent to bed for an hour before being taken to breakfast with the Abbot Arhatanghel. Like Cernica, Neamţ monastery is rectangular with a free-standing church in the middle. Some monks live in the rooms built into the monastery walls. Many more, including the abbot, live in bungalows round the grounds. The setting in the midst of mountains and hills is beautiful. The buildings are in a mixture of styles with attractive curved roofs, wooden verandahs, and balconies. Flowers grow rather haphazardly all around. Rather to our surprise the monk who showed us where the liturgy was taking place did not come in with us. Nor did the abbot ever appear in church though from our conversation with him it was clear that he was a very devout and sensitive monk from Sihăstria. We discovered later that the monastery was a very unhappy place. The former abbot, who had presided during the last years of communism when the monastery had functioned largely as a tourist centre to which even government officials brought their visitors, had been chased away by his monks immediately after the 1989 revolution. The new abbot found the recalcitrant monastic body too difficult to cope with and left after a year. This was sad, for Neamţ has a great history and was the final monastic community and resting place of the great Paisius Velichkovsky.[2]

We stayed only two days at this beautiful place and then went on to Agapia, a monastery of nuns. Agapia is one of the most famous and most beautiful monasteries in Romania. It is about two hours walk over the hills from Sihăstria, or somewhat further by road, and is set at the end of a valley with hills rising on three sides. The monastic buildings, built in the traditional quadrangle with a free-standing church in the centre, are surrounded by houses built in brick and wood. Most of these are occupied by nuns as

---

2. I visited again in April 1999 and found a much happier monastery under a new young abbot.

the style of life here tends to be idiorrhythmic. Five hundred nuns live here, but only a small number of them live in the monastery building. The others are gathered in these houses as monastic families and tend to live and worship there much of the time. Nevertheless Offices and the Liturgy in the monastery church are beautifully sung by teams of cantors, changing every week. The church is unusually large for a monastery and was decorated by Nicolae Grigorescu, in a very romantic nineteenth-century style of which the Agapia nuns are very proud.

The original monastery at Agapia, built for monks sometime before 1437, was locatred some way up the hill at Agapia Veche. The present monastery was founded by the nobleman Gavril, brother of the Moldavian prince Vasile Lupu, between 1642 and 1644. In the eighteenth century the monks left and were replaced by nuns.

Today the monastery is thriving. During the last twenty-five years of the Communist era it was governed by the remarkable Abbess Eustochia, a theologian and a woman of strong character. It has a thriving industry, fields, and workshops in which vestments, clothes, and icons are made and embroidery is done. There is also a large museum, mostly of ecclesiastical artifacts and additional paintings by Grigorescu. Agapia receives many visitors, including intellectuals and some government figures. Conversations at the guests' dining room table, often presided over by the abbess, can be fascinating. There is also now a school for teenage girls who receive an education based largely on religion and foreign languages.

Up the hill Agapia Veche continues to thrive, with about fifty sisters living in exquisitely beautiful surroundings and in an atmosphere which one is tempted to describe as charged with the spiritual. Their new wooden church, completed and decorated in 1995 by Fr Bartholomew of Sihăstria, is surely one of the most beautiful in all Romania. Old Agapia feels very much like one of the thin spots where heaven has trickled over onto earth.

Life begins early in Agapia monastery, even for guests. On a weekday the bells begin to ring at five in the morning for the service of *utrenie*. The bells are followed by the *toaca*—a nun walking slowly round the church carrying a carved wooden plank over her shoulder, beating on it with a hammer, a rhythm which has an astonishing, haunting beauty all its own.[3] By the time we visitors get into church the choir is in full song. We are ushered up to the front and made to take stalls next to the abbess. Gradually the dark church fills up with nuns, sixty or seventy of whom crowd in during the liturgy. At points of particular devotion they all begin to make prostrations with an amazing speed and gracefulness. The choir sings, often for three or four hours, seemingly without tiring. Gradually the dawn breaks through the windows and when the liturgy comes to an end and we are taken off to breakfast with the abbess, it is past seven o'clock and the nuns are beginning their own work of running this great monastic enterprise.

When one sees a monastery like this it becomes easier to understand the monastic system of Europe in the Middle Ages. The abbess has a large and beautifully appointed dining room and the food is excellent. She is, of course, a great power in the land. People gather at her table. Church dignitaries, foreign visitors, well-off Romanians are received with graciousness and important conversations take place. Sometimes these are political, sometimes theological. Quite often, while she is entertaining, services are being sung in church. She is not expected to be there, though she may lead her guests in for part of the service. Other nuns, too, are not in church for they also have 'obediences' which keep them away. For the most part, Orthodox monks and nuns love the Office and would like to be part of the liturgy more than they can. The fact that they are not always there

3. The *toaca* is itself a moving symbol of the survival of Orthodoxy through times of persecution. During the Turkish domination of the Orthodox churches, bells were forbidden and so the *toaca* became the means of calling people to prayer.

does not necessarily suggest a lax or individualistic regime.

On our first visit to the country it was possible to see only those great monasteries that had survived the decades of persecution and stood as castles of defence against the encroaching tides of atheism which were now fast receding. What does the pattern of monastic life look like in the country as a whole?

Cernica, Neamţ, and Agapia are amongst the best known monasteries. There are others equally large and equally famous. Varătec, just down the road from Agapia, is almost as big. Putna, founded by the ruler, Ştefan the Great, is very famous. Sihăstria we shall hear more about. There are, in fact, hundreds of monasteries for monks and nuns scattered round Romania, but a glance at a map shows that by far the largest number of these are in two places — Moldavia in the North East, and Oltenia in the South West. In Oltenia, and around Râmnicu Vâlcea particularly, are the monasteries of Curtea de Argheş, Frăsinei, and Cozia as well as a host of smaller houses. Many of these monasteries are very small indeed and are home to only a handful of monks and nuns. This is not unusual. Romanian monastic life has always tended towards an idiorrhythmic pattern, a few monks or nuns living in a small skete rather than in large monasteries. The monasteries are often to be associated with great Romanian figures. Curtea de Argheş was founded by Neagoe Basarab. In Râmnicu Vâlcea lived the great Saint Calinic of Cernica. In the mountains of Sinaia was Basil of Poiana Mărului, and monasteries today cluster around there. In Transylvania and the Banat there are far fewer monasteries than there are in the old Romanian territories of Moldavia and Wallachia.[4] These areas were ruled for centuries from Hungary and Austria, who discouraged monasticism as providing too fervent a centre of Romanian Orthodox opposition to their attempts to

4. Wallachia, centred on Bucharest and embracing Oltenia, is the southern part of the country.

catholicise the population. In the 1780s this policy of discouragement turned to violence when all the monasteries in this region were destroyed by cannon. Between the First and Second World Wars many were refounded, but during Communist times only a few were able to flourish. Rohia, near Baia Mare is one of the best known. Sâmbăta de Sus is famous for its founder, Constantine Brâncoveanu, who was martyred along with his sons by the Ottoman rulers in 1714. Since communism has collapsed many new monasteries have been opened and others are being refounded in places where they once existed. Partly to support themselves and partly under western influence, they tend to be more actively engaged in society or in the church than the Moldavian monasteries, which tend to be more withdrawn. It would be false, however, to make a western-inspired distinction between 'active' and 'contemplative' monasteries as Orthodoxy knows nothing of such a distinction. The life in all monasteries seeks to achieve a balance in which the Liturgy can be properly and fully celebrated, the monks and nuns can seek God in long hours of personal prayer, and the necessary work of the monastery can be adequately done.

Of these two aspects—prayer and work—the work is the easier to describe. In places where there are large monastic farms, much time must be given to traditional farming and to dealing with the crops and animal produce.[5] Several monasteries have industries which produce income. Nuns do a great deal of weaving and embroidering of vestments and in many monasteries icon painting, both on wood and on glass, accounts for the time of several of the artistically

---

5. This need led to an amusing misunderstanding on our first visit to Agapia. At one Liturgy, immediately after a few nuns had received Communion, the abbess stepped out and harangued the assembled company. We asked our Romanian speaker what she had said. He thought she had told the nuns that more of them should go to Communion. When we asked the abbess herself we discovered that in fact she had said that far more of them should be out in the fields bringing in the harvest!

gifted members. Many of the more famous monasteries, particularly those visited by tourists, have museums, mostly of church artefacts, of which they are extremely proud. These serve to remind the visitors of the important part which the monasteries have played in creating and preserving Romanian culture.

The monasteries are centres of worship. They are looked up to by the rest of the Church because they celebrate the liturgy with greater fullness than is possible in the parishes. However, there are variations depending largely on the size, and to a lesser degree on the tradition, of the monasteries. Two monasteries—Sihăstria and Frăsinei—are famous for being Athonite in their tradition. This means they never eat meat and they celebrate the night office. In Frăsinei the monks also do not allow women even into the monastic Church. The day begins with *utrenie*, which can begin at any time between 5:00 (as at Agapia) or 8:00 as at Sihăstria, and this is followed immediately by the Eucharist. Morning worship therefore lasts at least two hours, sometimes four. In the afternoon, *vecernie* (evening prayer) begins usually around five and also lasts for about two hours. Shorter offices are sometimes recited at the beginning or end of these major offices. In some monasteries a form of compline ends the day. In others this is subsumed into the night office which can begin at midnight, or (as at Sihăstria on a Saturday) begins at 8 and continues until midnight. In the more fervent monasteries there is also constantly a monk or a nun to be found in church, praying the psalms. So they keep the command of St Paul to pray without ceasing, at least as a community, if not as individuals. Meals are provided usually just twice a day; at midday is the main meal or dinner, and a lighter meal is provided in the evening. On Mondays, Wednesdays and Fridays as well as throughout Lent and the three other great fasts of the year no dairy products are eaten. Meals, in fact, are not very communitarian. Far from all the monks or nuns attend them, either because they are working, or because they live in smaller houses and eat with their monastic family, or because they are fasting. Guests, however, are usually well fed, as it is part of the Orthodox monastic tradition to allow guests to stay free for at least three days. Generally speaking a book is read during the meal, usually the life of a saint.

It is somewhat surprising to someone used to the Western tradition of monastic life to find the apparent freedom of eastern monks to attend meals in common or not, and to attend only such parts of the liturgy as they seem to choose. Those trained In the western tradition of monastic life, where the word idiorrhythmic tends to have a pejorative connotation, find it hard to realise that all Orthodox monastic life has an idiorrhythmic character to it. In the West, common life is strongly emphasised. A monk must put his community first, must attend all offices, meals and community activities unless he has very good reason not to do so. A monk (or nun) who tries to insist on his/her own pattern of worship or life, especially if this conflicts with that generally accepted by the community (and it need not), will be thought to be 'singular', trying to get his own way, and establish his own routine as a defence against that to which God has called him. In the eastern monastic tradition idiorrhythmic life carries no such pejorative overtone. There are disagreements and variations in the traditions of whether to live in large communities or in small sketes. There are differences of opinion over the relative merits of a prayer life centred on the psalms and the common liturgy, or on the prayer of Jesus, practised usually in an eremitical, or semi-eremitical way of life. But there is a complete acceptance that each person has his own needs, since each soul is an individual soul uniquely called by God along a path which only God, ultimately, can determine. This does not, however, mean that monks and nuns are left entirely to their own devices. As we shall see elsewhere in this study, every monk and nun is obedient to a spiritual father. It is the spiritual father much more than the community as a whole, or even the abbot, who is responsible for the monk's spiritual welfare. It is the spiritual father who must determine what devotional pattern is best for each monk. The spiritual father must see to it that spiritual growth is encouraged but individual whims are not simply indulged. People are not always at the same stage in prayer. People have different natures and so will pray differently. It is surprising to us Westerners to see monks standing round outside a church when the service is taking place inside. But they are likely fingering their prayer ropes, saying the Jesus Prayer. Others are busy at their books, their 'obediences', or seeing to the crowds of visitors who come to a place like Sihăstria for confession and advice. But these same monks will very likely be awake during most of the night saying the prayers they could not say during the day.

And why do these crowds of faithful Christians gather at the monasteries? To a large extent it is the monasteries themselves that draw the people. But certain monasteries have spiritual fathers whose reputation draws pilgrims from all over the land. The best known of these spiritual guides is Fr Cleopa of Sihăstria. To his life we should now turn.

CHAPTER 3

Father Cleopa of Sihăstria

A S BEFITS A GOOD MONK, Father Cleopa's life story is quickly told. He was born in 1912 into what he describes as a truly devout Moldavian peasant family and baptised Constantine. At the age of seventeen he arrived at Sihăstria, then a small monastery of only fourteen monks, with only the abbot in priest's orders. When he arrived he was made to wait outside the monastery for three days, and told to beat a piece of wood. After the three days he was asked, 'What did the wood say?' 'Nothing', he replied. 'That is what you must be like,' he was told. He was taken into the monastery but quite soon given charge of the sheep. For several years he cared for the monastery sheep, hardly ever seeing his fellow monks, but reading the *Philokalia*. In 1942 he returned to the monastery as deputy to the ageing abbot and was ordained deacon in 1944 and priest in 1945. In these difficult years after the Second World War (1944-1949) he was abbot.

Much of the monastery had burned down towards the end of the War and he was responsible for organising its rebuilding. At the same time he demonstrated a great gift for preaching to the country people round about. His sermons were very vivid and direct. His language was entirely Moldavian (a difficulty for his translator as many of his words do not appear in Romanian dictionaries). He speaks to the conditions of a people whose background is entirely rural and whose piety is very pragmatic. His preaching led

45

to a great revival in the monastery's fortunes and the number of monks increased greatly. But his reputation for holiness brought unwelcome attention from the Communists now governing Romania. In 1948 he retired to a hut in the forest for six months to escape arrest. He returned to Sihăstria but in 1949 the Patriarch asked him to take thirty monks from his monastery and to rejuvenate the monastery of Slatina. There he remained until 1956. Persecution of the monks began again in 1952, however, and many monks and priests were arrested. Fr Cleopa and his friend Fr Arsenie Papacioc[1] were taken in for questioning. After this, on the advice of his spiritual father, the two of them went into hiding in the mountains until 1954. In 1956 he returned as spiritual father to Sihăstria, but in 1959 a final period of persecution began, during which thousands of monks and nuns were expelled from their monasteries. Again Fr Cleopa disappeared. The monastery announced that he had died. Even his mother was told that, and went into mourning. In fact, he went off into the forest, dug a cave, and lived there for several years, seen only by a couple of shepherd monks who left him food. Only in 1964, when a sudden change of policy released the monks and priests from prison, did Fr Cleopa return from his forest hideout. From that time on he was one of the greatest of the Romanian spiritual guides.

Since 1990 a number of small books by Fr Cleopa have been published and are widely on sale in Romania. Only one of these, *De Vise şi Vedenii, (Concerning Dreams and Visions)* appears actually to have been written by him. The others are edited versions of talks and sermons given to visiting pilgrims and answers to questions put to him by fellow monks, chiefly his disciple, Fr Ioanichie Bălan. The account of his teaching which follows is drawn largely from three books: *Ne Vorbeşte Părintele Cleopa*[1] *[Speak to us, Fr Cleopa], Despre Rugăciune [About Prayer]*, and *De Vise şi*

1. See below, Chapter 8.

Vedenii (Concerning Dreams and Visions). His other books, listed in the bibliography, tend either to repeat what is said in these three or, in some cases (as in *Valoarea Sufletului [Values of the Spirit]*), consist largely of straightforward Christian teaching on a wide range of subjects. He teaches with great simplicity and directness; he is much given to long lists of good and bad things, some of which appear, as we shall see, a bit haphazard and others extremely well nuanced. His teaching does not attempt to be original or speculative, but aims purely at drawing his hearers into a deeper commitment and clearer knowledge of the spiritual life open to all Christian people. His message is firmly rooted in the *Philokalia.* In fact, so firmly rooted is he that when reading him and John Climacus side by side, for instance, one can easily forget which is which. But he has his own emphasis, different, as we shall see, from that of other well-known spiritual fathers like Father Paisie Olaru,[2] Father Teofil,[3] or a handful of others.

Fr Cleopa was the original inspiration of this study. When I arrived at Sihăstria along with a young Romanian friend in September 1996, it was with a sense of pilgrimage. That sense was enhanced by the long overnight train journey with the young Andrei chattering away throughout the dark, cold hours in a grubby compartment. It was not lessened by the pouring rain which soaked us as we tramped through the monastic gates after a bus ride from Tîrgu Neamţ. The monastery was shrouded in mist, surrounded by hills. It seemed to me at that moment a vast distance from anywhere. After finding our room we asked after Fr Cleopa. He lived in a separate wing apart from the monastery and near the guest quarters. Outside his room is a covered area with benches on which the faithful gather to hear him. While we were there it poured with rain, but the

2. A much loved spiritual father at Sihăstria. See below, Chapter 8.
3. A blind monk of Sâmbătă de Sus. Since Fr Cleopa's death he is probably the best known spiritual father in Romania. See below, Chapter 4.

faithful still came and crowded into a large room. That day
Fr Cleopa had just returned from a week in hospital and
was said to be very weak. Despite this he spoke for an hour
that evening to the gathered pilgrims, as he did on each of
the following evenings. On 23 September, by arrangement,
the delightful young brother Iachint, who cared for Fr
Cleopa, took me into the Father's room. It was a big room
and Fr Cleopa was sitting on the edge of his bed, fully
dressed and reading a large book in old Romanian script.
He looked better than I expected. He had a strong voice, as
I had heard previously in the large group. I asked him the
point of the monastic life. He replied that it was to live without marriage and even more to see paradise. We may die at
any time, he said, and we must prepare for death with prayer,
fasting, and vigils. I also asked about 'dispassion' (*apatheia*).
This, he simply said, was essential to the life of a monk.
Not wishing to tire him, I asked for his blessing, which he
gave me along with some incense from Mount Athos.

Simply to meet him and to hear him speak was a privilege. He is uncompromising in his teaching and speaks—
as he writes—without sophistication, (his books bear this
out) but his words come from a great depth, an infinity, of
love. Behind this large, battered human body one senses a
great depth. His words seemed to spill over from an ex-
traordinarily large vessel overflowing with his life in God.
It is this quality of his personality which makes his teaching so effective. Throughout his teaching is a sense of striving. Life is serious; salvation is not assured. 'Keep watch!',
his constant admonition to monks, underlies most of the
following summary.

KEEP WATCH!

With such a military instruction we will not be surprised to
find that Fr Cleopa sees the soul as a kind of battleground.
It belongs to God, but devils keep invading it in the form of

evil thoughts and temptations. All sin, he tells us, begins in the imagination; hence there is a need for a constant watchfulness over the imagination. As he explains it:

> According to Saint Basil the Great the imagination is a bridge for the devil through which he enters the soul of man. Therefore great attention must be given to prayer so that nothing deludes us, for the first point of entry (vama – the customs house) which the mind meets on the way to the heart is the imagination. No evil action, no devil, no passion passes from the mind to the feelings save through the imagination. For you cannot commit a sin unless you first imagine it.[4]

Most of us, on the other hand, tend to allow our imaginations great freedom, thus giving sin a place to get a foothold. It is not that the imagination itself is evil. Cleopa sees the imagination as a holy place which belongs to God. A sinful thought has no right to be there and is nothing less than an abomination.[5] At once we are warned, however, that the spiritual life is a battle we cannot conduct alone. The patristic doctrine of *synergeia* is strong in Fr Cleopa. We must work, but God gives the victory. So he reminds us that watchfulness itself has no power without Jesus.

> Saint Maximus the Confessor says: 'A person who believes is afraid, and whoever is afraid keeps watch.' Look , a thought has come! Now we must see whether it is bad or good. What should be done? The one who keeps watch must immediately cry 'Lord Jesus. . . ,' for watchful attention con-

4. Fr Cleopa, *Ne Vorbeşte Părintele Cleopa* 1:47.
5. *Ibid.*, 48.

> sists of three things—in keeping watch over
> our minds; in setting ourselves against sin
> when it appears in the mind; and in calling
> 'Lord Jesus. . . .' Our watchfulness has no
> power without Jesus.[6]

The whole motive for watching the mind is founded on
our fear of God. If we believe in the Lord, Fr Cleopa tells
us,[7] we will properly fear the Lord, and out of that fear is
born the knowledge that we must watch over our minds.
By keeping watch over our minds, we feel immediately the
approach of a sinful thought. We have the power to resist
the approach of the devil, yet the power is not ours but
given by God.[8]

This utter dependence on God is founded on an awareness of our own weakness. Over and over again Fr Cleopa
tells his disciples not to trust in themselves. Trusting i

n self brings catastrophic falls because we cannot do anything without constant help from God.[9] Evil thoughts must
be destroyed as soon as they arise, and they are destroyed
through the Prayer of Jesus.[10] No other prayer so completely and immediately expresses our willingness to turn
to Jesus, and to ask him to have mercy on us and to drive
out the offending thought.

Fr Cleopa's development of this point shows his dependence on the patristic tradition. Taking one of the most unattractive verses in the Bible, Psalm 137:9: 'Happy shall
they be who take your little ones and dash them against the
rock!', he identifies evil thoughts as the children of the

6. *Ibid.*, 51.
7. *Ibid.*, 32.
8. *Ibid.*, 34.
9. *Ibid.*, 37.
10. *Ibid.*, 40.
11. Ps 137:8.

daughter of Babylon[11] which must be flung against the stone which is Christ[12]. Then, like the great second-century theologian Origen, he leaps in his mind from one stone to another, linking the rock which Moses struck to draw water,[13] with the Christ whom the soldier struck to draw forth water and blood,[14] and then reminds us that this indeed is the stone rejected by the builders[15] which is now the head of the corner.[16] Even while Fr Cleopa stresses over and over again the weakness of the human spirit, he stands firmly by the freedom each person has to choose good or evil.

> Scripture says 'God created man and left him in the protection of his own advice'[17]. But in the day of judgement he will ask us to give account. We will say 'I could not, Lord'. 'You did not want to. I endowed you with the ability.' For the angels cannot force a man to do good, nor can the devils force him to do evil. When Satan tempted Eve in Eden he had to use great strength to shake the thinking power of man; that is, to urge him through his thoughts to do evil. But he could not force him.[18]

Every person has the power of free choice. Even in our moments of greatest weakness or temptation we have the power to turn to and run towards Christ, to trust in him.

12. 1 Cor 10:4
13. Nm 20:11
14. Jn 19:34
15. Mt 21:42.
16. *Ne Vorbeste Părintele Cleopa*, 37, 38.
17. . . . *l-a lăsat în mâna sfătuluï.* This Romanian expression, though a somewhat free rendering of what Scripture says, is difficult to put into English, but it expresses very beautifully the sense of God's tenderness and care – as one might leave a person in the care of one's mother or someone else equally trusted.
18. Cleopa, *Ne Vorbeşte Părintele Cleopa*, 1:41.

What then are the sins we must watch out for as they seek
to take root in the mind? The first of these is the love of
self.

LOVE OF SELF

Fr Cleopa tells us [19] that 'love of self' is the mother of all
sins.[20] Love of self refers to self indulgence. A soul which
does not set a proper watch over all the thoughts of the
imagination will inevitably become self indulgent. Without watchfulness the soul easily slips into the easiest and
most comfortable course of action or inaction. In this kind
of love of self, comfort and a refusal to be disturbed are the
motivating aims of life. A person avoids any real effort,
anything that will change the undemanding tenor of his or
her Christian life. In one sense this love of self is a generalised attitude, a kind of passive state, not actively entered
into. It is a kind of unconscious laziness in one's soul which
determines the other choices one will make. This desire to
feel all is well with us and nothing needs to be changed
leads to the sins with which Fr Cleopa is most concerned:
Vainglory and Pride.

Fr Cleopa insists there is a difference between these two
greatest of sins, but is not entirely clear on what it is. We
need to turn to a second book, *De Vise si Vedenii, [About
Dreams and Visions]*, on which this chapter greatly depends.
There he describes vainglory as the daughter of pride[21],

---

19. *Ibid.*, 35.
20. Kallistos Ware, in *The Art of Prayer*, p. 24, bears witness to the same
tradition of teaching: 'Traditionally the 'passions' are classified into eight
'demons' or evil thoughts: gluttony, lust, avarice, sorrow, anger, 'accidie',
vainglory, and pride. All eight spring in the last resort from the same
root— self-love, the placing of self first, and of God and our neighbour
second; and so of the eight, perhaps pride may be regarded as the most
fundamental.
21. Fr Cleopa, *Despre Vise şi Vedenii*, p. 48.
22. *Ibid.*, 61.

but elsewhere[22] he tells us that the difference between vain-glory and pride is like the difference between youth and old age, or between grain and bread. In other words, if un-checked, vainglory grows into pride.[23] Vainglory has about it a kind of immaturity, an unconscious acceptance of one's own worth which gradually hardens into pride as one real-ises, or believes, that one's own worth is much greater than that of others. Fr Cleopa is very clear about the nature and the danger of vainglory (or vanity: *slava deşarta* can be trans-lated as either). Tackling this failing first, therefore, makes sense.

Even to speak of vanity, he says, is almost impossible, so many forms does it have. Vanity destroys everything good because a vain person is serving, not God, only himself.[24] He alludes to a passage in which John Chrysostom sees vanity as a thorn hard to pull out and as a savage beast with many heads.[25] It is, Fr Cleopa says, a terrible sin which blinds the eyes of wisdom. Vainglory manifests itself in seven offspring: 1) the praise of self; 2) double dealing, trying to convince a person of one's own superiority over others; 3) finding new ways of wickedness in order to impress oth-ers; 4) envy, covetousness; 5) lawlessness *(neînvoirea);* 6) a love of quarrelling; and 7) disobedience. Vainglory begins, in fact, in childhood and accompanies us through life, mixed up in all we do, good or bad. Vainglory can even affect us after death, he points out, if we insist on having our corpses dressed in fine clothes![26]

Vainglory plunders all the good deeds a person has done. So, he tells us, John Chrysostom called it 'the moth of the treasure from beyond the grave' and 'thief of the riches of

23. As in most of his teaching Fr Cleopa is not original. Here he is teach-ing exactly what Evagrius teaches in *Praktikos,* 13-14, Cassian in *The Insti-tutes,* Bks 11-12, and Athanasius in the *Life of Anthony,* 5-6; and all those raised in this tradition.
24. Cleopa, *Despre Vise şi Vedenii,* p. 46. He refers here specifically to John Climacus, *Ladder of Monks,* 22.2 and 22.5.
25. The Chrysostom passage has not been identified.
26. *Ibid.,* p. 50.

heaven'. One of the most dangerous aspects of vainglory is that it feeds on the good things people do and on the good desires in people's hearts. In a moving passage in which an imaginary Brother John has described to Fr Cleopa his own feeling of the emptiness and pointlessness of his life in the monastery and spoken of his longing to go out among the people, where he can truly serve them and preach the word of God, Fr Cleopa identifies this apparent good desire as vanity.

> I have told you, brother, that vanity is a very cunning passion, very deceptive and very subtle; it works in many different ways, mixing itself up with and intertwining itself with all good actions and with all the spiritual works. Through a motive which seems good to you vanity has crept into your soul and under the appearance of good wishes to drag you out into the world so that you will be a preacher, and will live without an advisor and without direction; and in time you will come to the madness of the world and the laughter and mockery of the devils.[27]

Fr Cleopa does not actually see all life outside the monastery as 'madness of the world'. His highly successful and sympathetic preaching to lay people shows a great appreciation of lay Christian life. But a monk who leaves his monastery is, in his view, abandoning the call to holiness and turning away from the God he has chosen to follow. The strategy of the devil is to get the young monk away from his spiritual father and to encourage a false sense of

27. *Ibid.*, p. 62.

his own strength, and so to lead him to depend on himself and not on his spiritual father. Such self-reliance is very dangerous:

> Self-reliance. . . is 'for a monk to go where he wants, without being under a director, without submission and without obedience.' The Holy Fathers call this self-reliance a path which takes one astray and the source of all evil.[28]

The practice of depending on a spiritual father in everything one says and does is central to overcoming the spiritual danger of self-reliance.

A similar danger attends those who find themselves much moved by dreams or by a desire for visions. Dreams can deceive a person into believing he is in some way specially favoured by God, specially gifted by God. It is vanity that seduces him into believing this may be so.[29] Another of the dangers of vanity is a paralysing fear that can make someone reluctant to do even obviously good works for fear that they will lead him to vanity. Fr Cleopa counters this fear with advice from both the Gospel and the Fathers.[30] Clearly Jesus' teaching, 'Do not display your piety before men',[31] provides the key to resolving this problem, and Maximus the Confessor follows this up with the advice that we should work our good deeds in secret.[32] Ephraim the Syrian develops it still further: 'Do good deeds in secret

---

28. Fr Cleopa, *Despre Vise şi Vedenii*, p. 62. The phrase *depinde de sine*, which we have translated as 'self-reliance', does not refer to that mature independence which is a good quality in all people, but to that arrogant confidence in self through which a person who is inexperienced in the spiritual life can easily come to harm.
29. *Ibid.*, p. 72.
30. *Ibid.*, pp. 54ff.
31. Mt 6:1.
32. Fr Cleopa provided no reference, and I have been unable to locate the passage in the works of Maximus.

and pray unceasingly in the heart'.[33] And John Climacus describes the battle that must be waged all the time: 'Be silent and love dishonour, stop all the cunning thoughts of vainglory, humble yourselves before men'.[34]

Having drawn in the witness of Gospel and Fathers, Fr Cleopa then goes on to say that obviously not all good deeds can be done in secret. Deeds will often be seen, but what really matters about them is the intention behind them.

> ...every good deed has a body and a spirit.
> The spirit is the purpose for which it is done.
> The body is the deed itself. If someone does
> a good deed, whether openly or in secret,
> with a good intention, the good deed will
> not lose its reward from God; but if some-
> one does a good deed, whether openly or
> in secret, but his motive is bad, all his la-
> bour will be wasted and instead of reward
> he will be punished.[35]

Provided a good deed is done to please God, it is even right to do it openly that others may see the glory of God. In another passage quite reminiscent of Ignatius of Loyola we are advised that, to avoid vainglory, we should desire the honour of God and the riches of heaven, not the honour and riches of this world[36]. If someone does what is right with the intention of pleasing God, the fact that people praise him for it will not lose him his reward. We see Fr Cleopa's uncompromising stance on vanity softened as he agrees with John Climacus that it is possible to begin the spiritual life with vanity but to end it well.[37] In certain circumstances vanity can even encourage us to act well, and

33. Again, the source has not been identified.
34. John Climacus, *Ladder*, 22.39.
35. Fr Cleopa, *Despre Vise și Vedenii*, pp. 57f., and Mt 5:16.
36. Cp. Ignatius of Loyola, *Exercises*, 146.
37. Climacus, *Ladder*, 22.30.

the good action can lead us to virtue and a better understanding of the will of God; this in turn leads us to root out the vanity which we have now discerned as being a major motivation for previous good deeds. The same possibility of growth into virtue cannot be accorded to pride.

In his book *Despre Vise şi Vedenii [Concerning Dreams and Visions]*, written primarily for monks, Fr Cleopa considers most directly the problem of pride when dealing with the desire of the young Brother John for visions and other great spiritual experiences. Pride, as we have seen, is vanity grown up. Vanity may be a natural human tendency, a kind of unthinking assumption that everything one says, thinks, or does is of great value to everyone else. With pride comes the conviction that one is set apart from others, that one has achieved virtue and can stand alone in one's own strength. In the Gospels Jesus criticizes the pharisees because their very virtue has led them into pride. This is the greatest temptation for a monk. He has become virtuous. He has kept the rules; he has engaged in much prayer, in impressive fasting, and in costly asceticism. He has learnt much about the ways of God and the Gospel of Christ. It is easy for him to think he is a cut above other people. Most dangerously, says Fr Cleopa, he begins to believe he can stand alone; he trusts himself. That is what Lucifer did, and he fell from heaven.

The first aspect of pride's destructive nature is that it takes good things *(bunuri)*, good qualities of a person's life, and corrupts them[38]. It is founded on our natural gifts of cleverness, beauty, or a strong and determined will; or on our acquired knowledge or wisdom; or on such purely fortuitous goods as riches and honour. Most dangerously, perhaps, it is founded on one's growth in the spiritual life. Taking pride in them corrupts our life at its source. Pride enters when a person forgets that these gifts come from God and thinks instead they are his own, or when a person

38. *Despre Vise şi Vedenii*, p. 16.

wants these gifts simply to impress others, or thinks he has gifts which he does not in fact have. These are fairly obvious manifestations of pride. Fr Cleopa identifies two other instances of pride: when a person libels others and covets their honour; and when someone speaks badly of the saints and holy fathers. Pride here is the assumption that one has a right to stand above and criticize other people, particularly saints who have clearly surpassed us in truly doing the will of God; and coveting honour is a clear indication that one believes one should have honour, and for sinful human beings to stand before an all glorious, infinite and all powerful God and think they deserve honour can only be a delusion of pride.

In Christian mythology pride is always seen as the fundamental sin of Lucifer. Fr Cleopa picks this up, quoting Isaiah 14:12ff:

> How you are fallen from heaven
> O Day Star, son of Dawn!
> How you are cut down to the ground
> you who laid the nations low. . . .

This he identifies specifically with Lucifer[39] and describes the punishment of Adam and Eve who fell into disobedience when seduced into Lucifer's pride. For them the single act of standing apart from God, trusting in their own judgement, led them into catastrophic sin. Yet still Fr Cleopa makes the further distinction that pride of the mind is worse than pride of the will, for it is the mind which should keep watch over the soul.

> Since pride of the will is more easily recognised by the mind, it will be able to recover easily, being submitted more easily to those things which had fallen. But when the mind is proud and believes firmly that its judge-

39. *Ibid.,* p. 20.

ment is better than that of others, how can
it recover itself? Not having someone to submit it to the judgement of others it does not
consider another mind better than itself.[40]

Clearly, Fr Cleopa is convinced that self reliance and a refusal to submit to others' judgement are the cause of a potentially lethal pride of the mind.

HUMILITY

The most potent antidote to pride is, of course, humility
(*smerenie,* also translated 'meekness'[41]). In his discussion
of humility Fr Cleopa makes a number of important
points[42] which give colour and attractiveness to a virtue
which most people in the modern world find hard to accept. Humility he describes as the willingness to see oneself as more sinful and unworthy than anyone else. This
has a negative tone, but its positive aspect is that we should
look, not at other people's sin, but only at our own. Regarding other people's sin easily blinds us to our own and
easily leads us into the proud delusion that we are not as
other people are'.[43] By attending to our own weakness and
our own sin, we keep firmly in our place and have no cause
for pride. So it is that Fr Cleopa describes humility as 'the
only door to the kingdom of heaven'.

40.*Despre Vise şi Vedenii,* p. 16.
41. In English the words 'humility' and 'meekness' very often have pejorative overtones and need always to be explained when used in a good context.
In Romanian the pejorative overtones are entirely lacking. Indeed, *mir,* at
the heart of *smerenie* is the Russian word for 'peace'. The word itself is used
only in a religious context and is of great importance since humility is one
of the essential qualities of the spiritual life, the virtue which, above all, the
young monk must aim to acquire.
42. *Despre Vise şi Vedenii,* pp. 23ff.
43. Lk 18:11

A more attractive description of humility is the recollection that it is the clothing of the Incarnate Son of God. Humility was that quality that made Jesus attractive to all who met him and without his willingness to 'humble himself and become obedient unto death'[44]   there could have been no Incarnation. This central Christian belief makes it clear that humility is not a virtue which human beings can create for themselves. It is, says Fr Cleopa, a gift from God which crowns all other goodness in a person. Then he makes a quick tour of Holy Scripture,[45] showing how all the patriarchs and prophets, from Abraham and Isaac (a type of Jesus, carrying the wood for his own sacrifice) through Moses, Daniel, Gideon, David, Elijah, Josiah, Isaiah to John the Baptist, had this virtue of humility. The greatest example of all is Mary. She was prophesied through all the Old Testament, she is honoured by men, by angels, and by God himself, but she was chosen to be the Mother of Christ because of her humility.

How then is humility born in the soul? It comes, Fr Cleopa teaches, from a true knowledge of the self. This is more than the awareness of one's sinfulness mentioned above. One of the deepest truths we can know is that we are created good and are loved by God; therefore we have no need of the false claims pride makes for us. Another truth, says Fr Cleopa, is that we face death and judgement, and need to prepare for this with physical effort, obedience, and a righteous heart, with disgust at our sins and a sadness over the tragic history of the world or, in a passage he quotes from Saint Isaac the Syrian, humility comes from fear of the Lord, from temptation, from a feeling one has been abandoned by God, from fighting against nature and the devil, and from much prayer.[46] As humility

---

44. Phil 2:8.
45. *Despre Vise şi Vedenii*, pp. 26ff.
46. *Despre Vise şi Vedenii*, p. 34. Here Fr Cleopa is drawing on Climacus, *Ladder* and from Isaac of Nineveh, *Sayings* 58 and 21.

is so much misunderstood today we need to explore its real meaning as it is understood by the Christian tradition.

First of all, although humility is quite definitely a gift from God, we realize that it also requires very considerable cooperation from human beings. Moreover, the description which Fr Cleopa gives of humility is so wide ranging as to cover all of Christian life. Humility is not to be found in just one area of life. We cannot, for instance, simply be humble before God. Humility is a way of understanding ourselves in relation to God in a way that affects everything we do and think and every relationship we have with others whom God has created. More specifically, humility is a product of that true knowledge of self which, we have seen already, is *needful* for every monk. He must watch, and must recognise his *need* to keep watch constantly against the evils that will enter his mind if once he gives them an opening. He must realize he is weak and easily tempted, or he will not keep proper watch. The knowledge of death and the fear of judgement are essential means of concentrating the mind on what really matters.[47] We human beings can easily be carried away with the good things happening around *us*, with *our* achievements, successes, and joys. Death and judgement remind us that these joys are transitory, and in the divine perspective may not count for very much. Physical effort reminds *us* of the need strenuously to cooperate with God.

Obedience, moreover, is characteristic of humility and cannot really exist without it. Righteousness of heart—what might be described in the western tradition as the 'ordering of affections'–means that the heart is directed truly towards God in a way that makes all other affections fall into their true place. The righteous of heart do not destroy or devalue all other things, but view them as they really

---

47. See, for instance, *Ne Vorbeşte Părintele Cleopa*, 5:60: 'The two wings which take us to heaven are fear of God and fear of death.'

are in the light of God. Fear of the Lord is a healthy quality, and, as Fr Cleopa elsewhere expands the biblical passage:

> 'The beginning of wisdom is the fear of the Lord'. That is the foundation of all good acts. Wisdom has two heads: the first is fear of God; and the higher one is love of God, so that all good deeds begin from fear of God and end in love of God.[48]

Fear then denotes that proper kind of awe which may well be combined with the deepest kind of love. Temptation too has its place, and God will allow it when it will help the spirit grow.[49] Here Fr Cleopa describes the temptations that will attack the meek as idleness, confusion of mind, a conviction of the weakness of the flesh, loss of hope, darkness of thought, the loss of human help and the loss of what the body needs. From these temptations a person gains a soul which is lonely and helpless, and a heart which is crushed until it is very meek. Then, when the faithful servant feels he or she has been abandoned by God (and this is a common experience of those who serve God most faithfully), he becomes more deeply aware of an intense need for God and a longing that he return. Fighting against nature and the devil goes together with much prayer and guards the person against the kind of complacency which leads to pride.

Humility should not be seen as a negative virtue (as Westerners now tend to see it) nor does it serve only to prevent pride. It is the royal road to salvation since it is the road that Christ took and is itself a source of great joy. In a section where Fr Cleopa quotes both from Climacus[50] and Isaac the Syrian,[51] he tells us,

48. *Ne Vorbeşte Părintele Cleopa*, 1:30
49. *Despre Vise şi Vedenii*, p. 38.
50. *Ladder*, 25 and 17.
51. *Discourse* 6, 21.

Humility is so great that alone and without any other virtue it can open the gates of the Kingdom of Heaven, as it is written 'repentance raises him who falls, tears knock on the gates of heaven, but holy humility opens them.[52] Humility. . . is the source of that complete unconcern for self *(defăimării de sine*—literally, devaluing oneself) which prevents a man from falling. Humility. . . has the power to deliver a man from the righteous scourge of God, as it is written, 'A well controlled and humble heart God will not scourge'. (Ps 50: 18)[53]

Humility, he goes on, also brings our hearts to fear God and, of all virtues, humility along with love is most pleasing to God. Humility is a precious garment for the chosen of God and humility takes our words to God and gains forgiveness for our sins. Finally, although all people are tested with temptations that often come from God or are permitted by God, the meek, because they are friends of God, will not be tempted beyond their strength[54]. And as John Climacus tells us, humility is the one good quality which the devil cannot imitate[55]. When he does attempt to ape it, as in Dickens' Uriah Heep, the spectacle is so unpleasant that people quickly realise it is not the real thing. Unfortunately, in the modern world, false humility has given true humility a bad name. True humility is immensely attractive and gives virtue warmth and humanity. One of the ways in which humility can best be achieved is through the complete revelation of all our thoughts and temptations

52. *Ladder*, 25,16
53. *Despre Vise si Vedenii*, pp. 35ff. The variation on the English version of Psalm 51 is that of the Romanian psalter.
54. 1 Cor 10:13
55. *Ladder*, 25.17.

to a spiritual father who can help us to understand where they come from. To open ourselves in this way to another human being demands courage and a very sincere desire to seek the truth. It also presupposes a relationship of trust between the spiritual child and the father. Just such a relationship is seen in *Despre Vise și Vedenii*, where a charming dialogue between Fr Cleopa and the novice John, though attending to the matter of dreams and visions, is important in demonstrating the novice's trustfulness and openness and the gentleness and patience of his spiritual father.

In this discussion Fr Cleopa makes it clear that no one should desire spiritual dreams or visions, as to do so would almost certainly be a mark of spiritual arrogance or pride, or of a desire to gain special kinds of favour. If one does receive a dream or a vision, one should be extremely suspicious of its authenticity and tend to assume that it comes from the devil and not from God. This is clearly because dreams are easily used by the devil to foster feelings of pride and self importance, and their ambiguous nature makes the dreamer or the visionary particularly susceptible to deception. It is simply not true that devils can foresee the future, but they can guess at it in an attempt to mislead.[56] However, Cleopa does admit that there can be good dreams which, as Saint Diadoche of Photike says, leave the soul peaceful, longing for what has been seen, unlike demonic fantasies which are deeply disturbing.[57] It would be simplistic here to say that good dreams make one happy, but they can leave a kind of sweet sadness and tears without pain. These dreams can give a wise person an idea about the state of his soul.[58]

56. *Despre Vise și Vedenii*, p. 126.
57. *Ibid.*, p. 122, quoting Saint Diadoche, *On Spiritual Knowledge and Discrimination: One Hundred Texts*, 37, in *The Philokalia*, Volume 1, translated by G. E. H. Palmer, Philip Sherrard and Kallistos Ware (London: Faber and Faber, 1979). Saint Ignatius makes the identical point in his 'Discernment of Spirits': 'it is by the sense of peace or of disturbance that a movement's provenance may be known': The *Spiritual Exercises*, 329, 335.
58. *Ibid.*, p. 123.

More important than this description of dreams and visions, however, is the relationship we see in the book between Fr Cleopa and his spiritual child. Brother John is earnest, naive, and enthusiastic, and he tells everything that is in his mind to Fr Cleopa. Indeed, Fr Cleopa instructs him to speak all that is in his mind, for he will be 'speaking really to God who knows all thoughts'.[59] In this he is obeying the fundamental precept of spiritual fatherhood: that the spiritual child must honestly reveal all that is in his mind, all that happens in his prayers. He must not worry about whether this is making a good impression or not. He must simply tell all. This requires a great deal of trust in his spiritual father, and in this book at least we find Fr Cleopa worthy of that trust, never becoming irritated, angry, contemptuous, or impatient. Nor does he accuse the brother of wrongdoing. He simply explains clearly what is happening so that Brother John can see the error of his ways. In Brother John, on the other hand, we see four qualities which are essential for the relationship to work: honesty, humility, trust, and a real desire to grow in the spiritual life. It is this final quality which really motivates the other three.

Although it is often the spiritual father's role to urge on a disciple to greater things, he must also restrain him when he tries to go ahead too fast, or to take on practices which, perhaps good in themselves, are not appropriate to him at this stage of his spiritual development. Fr Cleopa tells the brother that those who take on unwise devotional practices without the advice of a spiritual father often go mad. People must not take on practices beyond their strength.[60] In this context it is important that a brother should know himself, particularly his weakness and sinfulness, and not aspire through arrogance or pride to that which is beyond

59. *Despre Vise și Vedenii*, p. 78.
60. *Ibid.*, p. 82. Saint Simeon the New Theologian, himself an extremely ascetic man, rebuked a disciple whose ascetical enthusiasm, going far beyond what Simeon had sanctioned, caused his collapse.

him. He must consider his unimportance and to help him do this he must first remember that he was created from nothing and exists only because of the goodness of God. Then he must build his spirituality on this knowledge that he is made from nothing; he must remember that he is born in sin and that we are fleshly, made from semen and blood during nine months inside a woman (Fr Cleopa's earthy references help to bring overly spiritual people down with a bump!); we must know that we are never without sin before God, nor can we ever understand our sinfulness; we should discover our weakness through temptation, which God permits; we should think that at death we will leave the body which we love so much and it will become foul and stinking and that this body will return to dust; once a day we should think of what we have said and done and see how weak, foolish and sinful we have been; and we must know the many bodily and spiritual passions we experience.[61]

THE PASSIONS

This brings us to that area which every spiritual father must deal with, the passions, and the struggle to achieve *apatheia,* or dispassion. Fr Cleopa recognises that there are natural and untainted passions—passions, that is, which are natural to the human condition and whose existence does not constitute sin. These are hunger, thirst, pain, corruption *(stricăciune),* tiredness, sadness, and fear. The sinful passions, however, have at their root the love of pleasure, the love of money, and the love of glory. These he names as

> gluttony of the stomach, insatiability, pleasure *(desfătarea),* drunkenness, secret eat-

61. *Despre Vise şi Vedenii,* p. 92.

ing, love of kinds of pleasure, fornication
(*curvia*), adultery *(preacurvia)*, lust, impurity, incest, the destruction of babies, asso-
ciating with fools, desire for that which is
against nature: theft, plundering holy
things, swindling, murder, anything
physically enervating and giving in to the
desires of the body, especially when the
body is healthy. Then fortune telling, ex-
orcism, potions *(farmacele)*, love of orna-
ments, flippancy, softness, wearing make-
up, games of chance, wrongful and self-
indulgent use of things which are sweet
to the world, a life which loves the body,
which coarsens the mind making it worldly
and foolish *(dobitoceasca)* and never letting it spread out towards God, or towards
virtuous things.[62]

The fundamental cause of this is the love of self which Fr
Cleopa describes in relentless detail as

love of appearances, laziness of the will,
hardness of heart, being self-opinionated,
valuing oneself, delusions about oneself,
sparing oneself, self-advertisement, pleasing oneself, self-satisfaction, hoping in
oneself, justifying oneself, hyper-sensitiv-
ity and insensitivity towards oneself, which
is a death of the mind and a killing of the
spirit, even before the death of the body.[63]

Such a detailed and exhaustive account of the sinful passions may seem to our eyes excessive, but if they are the

62. *Despre Vise şi Vendenii,* p. 94.
63. *Despre Vise şi Vendenii,* p. 94.

reality of human life then it is important that nothing be concealed. Indeed, this love of self describes a self-focussing which prevents us from seeing anything else. A person who is so wrapped up in himself and deluded about his own importance is quite unable to attend to the movements that God may be making within him. Such a mind is turned in upon itself and is unable to grow. Nor can it admit that anything is wrong. Only when it escapes from these passions and from the self-centredness which is at their root, will the person be able to see clearly. This 'enlightenment' of clear sight is one of the aims of the spiritual life, a goal which cannot be achieved as long as we are ruled by sinful passions. As Fr Cleopa recalls John Chrysostom saying

> Let us remember our nature, let us re-
> count our sins, that we may know who
> we are and arrive at humility.[64]

This helps us, too, to understand that the enlightenment is not a kind of extra-sensory perception but is that clear-sighted vision of the truth which is the possession of someone who knows truly who he is in the sight of God. A person whose sight is clouded by passion will not see God. These are the spiritual passions which are 'the fruit of our destructive and changeable nature: forgetfulness, unconcern and ignorance'.[65] In one of those lists which are a distinctive mark of his style, Fr Cleopa continues:

> But when the eye of the soul, that is the
> mind, is darkened by this, then it is taken
> captive by all the other passions, which are:
> impiety, distorted belief – that is heresy –
> blasphemy, haste, anger, bitterness, vio-
> lent conceit, hatred of men, remembering

---

64. *Despre Vise şi Vendenii*, p. 95. I have been unable to locate the Chrysostom reference.
65. *Despre Vise şi Vendenii*, p. 95.

evil, speaking of evil, being judgemental, sadness without cause, fear, cowardice, quarrelsomeness, rivalries, jealousy, vanity, pride, double-dealing, deceit, unbelief, meanness, love of material things, a desire for what is earthly, laziness, smallness of spirit, dissatisfaction, grumbling, cockiness, being self-opinionated, arrogance, being over-bearing, love of domination, wishing to please men, sinning, shamelessness, insensitivity, flattery, fraudulence, irony, duplicity, allowing the passionate sins of the spirit and thinking about them, about which I have said above that it is the mother and root of all evil.[66]

The holy fathers, says Fr Cleopa, describe the passions with which we fight as 'demons'. These demons remain in a person even after baptism, not in the heart but deep within the body. Only by calling on God and Christ can we drive the demons out of ourselves and to do this we need the four virtues of meekness, absolute attentiveness, resistance, and prayer. Resistance should take the form of good deeds—not really actions but attitudes of belief, gratitude, and discernment[67]. But passions themselves are overcome only through much prayer.

PRAYER

Sihăstria, where Fr Cleopa lived through much of his long monastic life, is a place of prayer. This does not mean it is a place of peace. The monks know that in coming to this place they will have to engage in warfare with the devil and

66. *Despre Vise şi Vendenii,* p. 95.
67. *Despre Vise şi Vendenii,* pp. 98ff.

all his works. Their first task is to learn to pray, to strip themselves of all the selfishness, the self-centred passion, the concern with the flesh and its comfort which prevents them from being raised up to God. It sounds self-centred to someone who does not understand the monastic life. It sounds as if they are concerned simply with nurturing their own souls and preparing for themselves a cosy place in the kingdom of heaven. This is very far from the truth. The rest of the Church sees prayer as their work and one frequently finds people saying specifically that monks should not work outside their monasteries. Their place is in the monastery, praying.

Praying for the world does not simply mean that monks are praying with lists of names, causes, or places in mind. Intercession is more than, though it includes, this. At Sihastria it is impressive to see monks always in church, working through piles of paper on which people have written˘ requests for prayer. They themselves say that behind this ministry of intercession there is the never-ending engagement in warfare for possession of one's own soul, to take it finally out of the devil's clutches and deliver it into the hands of God. This is what gives Sihastria its deep sense of purpose, the sense of busyness, of a kind of humming going on all around all the time. It also contributes to a certain sense of anxiety among the young as they strive to maintain an unfamiliar level of prayer.

The actual ways these monks pray, as we have seen, are usually quite simple to describe. Young monks are expected to read the Scriptures constantly and, in particular, to recite the psalms. This is an activity which must fill every free moment of the day so that the mind is saturated in Scripture and so that the words of the psalms become the words of one's own prayer. Most monks will continue the reading of Scripture all their lives. They will also take on a longer and longer recitation of the Jesus Prayer. The sheer simplicity of the words of this prayer—'Lord Jesus Christ, Son of God, have mercy on me a sinner'—conceals an inexhaustible depth of theology and largeness of meditation on the mystery of God's relationship with man.

Interspersed with this scriptural repetition are the prostrations, the fastings, the sleep-denying vigils by which the body is brought under control. Prayer is not simply an activity of the mind. That, indeed, is only the first stage of prayer. Prayer involves the whole body, and moves from the mind into the heart, where Christ engages the affections. It is in the heart that the real battle between God and the devil takes place, and it is here that the Christian must bear constantly in mind the injunction to 'Keep watch'. Watching always over the mind, examining every thought and every feeling as it enters the consciousness, is an essential part of this struggle to escape from the worldly life into the life intended for us by God. Fr Cleopa, and Eastern monks in general, easily slip into a language which suggests that the world is of its very nature evil. In this they follow the Gospel of John. A monk comes into the monastery to escape from the world and anything that turns his attention back to the world is a distraction from his real vocation to attend to God. In practice this dualism breaks down. Fr Cleopa himself was very understanding of the problems people faced in living as Christians in the world and gave them good, realistic advice. Monks themselves relate constantly to people 'in the world' and themselves run quite successful enterprises for their monastery or for the Church. To some extent the language of 'the world', as opposed to 'the monastery', is part of monastic rhetoric— which is not to deny that a real break between world and monastery is inherent in the monastic life and expected of monks.

Father Cleopa was, in the truest sense of the hackneyed phrase, a man of prayer. He was a person who had so devoted himself to praying that his life became one almost continuous prayer, and into this prayer he took all those who came to him; and through that prayer they felt blessed. And yet his prayer was always rooted in human life. He exemplified the truth that prayer should never appear to be an escape from human life. Prayer and action are indissolubly joined. 'Prayer is the mother of all good deeds,' he said, 'since it is prayer that brings love into our souls.'[68]

Fr Cleopa's teaching can sound harsh sometimes, and his prayer can seem based on the endless repetition of formulas. Yet in his teaching he constantly returns to the need for love. People will not do good deeds unless they love. It is as simple as that. Love is not a human quality. It is a gift from God. By engaging in fervent prayer to God we make it possible for God's love to enter our souls and to become the motivation for any good deeds we do. Good deeds themselves have a place in our movement towards God. They are not simply a fruit of it: 'All good deeds bring a man near to God, but prayer unites them.'[69]

There is a sense here that good deeds are isolated, relatively meaningless, acts which need to be gathered up into the prayer which gives them significance before God. This could be seen as a part of that larger process in which a fragmented, sinful world is drawn together into wholeness as it is taken up into Christ to be offered to God.

Another aspect of prayer which Fr Cleopa deals with is forgiveness. Behind a simple injunction can be seen a real theology of forgiveness: 'Pray for those who hurt us, that they will do good, and that we will recognise that we ourselves are sinners.'[70]

Forgiveness can be seen as more than a kind of forgetting that wrong has been done. Forgiveness grows into a real concern for the welfare of the person who has done wrong. We do not seek punishment or revenge. We do not simply remain unconcerned about the other person. He too is a child of God in need of salvation. We must be concerned for him, long for his redemption, and pray that he will do good, not just so that the kind of damage he may

68. *Despre Rugăciunea*, p. 62.
69. *Despre Rugăciunea*, p. 64.
70. *Despre Rugăciunea*, p. 63.

be accustomed to inflicting on those around him may cease, but that he himself may be saved. At the same time we cannot forgive unless we acknowledge that we ourselves share in his condition of sin. If we do not do that, we shall be forgiving from a sense of superiority and pride. Our forgiveness will itself be an act by which we set ourselves above the other person. As Christ himself became one with humankind in order to lead us to forgiveness, so we can only truly forgive if we enter into the other's sinfulness and, as a fellow sinner, seek to lead him to God.

As with most writers on prayer, Cleopa sees the journey as one that passes up a ladder towards God. At the bottom of the ladder (though not in itself despicable because of that) is prayer of the *lips*. From prayer of the lips one moves to prayer of the *mind*.[71] This is simply prayer prayed with some degree of understanding. 'If I pray set prayers with understanding I am now praying the prayer of the mind.'[72]

Once prayer has risen to the mind it has entered the soul, for, as Cleopa is able to tell us on the authority of John of Damascus, 'the soul has two ruling parts, the mind and the heart'.[73] The heart here represents the feelings, and the aim of prayer in the Palamite tradition of Orthodoxy is to achieve prayer of the heart, prayer in which the deepest parts of the personality are affectively directed towards God. Cleopa in no sense denigrates the mind. Both mind and heart are necessary to prayer. Although, as we have seen, he is concerned that prayer should leave 'the passions' behind, these are the sinful passions, not the feelings and affections which give life and meaning to our relationship with God and the world. At the same time, by putting the prayer of the heart above that of the mind he does not discount the importance of mind, intelligence, rationality, and learning. He simply puts it in its place. One does not need

71. *Despre Rugăciunea*, p. 65.
72. *Ibid.*, p. 66.
73. *Ibid.*, p. 66. I have been unable to locate the John of Damascus reference.

to be a learned academic to enter into the deepest kind of prayer with God. The simplest, uneducated person can do that. But an academic does not have to abandon his learning to come to God. His learning will lead him to a deeper and richer understanding of what he is praying, though it must not prevent him entering into the larger area of the affections where the whole soul begins to engage with God. For, as Fr Cleopa tells us,[74] prayer of the mind is 'a bird with one wing' until it moves into the feelings of the heart.

Prayer does not stop here. It does, however, change character. Up to this point prayer may be considered part of the natural world—the lips, the understanding, and the feelings through which God has made it possible for human beings to reach out to him and to join with him in real communication and a sharing in divine nature. Beyond that we enter into the realms of the more extraordinary, or ecstatic, prayer which is a special gift to the specially chosen servants of God. Cleopa identifies four stages in these further reaches of prayer:

First, there is the prayer which is automatic and goes on without words. This he describes as *de sine mişcatoare*, self-moving prayer.[75]

Second, there is a visionary prayer *(rugaciune cea văsătoare)* in which the person praying is able to see angels, demons, thoughts and the inmost hearts of those around him because his mind is utterly clean. Although it is clear that most of the great spiritual fathers have this gift, and indeed need it for really effective spiritual direction, Fr Cleopa hardly ever describes his own experiences of this nature, and in another book *(Despre Vise şi Vedenii)* makes it clear that this kind of experience should never be desired, because the possibilities of being deluded and led astray are very great.

74. *Ibid.*, p. 67.
75. *Ibid.*

Thirdly, the soul may be led into ecstatic prayer where the person at prayer is taken to heaven and seems to be on fire. One of the most famous examples in recent Orthodox tradition of such prayer is Saint Seraphim of Sarov, whom a young man, Motovilov, saw so on fire with the light of the Holy Spirit that he could not bear to look at him.[76] Finally, there is the spiritual prayer where the soul actually participates in heaven.[77] This, Fr Cleopa says, is beyond the real boundaries of prayer.

In his writings, which are mostly culled from his talks, Fr Cleopa does not expound to any great degree the nature of these levels of prayer which go beyond the prayer of the heart. This is not at all surprising, partly because of the ineffable nature of such prayer, partly out of a natural humility which lacks the more scholarly person's habit of reducing all knowledge to writing, and also because almost all his speaking was directed towards those who had never experienced this intense prayer. He would not have wished to suggest that this prayer is necessary to salvation. Nor is it something to aim at, as it is purely a gift from God. Instead, having briefly described this intensity of prayer, he returns to that to which all Christians can aspire, the prayer of the heart.

The heart, he tells us, is 'the inner room of the mind, into which one must go to pray'.[78] Two obstacles, however, prevent the thoughts of the mind from reaching the heart. These are imagination and reason[79]. Neither of them is wicked in itself, but they contain the potentiality of great temptations. Sin, as he tells us elsewhere,[80] begins in the imagination. This is why the imagination must be so carefully watched. And reason, though a necessary part of the

76. Zander, p. 90.
77. *Despre Rugăciunea*, p. 69.
78. *Despre Rugăciunea*, 72.
79. *Despre Rugăciunea*, 73.
80. *Ne Vorbeşte Părintele Cleopa*, 1:47.

human personality and itself a gift from God, can also give rise to pride, and the deluded rationality can refuse to give way to the affections which alone can lead us into the love of God. In a later book he speaks at greater length of this movement into the heart:

> When we go with our mind into our heart we must close three doors: the visible door of our cell, against men; the door of our lips so as not to speak with anyone; and the door of our heart against devils, placing the mind as a porter to the heart. When someone prays from the heart he is filled with love of God and wants no more than to remain thus for ever, as Peter wished to remain on Mount Tabor. The mind in the time of prayer ought to be blind, deaf and dumb so as not to see, to hear or to speak anything with anyone except Christ. Then the mind is taken by the Holy Spirit and given other short words of prayer.[81]

Taking the mind into the heart is a way quite commonly used to describe a stage of prayer in which prayer involves not just of the mind, the will, or the feelings, but the whole person. Fr Cleopa describes this quite vividly:

> The union of the mind with the heart consists of a union of spiritual thoughts of the mind with the spiritual feelings of the heart. The heart closes and opens with great difficulty. Then the heart swallows Jesus and Jesus swallows the heart. Then a prayer is conceived which is fire in the heart, without distraction and fantasies. Then a spiritual union is accomplished between

81. *Ne Vorbeşte Părintele Cleopa*, 5:78.

Bridegroom and Bride, between Christ and
the heart. Then indeed Christ stays with us
in the mansion of our heart and the devil
can no more overcome us.[82]

In seeking the prayer of the heart one should not worry
about techniques. Beginners on the road to prayer often
fret about whether they are using the right forms or adopt-
ing the right postures. Fr Cleopa firmly tells us, 'God wor-
ries about the position not of the body, but of the mind and
the heart'.[83] Likewise, in prayer one should avoid ponder-
ing theology or reflecting on Scripture. These are common temptations which the devil uses to distract us from
entering into real prayer.[84] Prayer burns the devil, says Fr
Cleopa in this context, so it is not surprising the devil wishes
to distract us from it.

By contrast with the scorching heat which prayer inflicts
on the devil, the soul will find that as the mind enters the
heart 'it is united with Christ in a spreading warmth that
brings tears of repentance. Repentance ("crushing of the
heart") is the foundation experience of prayer.'[85] In common with most masters of prayer in East and West, Fr Cleopa
invites us into experiences which seem to offend against
the natural human desires—experiences of weakness, help-
lessness, blindness, and the crushing of the heart. Only in
this way can we discover the love of God:

Go into the heart, blind, deaf, and mute,
and seek God in the only place he can be
found. What we find there is love, for grace
leads us in prayer like a mother teaching a
child to walk.[86]

82. *Ne Vorbeşte Părintele Cleopa*, 5:77.
83. *Despre Rugăciunea*, p. 74.
84. *Despre Rugăciunea*, p. 75.
85. *Despre Rugăciunea*, p. 77.
86. *Despre Rugăciunea*, p. 84.

Once we have experienced this love we will find that it is all embracing and can be recognised by its infinite longing for God and for all those others whom God also loves. This love is no longer a love coming from within ourselves; it is participation in the love of God:

> The signs that we have reached this highest form of prayer are: a great warmth in the heart, a constant longing and desire for God, an unspoken love for all men and for all creation, an ineffable spiritual joy, weeping for joy and a deep source of tears, of humility and a fearlessness of death.[87]

Prayer is a gift from God and the experiences which accompany prayer are themselves a part of the 'longing and desire for God'[88] which is characteristic of authentic prayer. What one meets in Fr Cleopa is not an excitingly new teacher on prayer, but simply a man whose years of commitment to God have brought him into very close touch with God. People came to Fr Cleopa in great numbers because they found that in him they met God. His advice, his instructions, his very presence had about it the mark of God. Even when he gave tough advice they felt invigorated and encouraged by him and clearer in their perception of the centrality of God in human affairs.

A HUMAN TOUCH

Like many people with a reputation for sanctity Father Cleopa has acquired legendary status. Stories, sayings and memories of him abound. People speak about his simplicity and the robust nature of his devotion, and if they seem

87. *Ne Vorbeşte Părintele Cleopa*, 5:61.
88. Ps 34:2.

to make of him something of a modern desert father, that in itself is his significance in today's church. His is a voice through which tradition speaks loudly, calling the Church back to faithfulness, away from the glittering attractions that threaten to seduce it into a world that has forgotten God. He has the same simplicity and utter radicality that makes the desert fathers both disturbing and attractive to Christians whose minds are tired of the subtleties and complexities of modern thought.

He had a great devotion to Mary, the Mother of God. It is easy for a westerner not to appreciate just how large a part Mary plays in the life of an Orthodox Christian, particularly of a monk. We may be a little taken aback to hear him say:

> Do you know who the Mother of God is? She is the Empress of the cherubim, the Empress of all creatures, bodily larder or pantry of God the Word, the door of light through which the perfect light came into the world. She is the door of life through which Christ our life entered into the world. She is the locked gate through which no one has passed except the Lord.[89]

His profound theology of a simple marian icon is perhaps easier to understand.

> When you see the icon of the Mother of God with the child Jesus in her arms, do you know what you see? Heaven and earth! The heaven is Christ, who is far beyond heaven; the creator of heaven and earth. But the Mother of God represents earth,

89. Bălan, *Viaţa Părintelvi Cleopa*, p. 175.

that is, all the peoples on the face of the
earth, as she is one of us.[90]

And he is one with the patristic tradition in loving to dwell
on the paradox of heaven held within the arms of a human
mother:

> The arms of the Mother God are much
> stronger than the shoulders of the cheru-
> bim and of the most blessed thrones. For
> whom does the Virgin Mary hold in her
> arms? Do you know? She holds him who
> has made heaven and earth and all things
> visible and invisible.[91]

Even when, although rarely, Fr Cleopa spoke about the
attacks made on him by the communists, what mattered to
him was the response God made to his prayer:

> Once I was arrested by the Security Police
> at Slatina monastery and was taken to
> Fălticeni. There I was beaten and thrown
> into a cellar in which hundreds of lights
> were burning. Everyone who entered there
> went out nearly mad. They threw me in so
> that I would lose my mind. I could not see
> with my eyes and I was helpless on account
> of the heat. Then I took my mind down
> into my heart with the Prayer of Jesus. Af-
> ter an hour they brought me out and they
> were all amazed that I could still speak and
> walk without anyone holding me up.[92]

Most of what has been recorded in print about Fr Cleopa is
his rather formal 'spiritual' teaching. In fact, he clearly ar-

90. *Ibid.*, p. 176.
91. *Ibid.*, p. 176.
92. *Ibid.*, p. 211.

ticulated much more than spiritual teaching and it was through his ability as a story teller that he caught people's attention. As one witness affirmed:

> You never got tired of listening to Fr Cleopa. Whatever he said was interesting. Stories from his childhood, about life in the monastery, about when he was being persecuted, or arrested, when he fled to the forest, or again in the service of the people, about his journey to Jerusalem, to the Holy Mountain and many other anecdotes. Often those who were listening wept. Sometimes even he wept. Everyone was spiritually moved, not only because of what he said, but primarily because of the gift of God which was in him. For simply his presence, through the Holy Spirit in him, changed people's hearts.[93]

Orthodox people love to be certain that their spiritual father is truly inspired by the Spirit. And one way by which this inspiration is made manifest is the father's knowledge of something which he could not possibly have known by ordinary means. Three little accounts are typical of many that have been recorded about Father Cleopa's demonstrating this kind of supernatural knowledge.

> When Fr Cleopa was speaking he spoke under the inspiration of the Holy Spirit. Once in a room full of the faithful he began to speak of something quite unconnected with what he had been talking about. It was something which did not concern the people. But at the end a woman came to him in tears and said 'Forgive me, Father,

93. *Ibid.*, p. 212.

for I am a sinner!' He had spoken for this woman.[94]

A brother, seeing Fr Cleopa sitting on the verandah, went up to him, kissed his hand, and asked for a blessing. But he did not disclose to him that he was battling with evil thoughts in his heart. The Father, looking into his face said: 'Brother, go to your spiritual father, confess yourself clean and ask for a penance that will deliver you from the unclean thoughts which are possessing you'.[95]

Two young people got married and had children, not knowing that they were related by blood. Their priest advised them to confess to a bishop and to follow his advice. Meanwhile the husband had been advised to ask the advice of Archmandrite Cleopa, whom he did not yet know. When he came to him he could not get near [him] as Fr Cleopa was surrounded as usual by many of the faithful. Therefore he waited his turn. Suddenly Fr Cleopa called him saying, 'Antony, come to me'. He thought he was calling someone else, and did not go. After a little while he called again 'Antony, come to me!' But not realising that he was calling him, again he did not go. Then Fr Cleopa looked directly at him, beckoned with his finger and said, 'You, over there, Antony, come to me!' Seized with fear, Antony said to himself, 'How does the Father know this when he has never seen me?' Then he went to the elder, who talked

93. *Ibid.*, p. 212.
94. *Ibid.*, p. 212.
95. *Ibid.*, p. 202.

with him for a long time and sent him away in peace.[96]

Young Brother Iachint, who looked after Fr Cleopa in his last years of illness gives a rather surprising testimony to his own agnosticism in the presence of the Father's gift of seeing more than was visible to others.

> I believe that Fr Cleopa was able to see with the Spirit. For he told me many things when he was alive and I did not believe them, but they turned out as the Father said they would. I believe that the Father used to see into my heart and would tell me what was of use to me. Then I did not believe. But it would have been better to have listened with more attention and belief. For he loved me and gave me what was useful for salvation. I believe that Fr Cleopa is a saint. I feel his help. I feel that he is with me. Thinking of him gives me peace, stillness, joy and hope that he is praying for me.[97]

Brother Iachint's testimony is more moving since it shows how his own love has been touched by Fr Cleopa's love and care of a young monk, in the midst of all his greatness. Earlier in this chapter we saw how gentle Fr Cleopa was with a novice whose enthusiasms were leading him astray. He could also be sharp when he encountered spiritual arrogance, which could be of great danger to the foolish enthusiasts:

> A young brother came, after only a few months in the monastery, and said: 'Father,

96. *Ibid.*, p. 201.
97. *Ibid.*, p. 213.

> I have a great hatred for devils. Give me
> permission to read the Prayer Book of Saint
> Basil the Great!' Fr Cleopa said 'You, too?
> Poor you! You hate devils? You will see how
> much hatred they have for you. Run away
> from here; don't do any such thing. . . . Lis-
> ten, just the other day he came into the
> monastery and now he wishes to curse the
> devil and to read the Prayer Book of Saint
> Basil the Great. Great hero!'[98]

Almost without exception, saintly people have no feeling of being holy. Generally speaking, they are aware only of their great failings. Once when a person came to him asking to see Fr Cleopa he simply directed him to a nearby field. There stood a donkey. On another occasion, while he was sitting on the verandah he looked straight at his disciple and said sincerely and clearly: 'I don't know why so many people seek me, a rotten old man.'

Although he had had little formal education Fr Cleopa was known for his intimate knowledge of the spiritual writings of the Orthodox tradition. This was the fruit of his years in the forest and with the sheep.

> Fr Cleopa often said, 'My boys, don't stand
> around doing nothing, wasting time. Take
> a book in your bag wherever you go, with
> the sheep or with the cows, or wherever
> you are sent, and read the word of God.'[99]

As we shall see over and over again in this study, a spiritual father's advice is not usually very complicated. Spiritual fathers trust the effectiveness of the simple christian life, lived with growing faithfulness and commitment. Typical

98. *Ibid.,* p. 205.
99. *Ibid.,* p. 194.

of this was Fr Cleopa's response to a brother who asked him, 'What shall I do to be saved, Fr Cleopa?' He replied, 'Listen, brother. You know how to pray, you know about going to church, you know about fasting, you know about being merciful, you know all the commandments of God. Want only to do them, for otherwise you cannot be saved.'[100]

Fr Cleopa took the Christian life very seriously and had an all pervading view of the tragic quality of human life, the urgent need for repentance, the catastrophic consequences of sin. Yet he had also a franciscan love for the world which, despite everything, remains good. Above all he loved birds:

> He often spoke of the 'youngsters of the forest', of owls, of pelicans, and other kinds of birds, showing us how they sang and what sort of voice each one had, delighting our hearts. Father used to tell us, 'Oh, what great joy I had when I received communion the first time in my hermitage, as a flock of birds came and sang so beautifully to me. . . !' And Father, when he could, lovingly fed the birds of heaven. This love never failed, for only two years before his death, after he had received communion in the church and was going back to his cell accompanied by two fathers, a flock of little birds came which twittered and settled on his shoulders, his head, his hands, and pecked at his beard and cassock without touching the other two monks. Then they flew into a fir tree and began to sing. Fr Cleopa sighed and said, 'How I would love to live once again with the birds in the forest!'[101]

100. *Ibid.*, p. 192
101. *Ibid.*, p. 211.

From the description of his last days in Ioanichie Bălan's *Life of Father Cleopa* it seems that Father Cleopa died as he had lived, surrounded by the faithful. In his last years he was often ill and had several spells in hospital, yet he kept returning to the crowds who waited for him at Sihăstria. Towards the end of November 1998, it was clear he was failing. Bălan tells us that on 29 November a young monk who had just entered the monastery came to him for a blessing and was told, 'From now on you have no father, or mother, or brothers, or relations, or fellow countrymen, or house. Nothing at all! Only Christ.' On Saint Andrew's Day he was able to sit with the crowds of visitors and give advice to them. On December first, he was found in the afternoon saying the prayers for the next morning. His disciples said, 'Father, it is evening and you are saying tomorrow morning's prayers'. He replied, 'I am saying them now because tomorrow I will go to my brothers.' His two brothers had died as monks sixty years earlier. Bălan remarks, 'The disciples received this, as usual, with disbelief.' That evening he went to bed quite late, 'showing signs of great tiredness. At 2.20 on Wednesday morning his disciple heard the father breathe more slowly. When he came to him, Father Cleopa sighed deeply and gave his soul into the hands of Christ.'[102]

---

102. Bălan, *Viaţa Părintelui Cleopa*, p. 168.

CHAPTER 4

Monasteries & the People of God

'What did you come into the wilderness to see?' (*Mt* 11:7)

WHEN JOHN THE BAPTIST PREACHED on the banks of the Jordan thousands of people came out of their homes in Jerusalem to hear him. What brought them? He was a challenging preacher who spoke brutally to them of their failings and deceits, but at the same time he showed them something of the salvation God offers. He exposed the emptiness of their lives and made them long for something more. This is often the response to a radical preaching of the Gospel. Monastic life does not aim at preaching the Gospel. It is directed primarily towards the praise and worship of God and the salvation of the monk's soul. To modern Western Christians this can seem a self-centred aim. In fact, praise and worship of God is the very opposite of self centredness. Saint Ignatius of Loyola begins his *Spiritual Exercises* by writing, 'Man is created to praise, reverence and serve God our Lord, and by this means to save his soul',[1] and these *Exercises* were the foundation of one of the greatest missionary orders the world has known. The goal of saving our souls puts us into a relationship with God which makes it possible for God to do far more for other people in this world than we could ever do if we made that our primary aim. By its living commitment to

1. *The Spiritual Exercises*, 23.

Christ, monastic life preaches the Gospel and does so in a form which people outside the monastery find intriguing. In Romania, as in most Orthodox countries, people come in great crowds to the monasteries. This is a particular feature of the great feasts and fasts of the Church, but is true at other times as well. What is it that they come to see? In some respects it is the attraction which John the Baptist had—the sheer otherness of his life exposing the futility of their own lives and calling them to a greater devotion to God. In other respects monastic life can be seen to be a thoroughly normal part of Romanian church life. It is integrated into the life of the parishes and monks have a respected place within the community. Even those who do not often visit a monastery express deep appreciation that the monasteries exist, convinced of their importance in the life of the Church.

Knowing this, we should not be surprised then that the first reason which people gave for their appreciation of the monastic way of life was the quality, quantity and intensity of the prayer. Laura Maruşter, a young computer science teacher in Timişoara, put it simply:

> Monks in a monastery pray and think about God and their life is dedicated to God. They pray for people who are in the world. People in the world do not have time to pray like this. People from the world come to the monks for advice and confession. There is a difference between parish priests and monk priests. That does not mean one is better than the other.[2]

2. Unless otherwise stated, all quotations come from interviews I conducted or from written responses made to a questionnaire which I gave to a few theological students. Most responses were in Romanian and were translated either by my assistants or by me. Most of the interviews took place in April 1997, a few in 1996 and 1998. Here they are identified only by their date and sometimes the place of the interview.

Three important points emerge from this testimony. The first is the perception of the vicarious nature of the monk's life. Not only do monks pray for the people in the world; that is simply intercession. They also pray on their behalf. They offer the praise and worship of God which other people would like to give but have not the time or the skill to do. This is, at least partly, the reason why most people were clear that it was a monk's job to pray and not to get involved in other more apparently useful activities which would take him away from his central vocation so important to their own lives.

The second point, which will be treated at much greater length below, is the expertise monastic counsellors are thought to have at least in the area of confession and direction of one's spiritual life. This leads on to the third point, the difference between married parish priests and celibate monk priests. Can there be distinction in role without difference in quality? Later we shall see some disagreement here. Most of the great spiritual fathers were monks—but not all. Some people do prefer to go to monks for important occasions, while others are insistent that married priests are better for them. The responses below may show that no distinction of quality can be drawn.

Fr Ioanin Chilan, a young priest in Ploiesti, expresses his appreciation of the monastic life very strongly in these words:

> In monasteries they have their *pravila*.
> Monks don't eat meat. They fast and pray
> continuously. It is very important that they
> keep this practice. Perhaps the world is kept
> alive by the monasteries. Although away
> from this world, they keep this world alive.
> Their prayer, their life, makes God look at
> us with understanding.

The *pravila* is the monk's personal rule of devotion and ascetical discipline. It covers the whole of his life and is given to him by his spiritual father. Prayers, fastings, vigils, devotional reading and his work are all included in it. All devout Orthodox Christians aspire to share in these ascetical disciplines. For them these have a sacramental quality which recognises that spiritual life is lived out in a material world and therefore includes every aspect of life, material as well as spiritual. It is the monk's special responsibility to live this sacramental life more fully than others can do; in this way the monks enable the sacramentalising of the whole world as they draw all parts of the world around them into their life with God.

Another young Orthodox layman, Constantine Fageţan lives a remarkable, quasi-eremitical life in a housing estate in Timişoara. He attaches the same kind of critical importance to monastic life:

> The difference of prayer in monasticism is
> simply its quality and intensity. Monastic life
> is the heart of the Church. It preserves the
> real tradition. Christianity might have dis-
> appeared without it.

His last remark refers to the gratitude people feel towards the monks for their uncompromising stance during the communist decades. Hundreds of monks were imprisoned. Many were tortured and killed. Thousands of monks and nuns were expelled from their monasteries, but few compromises were made. While lay people and parish priests could be more easily intimidated on account of their family responsibilities and vocational vulnerability, the monks were in a stronger position to maintain the life of corporate prayer on which the whole Christian Church at that time depended.

A student from Sibiu evidently sees this role of monastic life extending beyond the times of external persecution to the very nature of the warfare which is waged continually between the forces of evil and the forces of God:

> Without monastic life there would be an
> apocalypse. Monastic life stands between
> earth and the wrath of God.

Anişoara Carol takes up an aspect which is widely spoken of; the fact that the monks simply do pray more than other people and fulfil all the liturgical offices which others cannot:

> In the monasteries there is more prayer because the monasteries are founded precisely for that, so that those who are in them will pray more. Services are longer; Lauds and the midnight offices are prayed, which cannot be done in a parish.

It is not simply the quantity of liturgical prayer offered which counts. Orthodox people see the whole liturgy as having about it an integrity and a beauty which reveals the beauty of God and enables the salvation of man. It is therefore of more than sentimental or aesthetic importance that the whole liturgy should be celebrated wherever possible and in the fullest manner possible. Monastic liturgical prayer constitutes a kind of ideal form to which the prayer of the rest of the church can aspire and without which it might collapse. This quantitative aspect of monastic prayer was important also in Saint Andrew's parish in Ploieşti, where the congregation as a whole spoke of the value of the continuous prayer of the monasteries. This is even more striking in that this is one of the few parishes where the midnight service is offered two or three times a week, and is well attended.

What matters, however, is not, the sheer quantity of prayer but the quality of self-giving which the monastic life requires. It is this which should ensure that the monk's personal contribution to the prayer of his monastery is most effective That this self-giving is what gives value to the monk's personal contribution to the prayer of his monastery is reflected in the comment of Patriarch Teoctist, who commented:

> The monastery is made up of people who are specially committed to prayer, contem-

plation and the purest form of life—that is
the life summed up by the vows. In the
monastic life the Orthodox Church has a
spiritual elite.

Bishop Laurentius Streza extended this appreciation:
The person who devotes himself entirely to
God is able to fulfil all his commands. He
can pray more and love more for the world
and become an example in whom people can
see goodness, wisdom and gentleness.

Of course Bishop Streza would not think that a monk
automatically becomes such a paradigm. There is a clear
recognition that it is not the sheer quantity of prayer, or the
participation in the monastic life which achieves this sanctification, but the giving over of the heart and the will to
God. So Fr Cleopa adds to this:
A person who does good deeds, even if he
does miracles and speaks with angels, does
not achieve the heights of the monastic life
of silence, obedience, and poverty, for the
love of Christ. . . . Monks, by abandoning
themselves and renouncing their own wills,
bring themselves as a complete sacrifice with
all their being, that is with body and soul, in
the service of God forcing themselves, of their
own free will to take up the Cross of Christ
and to follow him.[3]

In the end what is important is that the monk should become more and more a person through whom God can
reveal himself and through whom others can feel they participate in the grace and power of God. It is this element
which Fr Marius Ioana, a student chaplain in Timişoara,

3. *Despre Vise şi Vedenii*, p. 68.

bore witness to when he spoke of his appreciation for monastic life.

> The light of the world is the monks. The light
> of the monks is the angels. The light of the
> angels is God. The monks succeed in set-
> ting themselves free from temptation and
> help us to pray. I feel the prayer of my spir-
> itual father in a very practical way, and he is
> a hermit.

Orthodox Christians regard the monks as standing between heaven and earth, reflecting the light of heaven down to the people in the world and drawing the people towards God. Fr Marius is standing in the ancient tradition exemplified by Theodore the Studite who considers monastic life to be the 'third grace':

> . . . understood as celestial life, as the de-
> scent to earth of the angelic world, as the
> attainment and realization in history of what
> by its very essence lies beyond the confines
> of history.[4]

At the same time, Fr Marius points to the aspect which is most appreciated in all the best spiritual fathers: that their prayers support their disciples in their daily lives. This is not a casual kind of support. We shall see again later that a spiritual father has a responsibility to see that his disciple attains salvation. His prayer plays a crucial role in his disciple's growing sanctification.

With such high regard for monastic life so widespread, parish life and parish priests might easily be thought to be secondary in their importance or in the quality of their Christian lives. Some Romanians I talked with were critical

4. As cited by Archimandrite Sophrony, 'Principles of Orthodox Asceticism', translated from the Russian by R. Edmonds, in Philippou, p. 261.

of individual parish priests and particular parishes. Yet despite their clear appreciation of monastic prayer in its uniqueness, people, when asked, were careful not to put monasteries and parish church in competition, nor to see monastic priests as necessarily better confessors than parish clergy. There was a clear awareness of their complementarity and of their different roles. Parish priests are largely concerned with the Christian life of lay people but, as Patriarch Teoctist himself insisted, theirs is not a lower form of life than that of monks, nor is a married parish priest less capable of being a spiritual father than a celibate monk:

> In Orthodox tradition monasteries represent spiritual power because the monastic life is a means of knowing God and is a means of personal perfection. There are two ways of purifying yourself. First there is the lay Christian's path, and second there is the monastery. Both have the same value.[5]

It seems, however, that having monks who are deeply engaged in purifying their souls is seen as having a good effect on the Christians whose souls are still largely controlled by passions. Fr Ilie Moldovan, professor of moral theology at Sibiu, made this link directly:

> Monasteries are of supreme importance. They are called to help living people to heal the wounds of the Romanian soul. Only pure souls can do something for the healing of souls.

Fr Moldovan was someone who felt very strongly that communism had done almost irreparable damage to the Romanian people, and that monasteries had played a crucial

5. Patriarch Teoctist, 1997.

role in repelling this destructive influence. This defence had made them particularly subject to communist attack. Even so, Fr Moldovan did not encourage monks to hear confessions outside their monasteries, but was clear that lay persons belonged in parishes and monks in monasteries. From this we conclude that monks are considered to have this effect on the Romanian soul at a distance, through example, but also simply through their prayer.

Fr Ioanin Chilan sees the value of these different roles:

> Parish churches and monasteries exercise their roles in the Church of Christ. The monastery does this through prayer and the possibility of providing an oasis for men in this desert of the world. In the parish the people can go to church Sunday by Sunday to receive communion, to be in communion with their fellows and with God. Parish priests keep the links with the people and have a large social role because they try to teach them how to live.

And although monasteries are very highly regarded, it is the parish churches which provide the focus for Christian life. Dr Zoe Popescu in Ploieşti saw the essential importance of the parish church for most people as the immediate and tangible centre of Christian life:

> The parish church is more important than a monastery for most people since the life of the people is in the church. The monastery is for special occasions. In church is the basis of our spiritual life.

PILGRIMAGE

One way of understanding the relationship between monasteries and parishes is to see it in terms of pilgrimage. Anyone who has been at a monastery in Romania during a time of pilgrimage will not easily forget the huge numbers of Christians of all ages and conditions who come to stay, often in considerable discomfort, or travel great distances, often at great inconvenience, in order to share in this time of enhancing their awareness of God's sanctifying activity in the world. Dan Borchina, a theological student in Sibiu, wrote:

> Pilgrimage is something usual for Orthodox believers, especially during times of fast and of the great feasts. Thus it happens that hundreds of thousands of people gather for the patronal feasts at the more important monasteries. It is something quite distinct and unique, an atmosphere like that of the Holy Easter when some hundreds of thousands of Christians sing the responses at the Holy Liturgy. The atmosphere is heavily laden with such communion and fraternal love that even those who have experienced it can scarcely understand. The monks at Nicula told me that before 1989 *Securitate* and the police made a cordon to block all the roads to the monastery but still the faithful gathered for the Dormition of Mary, to which Nicula monastery is dedicated, and walked through the forests in such numbers that the police could not stand in front of the torrents of people as they came to pray together to God.

Borchina recognises that lay and monastic Christians live fundamentally the same christian life but in different contexts. For a lay Christian to go on pilgrimage to a monastery deepens the commitment he already lives towards God.

This appreciation of monasteries as a centre for pilgrimage is taken up by another student, Lucian Colda, who includes as important aspects of the pilgrimage both the healing powers that certain monasteries, or relics and icons within monasteries, have, and the role of the living spiritual fathers whose holiness and reputation also attracts the crowds:

> The monasteries offer the opportunity for pilgrimages at the great feasts when thousands of people gather. Some monasteries have relics of the saints which are miraculous, which do, for example, heal the incurably sick. Certainly these healings are not free but presuppose on the part of the sick a strong belief and hope in the mercy and help of God. All this shows how much the monasteries are sought after by men. Sometimes people come who are possessed and seek healing. The spiritual fathers know how to calm them and to drive out the demons with the power of Christ.[6]

Holiness of place, hope of healing and holiness of life may be seen as three of the key factors which attract people to monasteries. Either because a monastery has existed a long time, or because it is associated with a particular saint or holy icon, people find there a sense of the sacred and come with an expectation that their prayers will be heard, and even that miracles will occur. They come in the hope and expectation of healing from physical and spiritual sickness. Holy places have always been associated with physical healing and in a society where medical resources are inadequate they will be particularly sought after by the sick. This is

6. That a twentieth-century student can speak here of demons indicates a link with the tradition quite different from that which a western student may hold.

undoubtedly the continuation of a practice which has gone on ever since monasteries were first founded in Romania. Yet this is no mere superstitious attachment to a reputed place of healing. Rather it is the reality of a living community providing an impressive example of lives given to God. Their self-giving, and the hours and hours of liturgy, which are multiplied at the festival times, create a sense of otherworldliness, or perhaps a sense of being close to the divine sources which irrigate and give life to Christianity in the world.

> In my mind the monastery is like a spring of cold water up in the mountains. In the town the water is warm and we have to put it in a fridge. When you drink the water up in the mountains with its natural coldness your thirst is completely quenched; you feel refreshed and calm and no longer anxious. In the monasteries the faithful find much greater help, for the people who go to the monastery are more concerned for the spiritual life and are those who have big problems. They are ill, distressed and they need a clinic for specialist spiritual treatment.[7]

The fourth attraction, as we have already seen, is the individual spiritual fathers, and each monastery has probably only one or two whose reputation for holiness is such that the people come specifically to them to receive from them the advice they need, the sense of absolute forgiveness of their sins, or quite simply the awareness of being close to someone who is very close to God and in whom God's presence can be felt. This raises the question as to whether monastic confessors are likely to be better at giving advice for the Christian life than married parish priests. Do peo-

7. Bishop Laurentius Streza. Interviewed in Caransebeș, 1997.

ple choose whenever possible to go to a monk for spiritual counsel and absolution in preference to a parish priest?

A common analogy used in respect of this question was that of the medical distinction between the general practitioners and the specialist. As Bishop Laurentius expressed it:

> I would compare a doctor and a priest. You see your own doctor regularly, but when you have a greater pain you will see the specialist. If a parish priest realises he is not able to solve a problem he will send the penitent to another confessor who prays more. The problem in a parish is that people come in great crowds to confession and all have to be confessed at once. A confession in the monastery is slower, deeper and tougher. It is like a very serious examination.[8]

Anişoara Carol made a similar point:

> In my opinion a parish church is the local hospital. If a sickness is serious it is necessary to consult the central hospital, where specialists are found. On the other hand parish priests can penetrate more easily into society in order to do mission. Monks ought to stay in the monasteries at their work and prayer.[9]

In her remarks, however, she made a clear distinction between the roles of parish priest and monk. A parish priest has a wide pastoral role caring for the people of God and even a missionary role in preaching to the unconverted. A monk belongs in his monastery. Fr Ilie Moldovan went

8. *Ibid.*
9. Written response in Bucharest, 1997.

further than this. 'A monk priest cannot do the parish priest's job. They are spiritual fathers for monks and not lay people.'
And a young deacon, whose father is a parish priest, said the same thing more forcefully.

> A parish priest must lead the people in this life, but a parish priest can tell you much more clearly about the secular society. A monk is confessor just for a monastery not for those outside. The parish priest is confessor for lay people. Lay people seek monks because they have no trust in the priest. Very occasionally they are right not to trust him. [10]

In all these remarks we may rightly see a definite limitation of the monk's role and a certain qualification of his fitness to give advice in all circumstances to all who come. There is a feeling, often expressed, that monks are not truly in touch with people and do not understand the difficulties under which people in the world live. So they may make unrealistic demands and unjustified criticisms. Only the relatively small numbers of truly great spiritual fathers are really trusted by the parishes to offer spiritual counsel and, as we shall see, there are often hesitations even about them. We must recognise that there is a natural tension within people's attitudes towards the monastic vocation. They value the life greatly for its example and the power of its prayer, but they have a healthy awareness that individuals within the life, for all their devotion, may not be well fitted to give advice to those outside. Individual monks do not always inspire trust.

In his remark, recorded above, Călin Sămărghiţan admitted, reluctantly, that some parish priests, too, cannot be

10. Fr Călin Sămărghiţan in Sibiu, 1997.

trusted as confessors. Some other people interviewed also complained many priests have simply been badly trained and many do not themselves pray much, or give real time to their own spiritual life. As Fr Eugene Jurca, a parish priest in a large housing estate and no great admirer of monasteries, said, no doubt with a touch of exaggeration:

> Priests' spirituality is weak. Most priests' lives are no different from anyone else's. They don't pray; don't confess; don't have spiritual exercise. They don't meditate on Scripture. They are not interested in spiritual achievement, only interested in money; they only give formal catechesis. They have no eucharistic awareness. They don't think of frequent communion for the faithful. They feel that pastoral work is a nuisance and just a way of getting money.[11]

Constantine Jinga made the same point though he believes that monks cannot give useful advice to people from outside the monastery.

> People go to monasteries for confession because they don't trust their priests. People should go to their own parish priests, because advice from monastic priests is useless for those who are not monks. It would be best if a parish priest himself took people to the great spiritual fathers when necessary.

And although Dr Jinga valued the quality of prayer in a monastery he did not seem to think this made monks better counsellors:

> Prayer is different there. The context is dif-

11. Interview in Timişoara, 1997.

ferent because everyone is there for prayer.
And you feel all monks are fasting and trying hard. Monks' prayer is deeper, but most
monks expect too much of lay people. Some
monks hate the world and hate people generally. Some go to the monastery just as a
way of finding a living. Christian life in this
world is more difficult than that in a monastery. In the world you must be flexible or
you frighten people off God. The monks'
image of cities tends to be that cities are
places where the soul is lost.

His rather negative view of the ability monks have to counsel married people was fairly widely shared. Another young
theological student expressed himself quite strongly on this
issue:

I will never confess to Fr Cleopa because I
don't like the monastic perspective. I don't
like the rigidity. Except for Fr Teofil, the
monks I have spoken with don't try to understand the problems of the world. They
just try to impose a pattern. A monk told
me off for getting married at twenty-one—
said I can't restrain myself with women.[12]

Not all people, however, share this negative view. Fr Teofil
of Sâmbăta de Sus was constantly cited as an exception to
any negative remarks about monks. Although he apparently says he cannot counsel married people because he
has no experience of the married life, this does not stop
married people turning to him. Fr Ioanin Chilan evidently
considered that the quality of a monk's prayer gave him
the ability to see more clearly than others, at least in matters to do with the spiritual life:

12. Daniel Sabău.

Monastic prayer is the same as parish prayer, but the volume and intensity is greater than in the parish, because purer prayer is found in the monastery. Monks understand people's lives even though they are out of this world. They may understand the world better than those who live in it.[13]

And even Călin Sămărghiţan, whose reservations about monastic confessors have been noted above, admits that monastic prayer could enable a monk to see more deeply than others, though one should not assume it:

Their prayer is the same as that in church. Monks' prayer may be much better heard by God, but in fact we don't know. We believe that prayer in a monastery is more devoted... I am afraid to confess to a monk because I cannot be a monk. Monks do understand, but not always. Certain monks can tell the truth about you that you don't know yourself. We must be afraid of the judgement of a monk and the judgement of God. [14]

Călin is clearly made uncomfortable by monks and is not sure whether that is because they speak a truth which he is reluctant to hear, a truth that comes perhaps from God or because their experience of life in a family is severely limited and so the advice they give ignores the realities of life as most people must experience it, or because they have no experience of life in the world. Monastic life clearly places a question mark over the value of life in this world. It exposes life's transitory nature and turns people's attention to the life to come; hence the frequent reference to death. Yet

13. Interviewed in Ploieşti, 1997.
14. Interviewed in Sibiu, 1997.

although this constant awareness of death is uncomfortable to lay Christians, it is authentically part of all christian teaching. So Călin would want to insist that monks essentially live the same life as all Christians live, but push out the boundaries, providing a challenge for the rest of us.

> Monks are the norm of christian life. There is the pure christian life and we try to be like it. The norm is the way of praying, way of work, way of obedience in family life. The monk pushes the Christian calling to the highest level. But saints can come from ordinary people too. Lay people can be as devoted to God as a monk.[15]

We have heard that same point made by the patriarch himself. Lay and monastic life have the same value. They are not different kinds of Christian life, but Christian life lived in different circumstances. All the same, it would seem that some parish priests do feel second rate, or are regarded as second rate, when judged against the more impressive commitment and devotion of the monks.

There may, however, be a particular reason for the higher regard in which monastic priests are often held. Under communism it was harder for married priests to resist the pressures to conform, or even to betray the Church, because of the ways in which their families could be penalised. This made parish priests often more suspect than the monks who represented for some a form of Christian life which communism could not infiltrate or suborn. (It did, but that is another story.) So Metropolitan Nicolae is clearly unhappy with some of the adulation given to monks:

> Monks are very famous for being confessors. Simply the fact that Fr Cleopa is a monk means that he is highly estimated by

15. Interviewed in Timişoara, 1997.

the faithful compared with a parish priest. This has long been the situation but it seems it is more emphasised now than ever before. The monk is seen by the faithful as having much more authority than the parish priest The monasteries are now being very much more visited by the faithful. Even a new monastery without the prestige of a Moldavian monastery will have many people coming to receive a spiritual light.[16]

This comment reveals the tension we have noted before between an acknowledgement that some monks do have a special quality of holiness and divine wisdom, and a feeling that, at the expense of the parish priest, more credit is being given to them than they really deserve. This tension is complicated by the significance which monasteries have had in Romanian national life beyond the areas of prayer and the spiritual life which may most naturally be considered their own. Anişoara Carol sums this up well.

Monasticism has been a source of culture and of spirituality. From the monastic houses rose the Romanian schools, literature, arts. The Romanian language was crafted; from there Christian values of morality were imposed on society; the State in earlier times was ruled according to the old Byzantine church laws. In times of war, monasteries with their walls and citadels became places of refuge. From their foundation they kept up a defence of the country against invaders.[17]

16. Interviewed in Timişoara, 1997
17. Written response, Bucharest 1997.

This identification of the monasteries with the national life and character also made it particularly difficult for the communists to attack them, both because of the resistance within the minds of the people and because Romanian communism was a particularly nationalist, not internationalist, form of communism and only the Russophiles within the Romanian Communist Party had a real interest in destroying Romanian national life.[18]

In talking to Romanians, therefore, one finds, that many have visited a large number of monasteries, particularly in Moldavia, as much for cultural reasons as for spiritual, though Romanian Orthodox would be reluctant to draw much of a distinction between the two. So Romul Petrişor, a former army officer and son of a priest, clearly has an appreciation of monastic buildings which goes beyond the cultural:

> The importance of monasteries is that you see a lot of icons and paintings. Some monasteries are wealthy and some are not. It is good that a monastery exists because you find there peace for the soul and many people go there for this. You feel close to God in that silence and peace. If you go outside the great feasts you can feel good in an empty church. You can pray better in an empty church than in a full church.[19]

And his view of this was supported by the managing director of an oil company in Ploieşti:

> Monasteries are our spiritual wealth. Monasteries were the storehouse for our traditions. People you can trust are formed there. These people are models. Church arts

18. Conversation with Prof Virgil Cândea, at Sihăstria in 1996.
19. Interview in Sibiu,1997.

are retained there—the painting of eggs
and icons for instance. Most important is
the sculpture in the human soul.[20]

In both these appreciations we see an easy movement from
an enjoyment of the cultural and artistic contributions to
the opportunity given in a monastery for prayer and spiritual growth. The former remark is typical of a Romanian
Orthodox searching for peace—not a nineteenth-century
romantic peace such as is found in nature poets, but the
peace that comes from being in a holy place, peace as a
contrast to the confusions, strife, and conflict, both spiritual and physical, of a life lived amid the warring nations
of Europe. The second remark is also typical in its frank
recognition that the soul has a priority—something that
the modern West would be reluctant to give it.

There is dark side to this, however, though only one of
those interviewed saw the danger of a monasticism too
closely identified with Romanian national life. He, as a son
of Timişoara, blamed this chauvinism largely on the monasteries of Moldavia:

> In Moldavia they don't understand that
> truth can exist outside the Church and the
> liturgy. They try to get rid of other traditions. A long monastic tradition supports
> this approach. This is an abuse of monastic spirituality. They exclude from life all
> sorts of quite normal things, TV, newspapers, etc. . . . In the Banat we are much
> more used to being in dialogue with other
> religions and denominations. . . . The negative aspect of monasticism is that most
> monks do not distinguish between national
> and Orthodox life. So Orthodoxy becomes

20. Lucian Staniu: Ploieşti, 1997.

exclusive of all others. Monks lose the universal meaning of Orthodoxy.[21]

His attitude was shared by another student from Timişoara, who was concerned that monastic life not hijack all of Orthodoxy and prevent it from speaking to a secular world in a language the world can understand:

> There is more to Orthodoxy than monasticism. Monastic spirituality makes its contribution, but attention needs to be given to those at lower levels. Parish church and monastic life are complementary. We should not see the monastery as a tank of spirituality. This suggests a weakness in parish life.[22]

Clearly many parish priests and Christians feel under criticism from the monasteries. How do the monks view the parishes? One must not forget that all of them come from parishes. In many cases, particularly again in Moldavia, there are close links between monasteries and parishes. It is not uncommon for several members of a parish, even of one family, to enter monastic life. The one is seen as a natural extension of the other. Monks look to the parishes, obviously as a source of recruitment, also as a source of financial support. In none of the research carried out for this project did a monk express negative views of parish life. One at least admitted that parish life might be more demanding than monastic:

> Parish life is more difficult than monastic because priests must work with people and understanding so many different people demands great patience. The parish church prepares people to go to the monastic life.

21. Robert Lazu in Timişoara,1997.
22. Florin Doboş.

> If a priest does his duty many will go to the
> monastic life. Not everyone is called to
> monastic life. They must first spend much
> time in parishes. They must get used to liv-
> ing under the rules of parish life. To be a
> monk is not a job. It is a gift to follow God's
> way.[23]

In this we see the essential role which a parish must play in
forming a potential monk or nun in the habits of devotion
which will be equally part of monastic life. Monastic life
does make very large demands on a person, both in terms
of liturgy and in terms of fasting, and in the attitude of
obedience which is at the base of monastic vocation. Unless this has been thoroughly learned, and indeed has become entirely natural to a person while living in the parish, he will find monastic life almost unendurably hard.
Although monks expressed appreciation of parishes in these
rather pragmatic or patronising terms, one did not feel there
was the same kind of reverence towards them as the parishes feel towards the monasteries. Differentiation of role
does appear to correlate with degrees of worthiness in the
minds of both monks and parishioners.

Generally, people interviewed felt that the monasteries
were a strength to the parishes, either through their prayers
or through the example they placed before the people. Undoubtedly, some priests find the monasteries a threat and
complain that they seem to take the worshippers away from
the parish churches. Bishop Streza felt that this was a false
opposition:

> I don't see a tension between church and
> monastery. The monastery strengthens the
> Church in the area where it exists. When
> the priests are not confident they feel that
> if people go to the monastery they will have

23. Fr Pantilimon of Ghighiu.

fewer faithful in church. But this is not so.
The faithful still come to the parish for serv-
ices such as baptism, weddings, funerals.
But the people need more.

Constantine Jinga, however, showed a high ideal of what
parish life could be:

> Parishes should be real centres of spiritu-
> ality and community life—a place where
> people can come to pray, talk together, a
> place where people can be community. At
> the moment parishes tend to be just the
> interface between people and the monas-
> teries.

This raises the question whether a parish should be a mini-
monastery, in which case it will inevitably be second rate in
comparison to the real thing. Or does life in a secular world
have a legitimacy which gives a parish church an authenticity which is not derived from its resemblance to a monastery? One of Jinga's friends, whose long and close involvement in parish life had given him a rather jaundiced view
of parish priests, could still feel that parish life was primary
in the nature of the life of the Church, and monastic life
dependent on it:

> Church life is parish life. Most people are
> in the parish. Monastic life is a minority.
> The only difference between monasticism
> and the parish is that in a monastery many
> are gathered together for the same purpose.
> Everything going on in a monastery should
> go on in a parish.

These remarks underline the fact that in Orthodox life monasteries are fully integrated into the Church. Bishops are
monks. Monastic life is not a kind of protest movement on
the fringes of the Church but very much at the centre. On

the other hand, it is the Church which enables monastic life. It is the generosity of the Church which sustains it materially and the sacramentality of the Church which makes possible its sacramental life. We should not be surprised, then, that Mircea had an ambivalent attitude towards monasteries. He both saw their value, while wanting them to keep their place, and perceived what many monks also realize, that the streams of pilgrims and penitents coming to the monastery easily distract the monks from their true vocation, which is to pray:

> I have been most disappointed in the best known monasteries. It is better to be in an unknown monastery. Great monasteries are disappointing because of the large number of visitors. Monasticism means reclusion. A monk should see very few lay people in his life. A monastery is for monks, not for lay people. A monk does not hate people, but becomes a monk because he can't stand life in the world.[24]

And this inherent conflict with the world was also perceived by one young student who had briefly lived in a monastery and still longed to return there.

> In monastic life, the fight is not against the body but for the body, because the body is the temple of the Holy Spirit.[25]

This brief comment in its insistence that monastic life is not a life against nature, points to a greater truth. It is not a life fundamentally opposed to the life which most Christians must live, concerned with the human realities of life, sustenance, and procreation. It is instead a life which is

24. This and the previous quotation: Mirca Szilagyi, Timişoara, 1997.
25. Christian Pavel, interviewed in Timişoara, 1997.

lived for others. Sacrifice is never selfish but must be for the sake of others. Part of the sacrifice is that one gains very little pleasure or sense of satisfaction for oneself. A monk who seems satisfied and comfortable is very likely missing the point of his life. Yet, while monastic life is, in one great respect, lived for others in the world, in another it is directed wholly towards God. There is an inherent otherness about the life, a difference in its standards and priorities which make it impossible for most people who have not embraced it to understand it.

In some ways the ambivalent attitudes in which we may see the potential for sharp disagreements may best be explained by an image which Constantine Jinga used to explain how he saw monasticism's role within the church. He compared it to a skeleton within a body. The bones of the skeleton need to be hard and rigid; otherwise the body collapses. But the body needs to be flexible, soft and warm and living; and that is the role of the flesh. This view was shared by Daniel Sabău who valued the rigidity, provided that the monks who lived this disciplined life did not try to impose it on others. On the other hand, he also wanted to see some monks involved in works of charity, learning, as he himself said, from the example of Roman Catholic religious orders. There is amongst Romanian Orthodox a human and natural ambivalence between wanting monks to live up to their 'desert' ideal of those who have withdrawn utterly from the world in order to live with God, and wanting them also to be available for spiritual counsel, for contact, and even for works of charity in areas where parish priests and other Christians cannot or do not reach.

Despite their love for the monastic life Romanian people are fully engaged in the world and have attitudes to family life much like those of any other nation. A simple question—would you like your child to become a monk or nun—produced a fascinating variety of answers, often quite unexpected. Fr Chilan, for instance, whose appreciation of monastic life is large and deep, said,

No. I would not encourage my child to enter a monastery. The feeling of the parent is attacked. You do not have the assurance that the vocation is true. A lot of young people go into monasteries not for a true vocation and are then disappointed. You as a parent cannot see your child disappointed. You see a separation between parent and child. You should really be glad about this, but I cannot receive this kind of joy. I have two little children and it would be difficult for me.[26]

Fr Călin Sămărghiţan expressed a similar hesitation:

As a parent I would be reluctant to see my child go into a monastery. Perhaps as a parent you can see whether this would be good for the child. Anyway I would tell him to wait and think about it.[27]

And his mother, the very devout wife of a priest, also would not like to see her children going into a monastery, because she saw the monastic life as a very difficult one.

On the other hand, Daniel Săbau, who expressed great criticism of the monastic state and wished to have no contact with monks himself, said he would be quite happy for his little daughter to become a nun, 'if her spiritual father thought she should'. And Robert Lazu, who admitted he regarded monks negatively, as being largely anti-social, was surprisingly positive in his response. 'I would support a child of mine who wished to enter a monastery, provided he could show me that it was his own decision, and fully understood what he was doing.' And Constantine Jinga

26. Interviewed in Ploieşti in 1997.
27. Interviewed in Sibiu in 1997.

said 'I think if my son wanted to become a monk I would
be shocked, but I would test it to see if it was real. If it
seemed real I would encourage it.'

Even for those whose regard for the monastic life is far
from uncritical, there is a recognition of the autonomy of
each person before God. God may call even our own children to ways of life we do not like or do not understand.
We can see in these young parents a desire both to protect
but also to recognise the child's right to answer a call from
God. Behind that perhaps is an attitude to christian life
which, more readily than in the West, admits the absolute
priority of God.

In this chapter we have glimpsed the cultural and religious background against which most of the great spiritual
fathers of Romania live. It is a multi-coloured background
with heights and depths, with great riches and some evident distrust. We need now to look at the spiritual fathers
themselves, many of whom, of course, are not monastic.
What constitutes a spiritual father? How must he live? And
what responsibilities do they have who call themselves his
disciples, or children?

CHAPTER 5

Duhovnic:
The Spiritual Father

THE TRADITION OF THE SPIRITUAL FATHER is one of the oldest traditions in the history of the christian ascetical life. Throughout the history of the Church from earliest times we see disciples gathering around holy men and women to learn from them, both through their teaching and through the example of their lives. Christianity has always been communicated by teachers, some of whom were recognised as men of prayer and holiness. In the environment in which Christianity grew up, both Jewish and Greek, there was a long-established tradition of disciples sitting at the feet of masters who did more than simply impart information; they also to varying degrees took responsibility for their disciples' moral life and in some traditions for their spiritual lives as well. It is likely that some such tradition existed in Christianity from the time of Jesus himself.

Clement of Alexandria seems to have been the first to advise any Christian who was wealthy and haughty to submit himself to some man of God who would be his director and trainer.[1] If this is so, then the tradition of seeking spiritual direction begins not among those seeking to lead

1. *Quis dives salvetur ;* PG 9:645C .Translated by W. Wilson in the Ante-Nicene Fathers series, Volume 2 (Edinburgh: T&T Clark–Grand Rapids: Eerdmans 1994) 591. A very good text in Greek and English, translated by G. W. Butterworth, is also available in the Loeb Classical Library.

an expressly ascetical life but in the lives of those who sought ways of making it possible to live Christianity in the world. It was, however, the desert fathers who made the practice famous, though they themselves generally tried to avoid having disciples either because they distracted attention from God, or out of humility, not believing they had any wisdom to teach. The great Antony, the most famous of the Desert Fathers, had a much more regulated idea than Clement of the demands a father could make on his spiritual son, demands which were appropriate to monks rather than to rich laymen. 'The monk ought, if possible, to confide to the elder how many steps he takes or how many drops [of water] he drinks in his cell, so as to avoid making a mistake in these matters.'[2] Antony, it seems, sought not only salvation from hell, but 'a radical healing of every disease of the soul together with fullness of life for the soul in God'[3]. Soon afterwards Basil the Great wrote of the cure of sin being undertaken with understanding by someone who genuinely loves,[4] and elsewhere insists that being a spiritual father to his monks is the first duty of a monastic superior.[5] Already in this brief description of the rise of the tradition of spiritual father, we may see a significant development in the understanding of his role. This is borne out by the experience of Romanian spiritual fathers in relation to their disciples. The richness and life-creating nature of the spiritual father turns on his being a father who loves. Clement described him chiefly in terms of training, stressing his role in leading a rich man to recognize his

2. *Apophthegmata Patrum*, 38; PG 65:88B; translated by Benedicta Ward SLG, *The Sayings of the Desert Fathers* (London: Mowbray–Kalamazoo: Cistercian Publications, 1975) 7.
3. Irénée Hausherr, 'Vocations chrétienne et vocation monastique selon les Pères,' Études de spiritualité orientale, Orientale Christiana. Analecta, 183 (1969) 405—cited by Turner, p. 72.
4. *Regula Fusius tractatae*, 34; PG 31:929A. See Saint Basil *The Long Rules* in *Ascetical Works*, translated M. Monica Wagner CSC (Washington DC: The Catholic University of America Press, 1962, rpt. 1990) 248.
5. *Regula Fusius tractatae*; PG 31:948C-1044; Wagner, 287-294, 319-320.

need to submit in obedience to another, something of which he is not likely to have much experience. Antony saw the father as a person to whom a monk opens his whole life that it may be so carefully examined that every aspect of that life is drawn into the struggle for perfection. Both of those features retain a considerable place in the tradition of spiritual fatherhood as it developed and as it is now practised. Basil's perception, over time, however, became determinative. The only person who can really help cure sin is someone whose understanding is informed by love. Spiritual fathers are loved by the men and women who come to them because they are themselves known to love. Everything about their teaching is imbued with love. Whether it be gentle or demanding, simple or far-reaching in its theological significance, it conveys the spiritual father's love for the penitent[6] and his longing for the spiritual child to share more fully in the love of God which he himself has come to know.

Fr Ioanichie Bălan, one of Romania's best-known writers on the spiritual tradition, tells us at the start something of the importance of the spiritual father in the Orthodox tradition:

> This is the traditional way of spiritual formation and growth in Orthodoxy: questions, advice, dialogue between spiritual father and disciple, between old man and beginner; between an experienced monk and a believer. Salvation through questioning, through prayer and humility, not through commandments and laws which are imposed, which produce fear and drive

6. There is a problem here with terminology. The Eastern tradition speaks of a spiritual father's disciple—*ucenic* in Romanian. In Western Christianity 'penitent' refers specifically to a person who makes confession to a priest. 'Spiritual child' has an infantilising flavour to it. 'Disciple' suggests something more defined.

love from the heart, which do violence to
the free will and freedom of a man.[7]

In this chapter, we will outline the role and work of a spiritual father in the Orthodox tradition and then to see how modern Romanians regard, and relate to, their spiritual fathers. Lest the term 'spiritual father' take on an inappropriate mystique, however, we need to remember that any priest who has been entrusted with the responsibility of hearing confessions can be considered a spiritual father.[8] A parish priest has this responsibility towards most of his people. But no one is compelled to have his parish priest as spiritual father. He, or she, can choose anyone. In almost all cases the spiritual father will be a priest, whether monk or married. This is partly for the obvious reason that priests generally are more concerned with the spiritual life than others are. In addition, it is usually the spiritual father who gives absolution and permission to receive communion. There is, however, a tradition in Orthodoxy that a spiritual father or mother may be lay. We came across a few people in Romania who looked to persons who were not priests for most of their spiritual counsel. Whether such people can absolve from sin is much more problematical. Simeon the New Theologian reckoned that a lay monk could be a spiritual father and give absolution where a priest might not. What one needed for this was not the grace of orders but 'a constant personal union with the divine Spirit, witnessed in visible charisms to validate and confirm the ministerial functions'.[9] Even at the time, however, this teaching caused Simeon great trouble and was not widely accepted.

There is, however, a distinction to be made in the roles of parish priest and spiritual father, which, though not ab-

7 Bălan, *Convorbire Duhovniceşti*, p. 8.
8. In Romania almost all priests have this authority. In Greece apparently fewer than half may hear confessions.
9. McGuckin (1982) p. 19.

solute, is still useful. The lay Romanian academician Virgil Cândea put this clearly:

> We make a distinction between an ordinary parish priest who must hear confessions in order to allow people to communion, and a *starets* of the Russian tradition who is a true spiritual guide.[10]

THE *DUHOVNIC* IN ROMANIAN TRADITION

Without wishing to draw too strong a distinction between these two aspects of the spiritual father's ministry, we need to bear this distinction in mind. When a person moves in the spiritual life from seeking forgiveness for specific sins in order to receive communion to a really serious engagement in living an ascetical life, he or she exposes the innermost self to the possibility of hurt as well as the expectation of growth. It is important that the spiritual father chosen to guide that person be pastorally sympathetic and a trustworthy guide. Such a person is called by the Russian term *duhovnic*, which, like the Greek *pneumatikos*, suggests a person who is both filled with the Holy Spirit and also loving and fatherly. Since the *duhovnic* is common to all Orthodox traditions we will briefly consider now the wider Orthodox tradition with some reference to Romanian writers. Then we will look at current Romanian attitudes to and relation with spiritual fathers. Finally we will consider the practice of confession insofar as it has not been dealt with in the previous discussion.

We begin by looking at what a spiritual father actually does. The need for a spiritual father is not limited simply to those who are in the monastic life. It is true that much of the literature concerning spiritual fatherhood is obviously

10. It is important not to be confused by terminology. In Romanian the Russian word *starets* refers to the abbot of a monastery and his role may be largely administrative. A spiritual father in Romanian is called a *duhovnic*.

aimed at monks in their more intense pursuit of virtue and their engagement in constant prayer. Both for his training and his protection a monk must have a spiritual father if there is one to be found.

Yet lay people too, who are taking the spiritual life seriously will also have a spiritual father whose responsibilities go beyond hearing their confession once a year so they can make an Easter communion. Usually their spiritual father will be their parish priest, but perhaps it will be a monk at their favourite monastery. Metropolitan Antonie Plămădeală makes the important point that Orthodoxy does not make a firm distinction between monk and lay person in terms of the spiritual life. 'What counts is a pure mind and a good heart, and not how one reaches it.'[11]

In a parish the priest is spiritual father to most of the people. He hears confessions, gives people permission to receive communion, instructs, exhorts, advises through preaching and through his own example. So, in a talk to seminarians[12] Fr Cleopa reminded them that as priests they must take great care to celebrate the sacraments properly and attentively, and that they must preach the Gospel with their mouths, with their hands (through writing), and in the manner of their lives. And in regard to his ministry as a *duhovnic,* the priest must be like a doctor who takes immense trouble to prevent people dying; so he must take immense trouble over a soul 'which is worth more than all the world'.[13] In this he must act with sensitivity, tempering the canons to the case, not overburdening people, but making serious demands of them.[14]

In a monastery, any priest who has his bishop's authority may hear confessions but there is generally a priest-monk appointed in each monastery to be spiritual father to

---

11. Plămădeală, *Tradiţie şi Libertate,* p. 77.
12. Cleopa, *Ne Vorbeşte Părintele Cleopa,* 1:90ff.
13. *Ibid.,* p.106.
14. *Ibid.,* p. 107.

the members of the monastery. He is responsible for the spiritual life of all the monks, but particularly for those who come to him and submit themselves to him as disciples. He will take on the role which in a western monastery is filled by the novice guardian—that is, he will instruct the young monk in the ways of monastic life and he will be responsible for saying whether and when a young man is able to move on into profession. The spiritual father's role in an Orthodox monastery cannot be underestimated:

> The *duhovnic* is the soul, the heart which gives life to a monastery. His moral authority, his experience, his gentleness and his skill in guiding souls towards eternal life are unquestionable. The *duhovnic* is a man of the spirit, who bears in himself the Holy Spirit and with his help struggles with evil spirits, for the salvation and redemption of his spiritual sons. Under his *epitrahil*[15] new monks are formed, souls grow pure for God, sins are absolved, and those who take the cross of Christ are guided. In the *duhovnic's* cell, as in a room of the Spirit, personal counsel is given, men's steps are placed rightly on the way of salvation, burdened hearts are opened, hidden wounds are healed, troubled souls are comforted and great questions of life are dealt with. At any hour of the day or night the *duhovnic* remains watchful, praying for his spiritual sons, opening the door for each: reconciling, quietening, absolving, blessing, sacrificing himself and placing his spirit as a guarantee for the spiritual son.[16]

15. Stole, the garment which a priest wears and places over the penitent while the latter makes confession.
16. Bălan. *Convorbire Duhovniceşti*, p. 13.

The responsibility of spiritual fatherhood is not a light one. In a sense, a spiritual father has in his hands the task of ensuring the salvation of his charges. He must always be available for counsel. The disciple should tell him everything he does, every thought he thinks, so that he may judge whether the disciple is progressing along the spiritual way. One of his responsibilities is to assess a disciple's readiness to receive communion and to give permission for that. The importance of this is rooted in the Pauline injunction against those who receive communion unworthily and therefore bring down judgement on themselves. Fr Cleopa tells us: 'I would give my whole body to be burned before I would give the most holy and most pure Body to someone unworthy. I would pour out all my blood before giving this fearful and most holy Blood to someone who is unworthy.[17]

He must also pray for his charges. Prayer is taken very seriously amongst the Orthodox and is thought by them to have an efficacy far greater than that which Western Christians generally perceive. A monk wants to believe that his father has taken complete responsibility for him, will defend him with his prayers and obtain for him the graces he is unable to gain through his own prayer. Clearly someone who can accept this kind of responsibility for another's spiritual welfare needs to be a special kind of person. How can a good spiritual father be recognised?

Normally, as we have seen, any priest can function as a spiritual father simply through his ordination and appointment to a parochial responsibility. Of those in the monasteries who are regarded as great spiritual fathers, however, much is demanded. Theirs is a grace which comes only as *a gift from God*. It cannot be learned or acquired by long study. This is the grace of discernment which enables a person to perceive deeply and to judge aright. In the *Conferences* of John Cassian, Abba Moses, after a long discus-

---

17. Cleopa, *Ne Vorbeşte Părintele Cleopa*, 2:23.

sion with other fathers as to what the key virtue is, concludes, 'it is very clear that no virtue can come to full term or can endure without the grace of discernment'.[18]

A spiritual father, however, will be expected to have a sound knowledge of people, a good understanding of psychology, and considerable personal experience of the spiritual life. These qualities can be gained only by experience. He will also have a profound and extensive knowledge of the Tradition, that is, of the teaching of the Holy Fathers. In practice this will tend to be derived from the *Philokalia*. People value their spiritual fathers for their learning as well as for their holiness. Thus Fr Cleopa is praised as a great, but self-taught, theologian whose knowledge was acquired particularly while shepherding in the mountains, or hiding from the communists. Fr Teofil, however, is recognized as a highly cultured man with a formal theological training.

Normally (but not always) a spiritual father will have a reputation as an ascetic. That is, he gives himself to prayer several hours during the night. He fasts rigorously and, as he tells his children to watch carefully every thought and image that comes into their minds, so he watches his own mind and firmly expels anything sinful or even just distracting because it does not belong there. He undertakes this asceticism not in order to become a great spiritual father, but out of concern for his own salvation. If he is being used as a spiritual father he bears the added responsibility of praying and fasting more than others do.

Beyond these largely human qualities of learning and behaviour there is also a need for the particular grace of being able to see beyond the surface appearances of a disciple's life. He must see what is really taking place in the person's soul. Fr Teofil makes this clear:

> For anyone to be a good spiritual father he
> must first have the special grace from God

18. John Cassian, *The Conferences*, 2.4; translated by Colin Liubheid, p. 64.

and also be able to see with the Spirit so that
he may know clearly the circumstances of
those who come to him for guidance. It is
not enough just to hear confessions. You
must know intuitively what is happening in
the spirit. This thing happens very rarely.[19]

This grace of seeing 'what is happening' often includes that
of knowing what is going on in a person's life even though
the spiritual father has not been told about it—as Jesus knew
about the life of the Samaritan woman at the well in John 4.
More urgently, he must be able to discern the activity of the
devil and give the right advice on how to ward him off.

In addition to this grace of discernment, many spiritual
fathers have the reputation of being able to speak exactly
the words of God for a particular person. Some believe
they are consciously given these words. Others (like Saint
Serafim of Sarov) simply trust that the words they speak
will be the ones that God wants the person to hear.

A spiritual father must be gentle. He should be meek,
because without that quality one cannot approach holiness.
But he will be gentle with those who come to him, never
losing his temper, never treating them harshly. This does
not mean that his advice will not be very demanding. He
will ask much and will make it clear that salvation, and
therefore heaven or hell, is at stake. But he will do it with
that particular gift of gentleness which enables him to be
called a father. So Fr Paisie Olaru describes the good spiritual father:

First of all, he must be a man of prayer, who
loves the Church and all people, who is
humble and gentle with those who are humble and who repent of their sins, and is
harsh with the lazy who do not go to church
and do not abandon their sins; he should

19. Interview at Sâmbăta de Sus.

not be a lover of money or of earthly things, nor should he be a lover of praise and honour. But the crown of all is that he should be ready in case of need to lay down his life and his soul for the Church of Christ or for his spiritual sons.[20]

In this Fr Paisie, a simple and godly peasant monk of Sihla, is reflecting the teaching of his namesake, the great Fr Paisius Velichkovsky, who wrote:

It is difficult to lead someone along paths of which one is ignorant oneself. Only he who himself has sustained a long combat against the passions and with the help of Christ has conquered the carnal desires, anger, vanity and avarice; who has healed his soul by humility and prayer, and who, with love, has followed his saviour in everything— only such a man can, without deception, show to a disciple all the commandments and virtues of Christ . . . But where will we find such a guide? They are not numerous, especially in our age. There remains for us a single way out: to study day and night the Holy Scriptures and the writings of the Fathers, asking counsel of like-minded brethren and elder fathers, to learn how to fulfill the commandments of God and imitate the ascetics of old.[21]

A favourite comparison with the spiritual father, significantly enough, is that of a doctor, and not, as one might expect, a teacher or a judge. Br Gheorghe of Sihăstria explains this comparison:

20. Bălan, ed., *Părintele Paisie Duhovnicul*, p. 52.
21. Cited by Sergius Chetvenikov, *Paisius*, pp. 82-84.

A doctor is an expert in disease and oper-
ates accordingly. A spiritual father is an expert on sin. With sin you think about it,
speak about it. Then you can't get rid of it. It
becomes part of your life. The deeper the
sin is the more skillful should be the confessor and the more people he has for confession the more skillful he is.[22]

In his book on penance, R.J. Barringer makes a similar
comparison when he writes, 'the clear intent of all penitential language is to heal the wounds of sin as these touch
both the individual Christian and the whole community'.[23].
Symeon the New Theologian, himself a demanding spiritual father, shows great sensitivity to the need to gain a
penitent's trust before applying 'hard' medicine.[24] One cannot over-emphasise here the need for the penitent to cooperate. The most skillful doctor can do nothing if a patient will not take his medicine. So, too, the best spiritual
father can do nothing if the penitent does not heed his
advice. The crucial factor in both cases is the trust that must
exist between the two, and, in the case of a spiritual father,
trust must be built on love. The need to cooperate is not
only an obvious *pragmatic* need. The doctor's patient will
probably not get better if he does not take his medicine. It
is the will of the spiritual father's penitent, though, which
most needs healing from the long established effects of
sin. His *willingness* to submit his *will* to another, to allow, in
the Romanian phrase, 'the cutting of the will' (*tăiere voinţa*),
allows the grace of God to work in the deep recesses of the
will. In a curiously paradoxical way, the more the penitent
surrenders his will to his spiritual father, doing what is

22. Interview, 1996.
23. 'Ecclesiastical Penance in the Church of Constantinople' (Oxford
D. Phil thesis, 1979) pp. 32ff.
24. *Tr. Eth.* VI.; *Traités Théologiques et Ethiques*, ed. J. Darrouzès. Sources
Chrétiennes, 129 (Paris, 1967) Volume 2:276-311. See also Turner, p. 102.

asked of him in trust and love, the more he makes possible the process of divinisation which is his deepest desire.

So we can see that the grace of spiritual fatherhood, though dependent on human skills and talents, is always perceived as a gift of the Spirit; most would go further and say that it is not simply a gift given by the Spirit, but the presence of the Spirit himself. Symeon the New Theologian put this strongly and controversially:

> Just as the children according to the flesh
> are not inseminated without the father and
> cannot be born without the one who sows
> them, so it is impossible for one who does
> not have the Spirit to be born from above...
> And as the earthly father brings forth sons
> who are likewise earthly, so also does a spir-
> itual man render spiritual those who wish
> to become his real sons.[25]

A spiritual father, then, is not simply a skilled technician. As well as being a man of prayer with long experience of the spiritual life, he must be a pastor who will need zeal, vigilance and above all love. It is this long-enduring love that will make him wait patiently even when his child is wandering abroad and, like the Prodigal Son's father, he will always welcome the wandering disciple back warmly.[26] It is his unending prayer and vigilance on the disciple's behalf, more perhaps than the advice he gives, which will bring the disciple to give himself truly to God.

It is not the spiritual father alone who has responsibility in this matter. The disciple himself is responsible for accepting God's call to seek salvation. In the first place, he must choose his own *duhovnic*, someone who will instruct him well, but in a manner he knows to be compatible with his own character. Young Brother Florin speaks very much for the ancient tradition when he says:

25. *Epistles* 4.121-126.
26. See Turner, 104.

> In the Orthodox Church it is better to choose
> your own spiritual father because characters
> are different. If you are very sensitive and
> find a spiritual father who is very strong and
> definite, he might try to change you to be
> like him and this would be bad.[27]

Since trust is a crucial factor in the relationship, as we have
seen, trust must be part of the choosing. The earnest seeker
after God must trust that God will lead him to the right
spiritual father. Then he will believe that the *duhovnic* really does speak the words of God to him. He must see in
his *duhovnic* the person of Christ. As part of this trust he
may follow the counsel of Saint Symeon the New Theologian: 'Never ask your spiritual father for anything. Wait
until he gives it. That will be the right moment.'[28]   This
trust will be based not simply on an intimate knowledge of
the father but on the conviction that God has led the disciple to him and that God will direct his actions and words.

> In choosing a spiritual father you have to
> allow the Holy Spirit to work in you. It is
> partly a matter of taste. Communication with
> your *duhovnic* provides a direct communi-
> cation with the vertical dimension. Usually
> an event in your life pushes you to your
> first real confession. This is the moment
> when you find protection from a priest. A
> confessor is given to you.[29]

After trust comes obedience, and this obedience must aim
at being total, unquestioning, and immediate. Only through

27. Interview at Sihăstria, 1996.
28. 'The First Chapters' 1.27; translated by Paul [John] McGuckin, *Saint
Symeon the New Theologian The Practical and Theological Chapters*
(Kalamazoo: Cistercian Publications, 1982) 40.
29. Dr Alex Popeuscu, Oxford, 1997.

this can pride and confidence in oneself be crushed. The young disciple must be open, willing to tell his *duhovnic* everything that passes through his mind, keeping nothing back. This is hard for a human being to learn and the disciple will be greatly helped if he can see his spiritual father as an icon of Christ, for 'icons are not visual aids but the actual means whereby a worshipper is brought into the presence of and into fellowship with heavenly realities'.[30]

At the same time, although he entrusts his salvation to his spiritual father, the disciple must also accept responsibility for himself. He must be determined to work hard, to pray, to fast, to keep vigils, and to do all that his *duhovnic* tells him to do that his soul may be purified and he may be saved. Above all, he must be truly motivated by a desire for God. A spiritual father cannot hope for success by providing training in conduct and character unless he has disciples who have begun ardently to desire sanctity.

At the same time as he cares for his individual disciples, the monastic *duhovnic* has a particular responsibility towards the wider Church. The Church sees the monasteries as places where the Tradition is most perfectly preserved and as places where prayer for the Church is particularly engaged in. The *duhovnic* must see that this state is maintained to the best of his monks' ability. In this the *duhovnic* provides a very important link with the Holy Fathers. He speaks their words, not just because he is learned in their writings, but because he lives their way of life. He is one with them in holiness and so their spirit speaks in him. Through the *duhovnic* the disciple and the wider Church are brought into direct relationship with the earliest age of Christianity, which is considered to be the purest age because it was closest to Christ and because the Holy Spirit was particularly active then in forming the doctrines and spirituality which became normative for later ages.

---

30. Turner, p. 191.

Holiness of life

In this regard, however, it is not enough that he should simply be a good patristic scholar. In line with what Plato, the Cappadocians, and the Eastern Fathers of the Church taught, the modern Orthodox believes you can only teach the truth if you are holy. Holiness is the essential quality without which any teaching will be vain. Holiness, too, is a gift from God. Indeed it is a gift of the very presence of God which transforms and in some sense 'deifies' man. 'The likeness of man to God in which holiness consists is exactly this continual submission of man in God, this increasing illumination of the consciousness of man by the light of the consciousness of God.'[31] Holiness is given only where it has been worked for, and 'continual submission' refers to the constantly active response the spiritual father gives to God. Holiness demands cooperation between God and a man.

How seriously this demand for holiness in a spiritual father can be, is articulated by Fr Paisie Olaru. In a rather charming fashion he accepts, and assigns to the *duhovnic*, responsibility for the world's continuing faithlessness. When asked to account for the decline in lay people's spirituality, he replied, 'The largest guilt lies with the spiritual fathers. If we were better, Christians would change.'[32]

The spiritual father also assumes the frightening responsibility not only of giving good advice when asked for it, but of being the kind of person through whom healing may come to the world. As Stăniloae remarks:

Through holy people and the generosity with which they give themselves to others and to Christ humanity is healed and renewed. This comes through their delicate

31. Stăniloae, *Rugaciune lui Iisus*, p. 65
32. Bălan, ed., *Duhovnicul Părintele Paisie*, p. 26.

empathy with all creatures and things as gifts of God.[33]

This brings us to the question of why we need a spiritual father. Men and women since the Renaissance have considered themselves to be their own best guides and are used to seeking out appropriate knowledge and adequate direction from wherever they think it may be found. The Reformed tradition of Christianity teaches that each person must answer directly to God without a human mediator and that in matters of the spirit one must be allowed that unmediated relationship with Christ. On the other hand, there is an almost infinite amount of hard experience to show that men and women deceive themselves very easily and are not always their own best guides, particularly in the Christian life where standards are very different from those of the surrounding world and where evil can easily deceive. Saint John Climacus was one of the first to say what has been repeated constantly down the centuries: 'A man, however prudent, may easily go astray if he has no guide. The man who takes the road of monastic life under his own direction may easily be lost, even if he has all the wisdom of the world.'[34]

Even so, the need for a spiritual father is not simply imposed from the outside. A monk entering monastic life seeks a spiritual father of his own accord, and his motive for entering monastic life and for choosing one particular monastery rather than another is very likely to be that he feels drawn to a particular spiritual father. Some see this in terms of seeking salvation, a conviction that their salvation cannot be assured without the guidance and prayer of a spiritual father. Others simply seek peace of heart. Monks and nuns have always been thought to understand the ways of prayer and the secret movements of the heart. This is why

33. Stăniloae (1995) p. 43.
34. *Ladder*, 26, translated by Moore, p. 259.

people have opened their minds and thoughts to them, hoping to find peace.

Then too the simple truth is that all men and women are sinners. Fr Cleopa never tired of speaking of the need for forgiveness. He cites as an example of this the monks of his own monastery, some of whom come to confession two or three times a week. Nor is it enough simply to 'go to confession', though that hearing of confessions and giving absolution is a large part of the *duhovnic's* responsibility. Stăniloae explores this sensitively in pointing out that forgiveness is essential, not only because we need to forgive in order to be forgiven, as the Lord's Prayer tells us, but also because other people need our forgiveness and we need theirs if forgiveness is to be truly complete. 'All sin', he reminds us, 'but all contribute to the cleansing [of the Church] through asking for forgiveness, through the gift of their forgiveness, through common and reciprocal prayer for their forgiveness.'[35] A good spiritual father helps a person to see the fullest implications of the sins he has committed and encourages the person to take all the steps necessary to eradicate the sin and its effects.

A spiritual father's responsibility does not end with death. Fr Cleopa is speaking within the tradition when he tells the penitent: 'Everything must be confessed to the priest so that he can answer for you at the day of judgement. He can't answer for what he hasn't been told.'[36] It is partly because priests are prepared to take on this awesome responsibility for another person's sins at the day of judgment that people love them so much.

A further part of the spiritual father's work is the direction of the disciple's prayer. In the hesychast tradition this will centre around the Jesus Prayer. Although the Jesus Prayer in itself is very simple, it aims at the prayer of the heart, that is the union of the mind with the heart which

35. Stănliloae, *Rugaciune lui Iisus*, p. 81.
36. *Ne Vorbeşte Părintele Cleopa*, 2:8.

leads eventually to the vision of the Divine Light.[37] 'The heart is master and king of the whole bodily organism', in the explanation attributed to Macarius, 'and when grace takes possession of the pastureland of the heart, it rules over all its members and all its thoughts: for it is in the heart that the mind dwells, and there dwell all the soul's thoughts; it finds all its goods in the heart. That is why grace penetrates all the members of the body.' [38] When one appreciates the importance of this prayer of the heart, it is easier to understand why parts of the tradition insist that it is actually dangerous to practise the Jesus Prayer without competent direction.

Spiritual Fathers in Romania Today

We have seen how great the spiritual father's role is understood to be in the tradition of the Church. Now we must look at how Romanians today consider it as they struggle after nearly fifty years of communism to live out this tradition in a very different world. Fr Ilie Moldovan, an elderly professor of ethics in Sibiu who was himself a parish priest for many years, sees the spiritual father's work as a particular grace given to him by God. 'A spiritual father has a vocation to this work', he believed. 'The vocation is verified by the fact that you can do nothing else'.[39]

In making this statement Fr Ilie begged a number of questions, which we must look at. We have seen already that the term 'spiritual father' covers at least two different roles. For some the spiritual father is the holy monk hidden in the mountains. For others he is simply the parish priest to whom one goes for confession. Spiritual fathers

37. See 'Hesychasm' in Cross-Livingstone, *The Oxford Dictionary of the Christian Church*, 3rd edition, pp. 763-764.
38. Pseudo-Macarius, Homily 15.20; PG 34.590A; translated by A.J. Mason, *Fifty Spiritual Homilies* (London: SPCK, 1921) 116.
39. Interview, 1997.

are, of course, men, not wholly unlike other men, not wholly unlike other priests. Each has his own characteristics, his own talents, which God has chosen to use in the building up of his faithful people:

> Spiritual fathers are not all the same. Fr Arsenie Boca of Sâmbătă, later of Prislop, was a good theologian. Fr Ion Iovan of Recea was different from Fr Cleopa. A spiritual father must be an organ of the Holy Spirit. He must speak from God and be taught by God. His greatest gift is the prophetic reading of the soul.[40]

Many of the interviews on which this section is based were carried out during the Great Fast before Easter. Those with whom I spoke had, for the most part, been taking the fast seriously and were now turning their attention towards their preparation for Easter Communion. In the Romanian Orthodox Church, Communion is a rare event for most people, being received only once or twice a year. This does not mean (as people in the West often think it means) a lack of devotion. Nor does it necessarily mean a kind of Jansenist spirit which keeps people at a distance from God. It does mean that people take their preparation for Communion with an impressive seriousness and the need to be truly purified in order to receive Christ's Body and Blood was clearly paramount in their minds. For such people, their approach to their spiritual father, be he their parish priest or a monk in a nearby monastery, would have about it the two-fold purpose: first to receive forgiveness for their sins; and secondly to be given permission to receive Holy Communion. Most people, when asked what they saw as the point of going to confession, said quite simply it was 'to receive forgiveness of my sins'. Some added to this a phrase such as 'to feel completely free of my sin'. Both clergy and

---

40. Interview with Fr Ilie Moldovan, 1997.

the more devout people believe such forgiveness should not be too easily given. As Bishop Streza explained:

A confessor should have the fear of God and a love for the penitent. If you fear God and feel pity for the suffering person you will not dismiss the person too easily and say 'Go away, you will be forgiven', for the forgiveness of God comes through the treatment administered by the priest. The priest must help the person and tell him what to do. If he fears God he will teach the penitent as if he is himself. He will say, 'This is the treatment you need. You must take these drugs. You must pray; you must give alms; you must help the needy. . . .' If he loves the penitent he will see him and support him continuously. My own family all go to the same confessor. He is very kind and warm and loves us all. But he says NO firmly when we ask for something we shouldn't have; and he goes on saying NO. If he did not say NO, but said 'God will forgive', God will not forgive, either the penitent or the confessor.

In this Bishop Streza raises three matters we need to look at more closely: the responsibility of the confessor; the treatment for the sin; and the confessor's attitude towards those whose confessions he hears.

A Moldavian priest[41] remarked that in their tradition a priest who allowed people to receive Communion unworthily would find that the people's sins came back onto him and he would either be condemned to hell or find that death, when it came, would be a long and painful journey. Clearly

41. Fr Dan Sandu from Iaşi, interview in 1997.

the priest there has a twofold responsibility: first to protect the holiness of God and not allow the sacrament of Christ's Body and Blood to be in any way defiled or dishonoured; but equally he must protect the penitents from receiving Communion unworthily and so bringing down judgement on themselves.[42] They rely on him to protect them from such a grave sin.

The treatment of sin, of course, is a matter of the ascetical life and will be taken up when we deal with this later in this study. Good spiritual fathers, however, though they take sin very seriously, are as warm and loving towards their disciples as the one Bishop Laurentius describes. All those interviewed spoke with great gratitude of the affection and support they receive from their spiritual father but said they wanted him also to challenge them.

One of the moving aspects of this research was my discovery of the relationship of love which exists between disciples and spiritual fathers. People's descriptions of what sort of person a spiritual father should be all witnessed to the love which they themselves had found. The first quality people singled out is that the father should by his nature encourage openness. One young woman said:

> I want to find in a *duhovnic* a father with
> whom I can speak openly. If the first step is
> made the rest comes from God. My spiri-
> tual father puts himself in my situation and
> always advises me wisely.[43]

A young man said much the same, with the important addition that in his *duhovnic* he wished to discern the nature of Christ:

> I want my spiritual father to receive me all
> the time. I don't want a feeling of fear. Be-

42. 1 Corinthians. 11.27ff.
43. Anşoara Carol, interview in 1997.

cause he loves me he is a model of Christ. Christ would not refuse anyone.[44]

As well as this sense of acceptance, there is also an awareness that a father has accepted responsibility for his spiritual children, and prays for them:

> A *duhovnic* should be warm and kind. He cares for you and will pray for you. You can feel that. To make confession you need to be in relationship with a person.[45]

And a theological student in Sibiu confirmed this expectation, saying:

> There needs to be a very close relationship between *duhovnic* and disciple. It is important that he understands you. It is not a teacher/pupil relationship. He is more like a friend. If it is based on friendship you can tell everything that is on your soul. The most important gift is that he can release us from our sin. He has a solution to each of our problems.[46]

And the same student added:

> One could take Christ as a model of the *duhovnic* since he was both judge, teacher and doctor.

Laura Maruşter gave moving testimony to the kind of *duhovnic* one monk is, at the same time pointing up by contrast the characteristics of other confessors which she found unattractive:

> Fr Teofil—he has a joy, he is full of life, of a good joy of God. Others are very dark. He

44. Christian Pavel, interview of 1997.
45. Constantin Fageţan, interview of 1997.
46. Lucian Colda, interview in 1997.

has an attractive simplicity. He is normal.
He has direct relationships with people. He
has a quality of the Transylvanian peasant.
I would like him as my *duhovnic* only he is
too far away. . . . Some priests and monks
are rigid. That may not be a bad thing, but
it frightens me. [47]

The quality of warmth and openness is more than a merely
human characteristic. It is regarded as a gift from God and
is part of the grace of true spiritual fatherhood and needs
to be conceived in theological terms. Fr Marius described it
in terms of humility:

What I look for in a *duhovnic* is *smerenie* [hu-
mility or meekness]. My own spiritual father is at a lower intellectual level, but he
doesn't need a higher level to save me from
different situations. I feel the power of the
Holy Spirit working in him. I would not
distinguish between a spiritual director and
a confessor, since you can't say the Holy
Spirit doesn't work outside the sacrament.[48]

This comment reminds us that most of a spiritual father's
contact with his disciple takes place in confession. So it is
here he must prove that he is trustworthy:

Duhovnics must convince the penitent first
that they will keep the secrecy. In this way
they must win the trust of that person. The
importance of the secrecy is winning the
trust.[49]

Metropolitan Nicolae of Timişoara had a very demanding
concept of what people expected to find in their spiritual
father:

47. Laura Maruşter in Timişoara, interview 1997.
48. Fr Marius, a university chaplain in Timişoara, interveiw 1997.
49. Fr Mihai Sămărghiţan, interview in Sibiu, 1997.

People's first expectation of a confessor is
his own example of life. They must offer to
the people a model of the life of Christ in
themselves. The faithful should see in the
confessor someone who strictly observes the
teaching of our Saviour Jesus Christ. The
second thing they look for is advice. He
must know how to give advice for everything that concerns the daily life of believers. He must give advice on how to be set
free from a sin which has been committed
because of the weakness of the flesh, but
also give advice for everything that constitutes daily life, especially concerning the circumstances which create the possibility of
committing particular sins.[50]

In this response one is aware of a recognition that the spiritual father works on two levels. One level is purely divine.
He must show Christ to his people, not just by his own
attempt to conform his behaviour to that of Christ, but by
allowing Christ to live in him. This, ultimately, is a work of
grace and is what makes the great spiritual fathers so immensely attractive to the faithful. In them they find Christ.
Through them the faithful feel they are in touch with God.
Irrespective of what the father might say, they will still feel
encouraged, warmed, inspired by this mediated contact with
the Christ who lives more openly in his chosen ones. At
the same time there is need for much advice about daily
life, and while some of this may come from the sheer holiness of the father, much must come from actual experience of life, of sin, and through reading the great spiritual
fathers of the Orthodox tradition. How then do priests prepare for their work as spiritual fathers?

50. Interview in 1997.

Since being a good spiritual father is a gift from God, no one can achieve it simply by study, though study will have its place. More important than any number of books read is the quality of one's own Christian life and the example of one's own spiritual father.

> To become a good *duhovnic* you must first be a good Christian, and to become a good Christian you must have had a good confessor. You cannot be a good confessor without having learned from a good confessor. A confessor should have models. Confessing cannot be taught in a lecture room. A confessor will confess the faithful in the same way as he was confessed.[51]

The need to have a good model is more than just having an example to work from. In the Orthodox tradition there is a real sense of a genealogy of spiritual fathers. Each great father hands on his gift to others, either in whole or in part. This provides a kind of apostolic succession which puts present-day Christians in almost direct contact with the earliest fathers of the Church, a link of vital significance to the Romanian Orthodox. As a confessor learns from the example of his own confessor, so also he takes upon himself the mantle of Elijah. The art of hearing confessions cannot be learned in a lecture room.

Even so, lecture rooms have their importance. The Patriarch of the Romanian Church himself was aware of this.

> Since the Church has many problems at the moment it cannot devote enough time to the preparation of confessors and we hope for a time when a priest, after he has completed his university training, will be able to

51. Bishop Laurentius, interview in 1997.

follow courses which will prepare him to be a confessor; courses in which he will be able to ask questions and be answered by his own bishop.[52]

The Patriarch spoke of a need for young priests to learn more about psychology and about how the modern world has impinged upon the traditional moral teachings of the Church. It is also true that, though in principle the Orthodox Church is rooted in the teaching of the Fathers, in practice, because of poor teaching and inadequate libraries, actual knowledge of the Fathers is quite sketchy and one often hears the same patristic quotations or fragments of spiritual advice repeated with perhaps little real understanding of the context.

And Metropolitan Nicolae spoke of the inadequacies of many of the present-day priests as well as of his own attempts to give them some help.

> The sacrament of confession suffers very much in the present day since priests are not always able to confess people properly. There is a regress in the spiritual life. We have gone as far as to believe it is enough for a believer to be confessed and to be given communion only once a year. I realise this regress from seeing (not hearing) how some priests hear confessions. I have been in a church where one priest celebrated the liturgy while another heard confessions. I've seen people kneeling there for just one minute. I doubt whether they could have said anything important, or said what was really on their conscience in one minute. This is why I got a professor from Bucureşti to translate from

---

52. Patriarch Teoctist, interviewed in Bucharest, 1997.

the Greek a book called *The Very Useful Book for Souls* by Saint Nikodim the Hagiorite.[53] He wrote this book using not only eastern sources but western ones, especially catholic ones. We only printed a few copies twelve years ago as the censor would not allow more. And the censor insisted we take out chapters speaking of sin and the moral life, pretending we were living in a golden age in which people are all new. We could not refer to the sins people can commit. Now we will print it again in full. This will tell priests that confession should not be done in a hurry because this is important in a believer's life. I think one of the greatest things people need today is a good confessor. The ethical level of the people is very much influenced by the confessors. While we don't have good confessors the spiritual life of the people is low. [54]

The amount of time clergy spend hearing confessions was referred to quite often during our discussions. Fr Eugene said he was prepared to give any amount of time to the matter, and this was borne out by his own practice of staying in church, sometimes till after midnight, hearing confessions. The Patriarch, too, recognised as a problem that too few confessors were hearing too many confessions:

Here at the patriarchate we also have very good confessors, but they don't have special training. Fr Sofian from the Antim monastery can't cope any more with the flocks of people who come to make their confessions,

53. An English translation is available as *Nikodemos of the Holy Mountain: A Handbook of Spiritual Counsel,* translated by Peter A. Chamberas (New York: Paulist Press, 1989).
54. Interview in 1997.

and in order to make a confession you need
more than ten minutes. There is a great deal
of work in this respect and when the training of priests improves, when they become
more missionary, they should teach people
that the absolution of a confessor like Fr
Sofian, or Fr Arsenie, or Fr Grigorie is not
more efficient but has the same value as that
given by the parish priest.[55]

Since many priests and bishops regard it as a regrettable
state of affairs that people go to monastic confessors rather
than their own parish priests, we need to ask why this happens and whether, in fact, there is something unsatisfactory in the training of the parish priests for the Romanian
Church. With large numbers of students in the theological
institutes, preparation for ordination is largely academic
and lacks a consistent pastoral or spiritual training. Well
motivated students ensure they get experience in their own
parishes, if they have good parish priests, and learn a great
deal from good spiritual fathers, if they have them. But,
not surprisingly, we found that there is a huge range in
competence and trustworthiness amongst the parish clergy.
Some are greatly respected and much sought after; others
are seen purely as cultic figures whom no sensitive or serious Christian would ever consult.

One priest who, as Professor of Moral Theology at Sibiu,
was intimately involved in the training of priests, was emphatic about their need for a more extensive preparation
for this vital ministry:

To prepare for this work one needs a good
knowledge of Holy Scripture, of the Holy
Fathers, of great spiritual fathers and a special experience of how God communicates
his will. This is the work of prayer. More

55. Interview in 1997.

than half the priests should not be *duhovnics*
because they don't know the spiritual
fathers.[56]

To become a good spiritual father, a priest must have done
more than simply have studied a lot, or even have had long
experience as a parish priest. A spiritual father needs to
know himself, for it is largely through his own experience
of the ways of God that he will be able to help others:

> One needs a long preparation to be a good
> *duhovnic*. It depends on how you see real-
> ity. Your own character says something. It
> is important to prepare yourself and to know
> how God works in you. Real spiritual fa-
> thers are those who cut any trace of subjec-
> tivity out of their relationship.[57]

Why does Fr Moldovan speak of cutting subjectivity out of
the relationship, when the entire tradition asserts that spiritual fathers need to draw heavily on their own experience
of God? In fact, the demand for objectivity accentuates two
characteristics required of a spiritual father: he must be able
to stand back from his own experience and from the
affection or friendship he has for his disciple, if he is to be
able to do what is really necessary for that person's spiritual
welfare. In this way he should be like a doctor—a favourite
analogy, as we have seen—whose clinical work must not
depend on or be hindered by his feelings for a patient. At
the same time a spiritual father must keep in view his goal,
which is neither to make his client happy nor to achieve a
human kind of success, but to save souls. As Robert Lazu[58]
wrote:

> I think a *duhovnic* must have a single preoc-
> cupation—the salvation of believers. Some

56. Fr Illie Moldovan, interview in 1997.
57. Sibiu students interviews, in 1997.
58. A young theological graduate in Timişoara, interviewed in 1997.

priests should not be *duhovnics* because spiritual fatherhood presupposes an experience and a knowledge of the 'science' of salvation which cannot be gained within a year.

This 'science of salvation' is to be learned both from books and from one's own prayer:

For preparation of a *duhovnic*, fasting and prayer are most important as this helps him to be in communion with the fathers who gave the teaching we read about. Other important books are Saint Nikodemus of the Holy Mountain, Basil the Great, John Chrysostom, Gregory of Nazianzus' Pastoral Advice. I also read the works of people like Fr Cleopa and Fr Teofil.[59]

Your preparation needs to be continuous and without end and you learn all the time from books. The books of the Holy Fathers are very useful, as are contemporary studies. These show how the spiritual father can teach himself and teach spiritual guidance to those whom he guides. Of contemporary writers Ioan Buga [and] Ilie Moldovan are particularly good. Also Evdokimov and Stăniloae, Vasile Mihoc and Antonie Plămădeală. In Romania we have a great value for the person.[60]

---

59. Fr Marius Ioana.
60. Fr Ioanin Chilan. See the Bibliography for this and some of Staniloae's dogmatic work; neither his commentary on the *Philokalia* nor his writing on prayer are available in English.

FINDING A SPIRITUAL FATHER

The process of finding a spiritual father is something of a
mystery and various people go about it in various ways.
Some people we interviewed simply went to their parish
priest and were more than happy with what they found.
Others searched around until they found a person who
was truly sympathetic to their needs. Sometimes there is a
clear sense of choice. On other occasions people are convinced that God has done the choosing. To some extent
one's choice will be determined also by one's expectations.
One young woman told me:

> I had difficulty choosing my *duhovnic*. At first
> I tried sensible reasons. This failed. Then I
> just went to a particular person. I expect for-
> giveness of sin first of all. I have many prob-
> lems relating to faith. He is a support in re-
> solving faith—and problems between
> people. He is very gentle. With a problem
> he invites me to state the problem. He helps
> me find a solution. He gives me teaching
> and books—Paul Evdokimov; *The Sacrament
> of Love*. The Holy Fathers. Sirach.[61]

This young women, it would seem, went in search of a
priest who could simply hear her confession and give her
absolution, feeling this was her primary need. But from
the relationship she found spiritual counsel and support.
Another student found his *duhovnic* more by accident than
by intent, yet the encounter turned out to be an event of
continuing significance in his life:

> I found my spiritual father by God's will.
> When I came to Timişoara I was looking
> for something else. I was working and found
> work in a monastery where I stayed for

61. Laura Maruşter.

seven months as a brother. I didn't remain
there because I felt that several monks did
not understand their vocation. I feel rather
guilty about making such a judgement, but
that's how I felt. I also found it difficult to
live in the mountains instead of in a town.

Subsequently, this young man left the monastery to study
theology, but he continues his relationship with the spiritual father he had in the monastery. 'My spiritual father
supports me in doing theology,' he goes on, 'but really wants
me to come back. He gives me more freedom than I can
handle.'[62]

Another young man shows how high an expectation he
has of his spiritual father and also the responsibility which
he feels towards the father he has chosen:
I would expect to be warned, admonished.
He must lead you and may show you things
you didn't see or were not aware of. To be
like an objective judge. He must be an understanding man. There is also some kind
of election. A spiritual son chooses his confessor. When you are sure he is the spiritual father for you you must do everything
he says. The ideal relationship is that between father and son. The worst thing is
for the spiritual son to judge the father and
criticize what he says. The penitent must
have right judgement (*bună socoteală*). Antony the Great said this is the main virtue
which links humility and prayer and can
give you the ability to choose between spiritual fathers but not to judge them. The peni-

62. Christian Pavel, interviewed in Timişoara, 1997.

tent should do what he is told even if he doesn't agree with it.[63]

The reference here to Saint Antony makes it clear that the quality of right judgement or discernment is not one that comes by cleverness or learning, but is a gift from God. Discernment can only be exercised against a background of humility and prayer, because one is seeking to discern the will of God, not one's own private good. A person who wants to hear the invitation which God is offering needs to set aside self-centred desires—and these are very good at hiding themselves. A spiritual father can generally spot the self-centred movements better than we can ourselves and so can help us make a God-centred response to the crucial choices of life.

The director of a large oil company told how he found, rather than looked for, a really good spiritual father:

> As a child my *duhovnic* was the parish priest. For quite a long time here it was Father Chilan. Then I met a special *duhovnic* at Cernica, Fr Ilie. He is a very warm person and you feel the urge to tell him everything.[64]

Another young man, whose relationship with the Church was fairly critical, found this responsibility of choosing a spiritual father a real problem, admitting, 'I am confused about this. I cannot search for a spiritual father because the teaching says I cannot judge my spiritual father. Searching means judging.'[65] And a fellow student, who had very strong awareness of his need for a confessor who could give him absolution from his sin, was ready to find spiri-

63. Călin Sămărghiţan, interview in Sibiu, 1997.
64. Lucien Stanciu, interview in Ploieşti, 1996.
65. Florin Doboş, interview in Timişoara, 1997.

tual counsel anywhere, pointing out that, 'A spiritual
father can be a layman—anyone who can give advice. He
leads a person in the spiritual life through his experience'.[66]
There is, then, a certain hit-and-miss factor in finding a
spiritual director. Some people go to the most available priest
until another, who is more clearly the right director for
them, appears. Others move around various priests until
they find themselves settling with one whom they can really trust and respect. Yet they have a clear sense that God is
involved in their search. They cannot simply look for someone sympathetic to what they desire. In the end the director they settle on is the director they believe God wants
them to have.

Finding a good spiritual father may prove a difficult un-
dertaking. Romanian spiritual fathers who are nationally
known live in isolated places and cannot be consulted very
often. During the decades of communism very few really
able men were allowed to go into the monasteries. This
has left the Romanian Church with a great shortage of
middle-aged, experienced leaders, either for the episcopate
or for the work of spiritual fatherhood. This is a lack of
which the Church is well aware and her leaders often speak
of it. The problem has been compounded by the nature of
theological education, which has tended to focus on learning by rote. As a consequence it has avoided a critical approach common in the West and has not always dug very
deep into the teaching of the Fathers. Clergy give a superficial appearance of 'knowing the Fathers' because they quote
from them very readily. One realises quite soon, however,
that everyone is quoting the same fairly small range of texts.
A shortage of books and an official communist discouragement of independent and creative thinking has made it
difficult for the Romanian Church to produce parish priests
who can face up to the problems of the modern age and
meet the intellectual and social challenges which confront

66. Mircea Szilagyi, interview in Timişoara, 1997.

their penitents, or provide the kind of theological insight and wisdom which their people need. Professor Cândea had a different and most interesting perspective on this problem, however:

> People complain today that they cannot find a spiritual father. It is particularly interesting how it has always been difficult to find a spiritual father. What is needed is good will and sincerity of purpose—two people seeking God together. Paisius and Vissarion[67] on Mount Athos were unable to find a spiritual father, so they agreed to obey each other totally and talked with each other, opening themselves totally. This is the essential mark of spiritual fatherhood and demands total good will on both sides. In fact we find our own counsels in Scripture and books. Beyond that we seek spiritual friendship. For this, goodwill and sincerity are essential.[68]

The good will of which Cândea speaks is essential to any relationship between a Christian and a spiritual father. Anyone seriously wanting such a bond must surely believe that it is indeed the activity of God which is guiding the relationship. The spiritual father must assume the goodwill of his penitent and believe the penitent is genuinely seeking God. The penitent needs to believe, really beyond a shadow of doubt, that his spiritual father loves him and genuinely wants what is best for him. Both persons are bound up in the good which God wills for them, and God's longing for both of them to discover the fullness of his love guides them as they seek direction together. It thus makes sense that where a spiritual father is lacking, good

67. Paisius' first disciple on Mount Athos; 'a young Romanian monk, who had begged him "with tears" to take him on'—Joantă, p. 138.
68. Interviewed in Bucharest, 1997.

will and sincerity of purpose in seeking God will still enable God to work within that person. This conviction helps us to appreciate that in Orthodox tradition, however good and holy the spiritual father may be, the real work is still God's.

SPIRITUAL ADVICE

We have seen that people's expectations of their spiritual father go beyond the absolution of sin, though even for this one needs a father who through the warm generosity of his nature will both encourage penitents to make a good and full confession and be able to make right judgement about the adequacy of that confession. We shall take a brief look now at the kind of advice a spiritual father usually gives, and the kind of problems with which he must often deal. Three responses from three different lay persons sketch out the areas of counsel which other people will then fill in:

> In crucial moments of our life the *duhovnic* is of great importance to show us the proper way to live as a Christian. The spiritual father knows our soul in some way; he knows our preoccupations and knows the shortcomings in our Christian education.[69]

> My spiritual father tries to increase my faith and calm my soul against misfortune. A spiritual father gives you courage.[70]

> I go to confession for forgiveness and also for advice in Christian life. I expect a *duhovnic* to teach me how to pray, to be more devout,

69. Dr Zoe Popescu, interviewed in Sibiu, 1997.
70. Romul Petrişor, interviewed in Sibiu, 1997.

to be gentle in spirit and to have the power
to overcome all difficulties.[71]

Clearly a large part of the *duhovnic's* responsibility is to deal
with the problems of daily life as they arise and as they
impinge on a person's Christian faith. A student in
Timişoara was more specific about this:

> From a *duhovnic* I would expect advice on
> the difficulties of life, and in taking decisions.
> In general he helps me to consider my own
> acts and deeds. He leads me through a con-
> sideration of my life. I would not trust him
> if he claimed to know what God wanted for
> me. Normally I go to confession monthly if
> possible, and mostly to seek advice. So I
> see the purpose of confession as first, guid-
> ance; second, forgiveness of sin; and third,
> preparation for communion. Forgiveness
> cannot improve my life with God if I stay in
> a state of sin, for then I cannot see my path
> towards salvation.
>
> The sort of advice I seek is about my reac-
> tions to society—getting angry. I find it
> difficult not to lose my temper. It is the man-
> ner of being angry which is at fault—not
> diplomatic but very rude.[72]

Secondly, there is the area of prayer in which (not surprisingly) Romanian Orthodox suffer from the same problems
as other Christians: distractions and the danger of prayer
becoming a mere formality. Anişoara Carol was given standard advice on this matter:

> My spiritual father encourages me to keep
> praying that God in the end will enable me

71. Mrs. Carmen Sămărghiţan, interviewed in Sibiu, 1997.
72. Daniel Săbau, interviewed in Timişoara, 1997.

> to pray not only with the lips but with my
> heart; he tells me to pray the prayers slowly,
> in thought so that I will understand what
> they mean and so that my mind will become
> attentive to the prayer.

We will see later how this advice conforms to the ideal of praying with the heart as well as with the head.

Thirdly, we see the role of the spiritual father in 'calming the soul'. This phrase was used quite often. In the Orthodox tradition, having a troubled or turbulent soul is seen as a particular hindrance to the spiritual life. Present-day Western Christians may disagree, regarding a troubled soul as perhaps a necessary stimulus to attack a problem in the world or in the self. In the East calmness of spirit is viewed as an essential quality of a true Christian life.

THE PHYSICIAN OF SOULS

Since the time of the Gospels themselves medical analogies have found their way into christian teaching. They have been commonly used as illustrations of the spiritual life and hearing them in conversations about the work of spiritual fathers comes as no surprise. What did surprise me was just how often I heard them in Romania. A young priest, for example, said:

> A good spiritual father will understand the
> man and will know how to offer the proper
> medicine and to make a true diagnosis. He
> must be sensitive to the possibilities of con-
> version within the person. The spiritual fa-
> ther must be able to extract the bad things
> from each situation as a doctor does when
> he cuts out disease.[73]

73. Fr Ioanin Chilan, interview in Ploeşti, 1997.

In this we see the emphasis on right knowledge. A spiritual father, like a doctor, cannot afford to be ignorant. He must know how to adapt the diagnosis and the medicine to the individual rather than treating all 'cases' as if they were the same. In this there is a recognition that the spiritual father's treatment will not always be pleasant. There are times when disease must be treated with harsh remedies or firmly cut away, and the spiritual father cannot be sentimental or unrealistically optimistic.

The Patriarch of the Romanian Church made a similar comparison:

> As a doctor will get into your body and try
> to find the sickness, so the confessor will
> enter your spiritual life and make it possible
> for a new life to be born in you.[74]

Patriarch Teoctist was the only one to speak directly of 'new life' being born in a person, yet the image is implicit in the whole experience of spiritual fatherhood. This aspect of fatherhood refers to more than the loving care which a father should be expected to show a child. There is an assumption that the spiritual father helps to give birth, and has a real generative role in the coming to birth of a new Christian soul. So far we have heard the father spoken of as teacher, begetter, midwife, and healer. When we come to look at confession and penance within the Romanian tradition we shall discover the medical analogies appear again. Now we must look briefly at the spiritual father as someone who supports and protects his disciple in a dangerous world.

TOWERS OF THE CHURCH

In the Western Christian tradition, the spiritual father tends

74. Interview in Bucharest, 1997.

to be thought of as having only a private, personal role in the Church. In the East, at least in Romania, his role is public. During the dark days of communism the knowledge that Fr Cleopa, Fr Arsenie, and a handful of others were alive and praying for the Romanian people was a source of great encouragement and strength to believers who felt themselves under relentless attack. Many people attribute the survival of the Romanian Orthodox Church to their prayers. Now that communism has passed, Romanian people feel immensely insecure as their society undergoes massive economic change and comes into contact with the secularisms and religious pluralisms of the West. The resulting search for stability and security, as described by a Sibiu theological student, again looks to the spiritual fathers as models and sources of strength:

> Great *duhovnics* are the towers (*stâlpuri*) that support the whole church. They are a model, a model of sanctification.[75]

Laura Maruşter used the same word:

> The *duhovnics* are the towers of the Romanian church. There are a lot of old fathers unknown who support the Church by their prayers.

These 'towers (*stâlpuri*) of the Church' exist not only in modern, post-communism Romania but stretch back to earlier ages, joining the generations together and providing a living channel of the Spirit. When talking with one of these great spiritual fathers, one has an extraordinary awareness of moving out of the present into a timeless past. The same words, with the same spirit of gentleness, the same freshness—as of a Christianity newly discovered—come to us as they did to the Christians of the fourth and fifth centuries when the sayings of the Desert Fathers first began to

75. Lucian Colda, interview in 1997.

find their way into the wider church. This observation by a Westerner did not surprise the Romanians. To them the living presence of the past was an entirely natural and wholly desirable feature of life in the Orthodox Church:

> Great spiritual fathers are like candles in the life of the Church. It is very important to receive advice from these fathers because you feel their power and authority. . . . Our Lord says, 'I will be with you', and he is with all spiritual fathers. Since his presence is the same in all of them you feel you are in touch with the earliest days of Christianity. There are differences among different spiritual fathers, but this is the same difference that existed among the Apostles. . . . The Holy Spirit is the same Spirit as in the time of Basil the Great so we can expect the spirit of the spiritual fathers to remain the same over the centuries.[76]

The Gospel of Christ begins with the preaching of John the Baptist: 'Repent'.[77] And at the beginning of any serious engagement with God is the need to repent of sin, not once, but constantly, for the tendency to sin is deeply rooted in all human beings. So every spiritual father must concern himself with his disciple's need to examine himself, or herself, constantly, to discern the sins that lurk in the secret places of the heart and to bring them out before God. Saint Symeon the New Theologian told his novices, 'Every day you are to confess every thought to your spiritual father',[78] and in one of his Hymns he said bluntly, 'Tell [your father] your thoughts, including any temptation, as if you

---

76. Fr Marius Iona, interview in Timişoara, 1997.
77. Mt 3:2.
78. Turner, 138, citing *Chapter 122; Chapitres théologique, gnostiques et pratiques*, edited with French translation by J. Darrouzées. Sources Chrétiennes 51 (Paris: Cerf, 1st edn. 1957, 2nd 1980) 669C.

were speaking to God, and do not hide anything'.[79] In the same way the modern day confessor will encourage his disciple to confess regularly and fully so as to approach Holy Communion with no stain of sin upon the soul and to be able to draw nearer and nearer to the God who is the goal of the Christian life. The sacrament of confession makes up a great part of the spiritual father's responsibility for the men and women for whom he cares. As we now begin to look at the way Romanian Orthodox use and regard the sacrament we shall find differences from some of the stereotypes of confession in the West. We shall find people going to confession with great care, with reverence, and with gratitude that their spiritual father can deal so well and so compassionately with their sin. Without confession, spiritual fatherhood would have no edge. It would become vague and undefined. It would lose touch with the reality of human life. Without confession spiritual direction easily wanders into an area which has not much to do with God, but a great deal to do with human desires and illusions. As we shall see, a spiritual father must not flinch from the task of exposing the sins of those whom he cares for. And if he is successful, they will be grateful, as to a doctor who has taken away their disease.

79. Turner, 138, citing Hymn VI.27f from *Hymnes I*, edited by J. Koder, French translation by L. Neyrand. Sources Chrétiennes 156 (Paris: Cerf, 1969) 192.

CHAPTER 6

'Father, Forgive'

A LARGE PART OF THE *DUHOVNIC*'S RESPONSIBILITY, as we have already seen in previous chapters, is related to hearing confessions, absolving people from their sins, giving them advice as to how to overcome their sin, and giving them, when appropriate, permission to receive Holy Communion. When asked why they went to confession, most people replied—not surprisingly—that they wanted to receive forgiveness of their sins, to have that sense of freedom and joy which comes from knowing that sin is forgiven, and to be allowed to go to Communion.

In Romania most Orthodox lay persons, even the most devout, go to Communion only once or twice a year during the time of a major feast—usually Easter or Christmas, and receiving communion is therefore preceded by several weeks of rigorous fasting. A priest in Timişoara expressed what proved to be a common metaphor for an Easter confession and communion:

> Before Easter you clean yourself up to receive a guest of honour. The paschal guest must be received into a clean house of the spirit.[1]

An accountant with an oil company in Ploieşti admitted that he does not go to church with great regularity, but

1. Fr Eugen Jurca, interview in Timisoara, 1997.

159

does go to confession once or twice a year. In the same parish a medical doctor who is very active in the Church, does the same, but admits that she had returned to the practice only after the fall of communism:

> I go before Christmas and Easter. This was the custom during my childhood. From the 60s to the 80s was a long period when I did not make confession or communion.[2]

The communist authorities made it very difficult for professional people to be obviously involved in the Church.

Parish priests, on the other hand seem to have a regular practice of confession every three months.

> As a priest I go to confession four times a year. It is a chance to review, or examine one's life. The aim is to tell God your sins with sorrow so that he can restore life to righteousness.[3]

As a priest, of course, he receives communion every time he celebrates the Liturgy, so confession for him does not have the same immediate link to Communion it does for a lay person.

One elderly monk-priest with whom I spoke went more often than this.

> Usually I go to confession twice in each great fast—six times a year—but I can go any time if I feel the need. Fr Arsenie used to advise us to go to confession each evening.[4]

Daily confession may seem a little extreme to us, but is also

2. Dr. Zoe Popescu, interviewed in Ploieşti, 1997.
3. Fr Ioanin Chilan, interviewed in Ploieşti, 1997.
4. Fr Pantilimon, interviewed at Ghighiu monastery, 1997.

spoken of by Fr Cleopa and would seem to be a not uncommon practice within the monasteries where monks,
especially young monks, are continually urged to constant
vigilance over their souls. If they are unremittingly on guard
to spot evil thoughts as soon as they appear, they will be
equally ready and eager to get rid of these as completely
and as swiftly as possible.

Amongst the young, however, there seems to be an increasing practice of more frequent confession and communion:

> I go to confession as often as possible—
> weekly or twice a month. Under the influ-
> ence of Bishop Serafim and Fr Teofil I re-
> ceive communion every Sunday, if I can. I
> feel very sad if I don't receive on a Sunday
> · as if Christ has offered himself to me and I
> have refused.[5]

There may be particular reasons for this increased fre-
quency. Many of the young people interviewed were theological students at a particularly sensitive stage in their lives.
A number of these have wider contacts with the West than
is usual in Romania and they may be consciously or un-
consciously influenced by Catholic patterns. Clearly, as the
interview reveals, Bishop Serafim and Fr Teofil are widely
influential among the young, and both (but particularly
Bishop Serafim) advocate more frequent communion,
though always with thorough preparation and confession.

The seriousness with which several of these young people
approach confession is well illustrated by what one theological student in Sibiu wrote:

> I go to confession once a month. It is good
> that a person should confess as often as
> possible. But it is essential that a person
> should come back from confession better,

5. Constantine Jinga, interviewed in Timişoara, 1997.

closer to God and to his brethren. Certainly, then, when we go to confession we seek total forgiveness of our sins; but the forgiveness offered by a spiritual father has no effect if the man is not sincere. There he must confess all his sins in a deep condition of humility and repentance. He must try not to commit the sins he has confessed, as far as this is in his power. If he confesses serious sins the priest will not give him permission to share in the Holy Eucharist until after a particular time has passed and after he has fulfilled a particular canon: prayer, an act of charity etc. He has the right to share in the Holy Liturgy but he cannot receive the Body and the Blood of Christ without permission from his confessor. A person must be aware that at confession he stands in front of Christ himself in an invisible manner and the confessor is only a witness. The forgiveness of sins which the confessor offers comes in fact from Christ. Through confession and the other sacraments a person succeeds in making Christ come into him in a mystical, sacramental fashion. A person communicates with Christ in the measure in which he is open to receive Christ. Through the Holy Sacraments a man is able to arrive at *theosis,* through the transformation which he undergoes which produces in him the uncreated divine energies. In this way he can come to contemplate the uncreated, divine light. He is entirely filled with Christ, making him live in himself as Saint Paul said, 'Not I who live, but Christ who lives in me'. Therefore a person with a special spiritual life is always dissatisfied with himself

and will seek together with his spiritual father to advance further along the way of
perfection, step by step. He finds himself in
a continual epictasis[6], as Saint Gregory of
Nyssa shows. As much as he wants to do
the will of God, so much the more will he
contemplate Christ and make him more
present in his life.

Five points of considerable importance stand out in the
comment. The first is the need for sincerity, not just in wanting forgiveness but in contrition, which is the readiness to
do whatever one can to put right what is wrong and to
avoid further sin. The insistence on contrition assures us
that this penitent at least does not regard forgiveness as
automatic, or as a formality. A sacrament is not efficacious
if participation is not actively willed. The second point: permission to receive Holy Communion can itself be delayed
until the priest is sure that the penitent is truly contrite. For
grave sins this delay can last several years. Ordinarily, it is
more likely to be much shorter. One priest said he often
delayed people for up to a week just to show them that they
can, if they try, abstain completely from sin for that length
of time.[7] Thirdly, the penitent is clear that, despite the presence of a priest, it is Christ to whom he is really confessing
and Christ himself who gives him absolution. This attention on Christ helps to ensure that the sacrament of penance is part of a growing relationship with Christ and not
simply with the confessor. Fourthly, though the mention is
brief, the recognition that the penitent must come back
closer to his brethren reminds us that the penitent's
relationship with fellow Christians is a central part of this

6. 'A striving forward': see Gregory of Nyssa, *Commentary on the Song of
Songs*, Homily 5; PG 44:888A; translated by Casimir McCambley ocso,
Saint Gregory of Nyssa: Commentary on the Song of Songs (Brookline, Massachusetts: Hellenic College, 1988) 128.
7. Fr Eugen Jurca, interviewed in Timişoara, 1997.

sacrament. Finally, we see that confession plays an integral role in the process of sacramental growth which leads a person on to that participation in the life of God which is the goal of all Christian life.

Another student, saw his practice of confession once a month as being less than he would like:

> Before, when I had a spiritual father near me, I used to confess more often. Now I have a spiritual father who is a hermit in the mountains of Oltenia and comes down to the monastery only at the end of the week. Moreover, I am very busy being in my final year of studies, therefore I go just once a month. When I go to confession I am looking in the first place for forgiveness of sins. The spiritual father is a real father to me, full of understanding, with whom I can discuss all the problems which worry me. His fatherly advice is very useful to me in putting me right on matters, in giving peace to my spirit and order to my thought. He is not a mere psychologist who teaches me a series of counsels and makes a kind of therapy in me. Before going to him I ask that God will enlighten him and that through him God himself will speak to me.[8]

In these comments we see the broader role of the *duhovnic* merging with that of the confessor. Clearly, this student has chosen to go to the father who can be of most help to him, even though this is less convenient that he would like. Although any priest can absolve from sin, the particular priest one chooses as a confessor needs to give one the confidence and inspire the trust that encourages a full unburdening of the heart.

8. Dan Borchina, written response in Sibiu, 1997.

This same student also makes clear the important part that discussion of problems and fatherly advice play within the sacrament of confession. In this he draws a clear distinction between a spiritual father and a psychotherapist. He assumes that the spiritual father's advice comes from God. It is not mere human counsel, however sensible that may be. A meeting with one's confessor is an encounter with God; of this both parties are firmly convinced and acutely aware.

We see amongst the young a clear tendency to go to confession once a month, therefore, even though the current practice in Romania tends to be once or twice a year. The Patriarch himself thought this practice of monthly confession struck the right balance between laxity and the danger of formalism:

> The liturgical confessions enter into the rhythm of the spiritual life, for confession is not meant to be done just once a year, or during every fast, but should be done more often. Nevertheless it is not good to have it too often, for there is the risk that it will become a formality. We think that once a month is about right.[9]

His reference here to the fasting seasons of liturgical year[10] underlines the importance of confession in relation to the times of fasting and the common times for communion. These seasons, when all Orthodox are engaged in preparation for or celebration of the great feasts of the year, help to build up a sense of solidarity, of striving together for the Kingdom of God. At the same time, every faithful Chris-

9. Patriarch Teoctist, interviewed in Bucharesti 1997.
10. In the Orthodox Church there is a four-week fast before Christmas, a seven-week fast before Lent, up to two weeks of fasting before the Feast of Saint Peter (29 June) and a two-week fast before the Dormition of Mary (15 August). Wednesdays and Fridays are kept as fast days. Monks also fast on Mondays. In times of fast people abstain from meat and dairy products, and in the monasteries there is only one meal a day instead of two.

tian needs to progress at his or her own pace and to deal
with sin as it appears. Monastic life tries to keep a balance
between the community obligations which help to make
the monastery healthy and the differing spiritual needs of
individual monks. The variety of confessional practice
amongst the laity shows a similar and parallel flexibility.

In all religious practice there is the danger of an unthinking formalism taking the place of a genuinely affective
relationship with God. The relationship between human
beings and God is seriously damaged by sin, and it is the
awareness of this damage and of its catastrophic consequences which creates within the human soul a desire for
forgiveness. This experience of sin, this consciousness that
one needs forgiveness, is central to the sacrament of confession. Without it, confession becomes a mere ritual, a
duty to be performed because the Church requires it. In
Romania today people are well aware that communism has
left them a devastated society. Amongst Christians this
devastation is seen often in terms of sin, both because communism led people into sin by encouraging deception,
financial corruption and an atheistic philosophy, and because the decades of communism prevented the Church
from educating Christians properly in understanding and
accepting their responsibility for sin. Romania is not unique
in this awareness that a sinful people is ill-educated in accepting responsibility for sin. Western countries, one may
argue, are even more afflicted. But the Romanian awareness of the problem has a moving quality about it, particularly among the young. Before looking at how the younger
generation of Romanians think about it, however, we will
begin with the old, an eighty year old monk who spent ten
years in communist prisons. He spoke sympathetically about
the problem people have with sin, and he identified a crucial aspect of this as loyalty to Christ.

The Orthodox church is Christ's Church,
and Christ accompanied the Orthodox

Christian [during the communist years] so
that the Church could not be defeated. The
young people are very confused after communism. They come to church hoping for
salvation. They cannot blame others for their
sin. They need to understand their responsibility. Nobody can force you to do something. It depends on your own will whether
you stay with Christ or not. . . . The most
serious sin is to deny Christ. People gave
him up in communist times to get advantages in life, not because they had to.[11]

Despite the pressures of life under communism, he points
out, people did not have to sin. In the new Romanian
society, it remains true that nothing compels a person to
sin. Sin—as the spiritual fathers of Romania, like saints
through the ages, teach—is something we *choose* to do. We
can equally well choose to do right as to do wrong. Orthodoxy is fundamentally optimistic about people's ability to
avoid sin. As a tradition, it does not appear to have been as
much influenced by pessimistic views of the corrupt
nature of the human will as the West, both Catholic and
Protestant, has tended to be. For Orthodox Christians the
doctrine of synergy, of God working with his people and
people cooperating with God, is fundamental. Without God
we can do nothing. With God we must fight the battles of
sin and must try to do good rather than evil in every part of
our lives. Confession helps people to accept personal responsibility for their sins, and it is vital that the confessor
make sure that a person does not refuse this responsibility.
One priest who has heard many confessions said of his
village people, 'People try to find excuses for their sins.
Sometimes they try to show sins are not their own.'[12]

11. Fr Pantilimon, interviewed at Ghiughiu monastery, 1997.
12. Fr Vasile Fodoruț, interviewed in Sibiu, 1997.

Later we shall see that one of the motives for giving people appropriate penances is to ensure that they do accept responsibility. The confusion many people feel about what constitutes sin in a world which is becoming increasingly secular, underlines the need for sensitive education. Even the secular world contains much that is good and freeing for the human spirit, yet the Church, and particularly the monks often fail to recognise this. Florin Doboş, a theological student who found it difficult to reconcile the Orthodox Church with the modern world, spoke for another group of Orthodox believers who could not simply be dragooned into a monastic attitude of rejection of the world. 'I suffer from modernity,' he said.

> I am on the perverted side. If Orthodoxy is a generalised monasticism it is wonderfully strengthened. But there is a devastated part of Orthodoxy to which monastic spirituality cannot apply. You can't talk about authority and obedience. You can't just make people feel guilty. . . . I go to confession to receive advice because I don't feel guilty. I go to receive advice in order to feel the need for forgiveness.[13]

The 'devastated part' of which Florin speaks is more than the result of forty-five years of communism. He, like many of his young contemporaries, especially in the west of Romania, feels very much a part of Western Europe and is both sympathetic to, yet apprehensive of, the freedom and autonomy which characterise the literature and philosophy reaching Romania from France and Germany. One of his colleagues, on the other hand, had no such doubts about his need for confession:

13. Florin Doboş, interviewed in Timişoara, 1997.

I have a deep sense of my own sinfulness. I look for forgiveness of sin. I expect advice as well, but absolution is first. It is even more important than Communion. In my spiritual life I don't rely so much on my spiritual father. I find advice elsewhere, in conversation and in books. But I feel my sins are very deep. I compare confession to a child who is dirty and comes home to be cleaned up. When I commit a sin I feel this so deeply I cannot pray. I feel unable to talk to God. It is ridiculous talking to God when you feel such a sin. I understand why some people go to confession more than once a day. Without absolution I could commit suicide.[14]

In this we see a quite different perspective on confession. This particular young man has had a long and close relationship with his parish church and clergy, and for this reason was able to be very critical of the clergy. He did not automatically regard them as fountains of wisdom and, as we see, was quite willing to look for spiritual advice and counsel in books or from friends, in whom, he was convinced, God could equally be at work. Yet, with his deep sense of sinfulness, he felt the necessity of a priest who alone could assure him of God's forgiveness and give him freedom from his sin. And he recognised that in the dispensation of God it is precisely because a priest is also a sinful man that he can exercise this extraordinary ministry of forgiveness:

A priest as a human may be deeply sinful, but his power to forgive sin is most wonderful, more even than that of making bread and wine the Body and Blood of Christ. . . . There are stories of priests being

14. Mircea Szilagyi, interviewed in Timişoara, 1997.

replaced by angels for all sacraments except
confession. A person's confession must be
received by a human being.[15]

Fr Dumitru Staniloae makes this point when he says that
only a human being can minister forgiveness to another
human being, because it is essential that confession should
be made to someone who shares the condition of sin. No
angel could do this. This same point was taken up by a
student and elaborated in a way which indicates the strong
sense of relationship which exists amongst Romanian
Orthodox and between them and God.

> The deepest confession between man and
> God was given by God. God spoke to Adam
> face to face. Adam replaced the relationship
> with God with an image. We always want to
> be next to God and to love him directly. In
> confession you have one foot on the ground
> and one in heaven. When you love some-
> one you want something for him. Even rig-
> orous demands come from love.

This recognition of God's confession of love reminds us
that confession is fundamentally about love, God's love for
us and our love for God. Confession deals with sin, but
does not start with sin or finish with sin. Confession is
often a frightening and costly exercise for a person to engage in. Yet if we want to come before God in truth we
cannot avoid it. Saint John tells us that we cannot with truth
deny our sin and we cannot come to God with a lie.[16] Yet
God himself longs to restore the damage done by Adam.
God showed his love by dying on a Cross. Man needs to
respond to this offering with all he has in order to receive

15. Mircea Szilagyi, interviewed in 1997.
16. 1 John 1:8,9.

fully the love which God offers. The recognition that man and God can, in the end, speak face to face is one of the glories of Christianity. That this inevitably will happen, however, should not be too lightly assumed. To think we can speak face to face with God before we are ready betokens pride and suggests the very *hubris* for which man was cast down from Eden and which continues to undermine his attempts to be restored to the lost relationship with God.

> Jesus is a bridegroom who invites me to be a bride, but I behave like a prostitute. Yet Jesus never ceases to be a bridegroom. When I sin I cannot pray because I know I am not fit to talk to God. All I ask is his mercy not to turn away his face. . . . I feel ashamed before my spiritual father when I take my sins to him. A man confessing directly to God would be superior to one confessing through a priest. We cannot speak face to face with God. . . . But a priest is not like a pipe through whom grace flows. God becomes real and obvious in the person of the priest.[17]

Ion Buga, in his study of pastoral theology, supports this student's conviction that the refusal to confess is a form of human arrogance: Not to confess to a priest, but to think one can defeat sin without the sacramental help God offers is simply pride.[18]

This student's remarks actually show a maturity which is surprising in a young man whose experience of the spiritual life, though intense, has not been extensive. In fact, it is very likely he is repeating what his spiritual father has told him. As one moves around Romania one hears simi-

17. Christian Pavel, interviewed in Timişoara, 1997.
18. Buga, *Pastorala*, p. 104.

lar nuggets of spiritual teaching repeated by many different people. This in itself demonstrates the respect in which the spiritual fathers are held and the influence they have in forming the minds of their disciples. The fact that the same teaching circulates widely throughout the country can rightly be used to suggest that the truth and depth of the teaching is widely recognised and valued; or it can indicate how the Orthodox in Romania have had to survive on a fairly narrow range of resources and that this has led to considerable repetition of the same teachings. This can make them suspicious of originality and change—which again gives them stability in contrast with the constant desire for new things that Western Christians often demonstrate—but it also militates against a sensitive response to the insights and movements of the post modern age.

One aspect of Christian teaching which spiritual fathers now and in the past have wanted to make very clear is the catastrophic nature of sin. Sin must be taken very seriously because it corrupts the human spirit in ways which are often hidden from us and the activity of the devil must never for a moment be underrated. And yet the spiritual father must remind his disciples constantly that they are strong enough, in Christ, to resist. They do not have to sin. Like Jesus, they can resist temptation, no matter how great that temptation may be. As an old spiritual father in Timiseni monastery put it:

> Jesus was tempted in Gethsemane. If we are tempted by the devil we must turn to God. Everyone can resist sin by the power of God. We must confess from the heart, with all sincerity, hiding nothing. Tears are an excellent detergent for sin. We must feel disgust (*scârba*) for sin and not sin again. Sin, a single sin, is the only obstacle between man and God when someone comes to communion. It must be confessed. He has Christ in him. The Body and Blood truly are Christ.

Receiving communion unprepared makes a person like Judas. . . . Our Lord remains inside us as long as we don't make him go away by our sin. As soon as you sin, Christ leaves you, so you need to confess and communicate again. Make confession and communicate as often as you need.[19]

Here we see a shift in the perception of confession and communion. Rather than being a special event seldom experienced, confession and communion are intended as a mean to bring us to perfect unity with Christ. Fr Negrutiu sees this unity with Christ as something we can hope to experience in our present life on earth. His assertion that Christ leaves us as soon as we sin would not be shared by most Christian teachers since it would make nonsense of a doctrine of baptism, which incorporates us once for all into the Body of Christ. What Fr Negrutiu may mean here is that what departs is the intense experience of Christ's presence which Orthodox are not ashamed of wanting to experience after confession and communion.

In the response of a young deacon, we see a slightly different attitude to this relation between confession and communion:

For a deacon or priest confession and communion are not so immediately linked. This is not because priests are better than layman. A priest knows more about the Eucharist and can control himself better than a layman. Most Orthodox lay people should not receive communion too often or they lose the sense of sacredness of communion. A priest sees all his life through Christian eyes. As a deacon I try to see each

19. Fr Negruţiu, interviewed at Timişeni Monastery, 1997.

moment of my life through Christian eyes. Communion does not make people righteous—it is the goal of righteousness.[20]

At first sight this may seem a case of clerical arrogance, but it expresses the priestly ideal of staying sufficiently within the awareness of Christ's presence to be able to receive him sacramentally at any moment. One aspect of staying within Christ's presence is keeping oneself free from the sin which places a barrier between oneself and Christ. With lay people it may not be sin itself that keeps them from Christ, but their sheer concern with earthly, material things, and the business of working in environments that are not obviously centred on God. Given the reality of sin and the reality that most people live lives inextricably entangled with a disordered world, it is moving to see the sensitive manner in which many confessors maintain the ideal of perfection along with the practicalities of life.

Amongst the Romanian Orthodox, for instance, there is great criticism of the West's toleration of sexual relations outside marriage, and a very widely expressed disgust with the toleration of homosexuality is rooted in the strong conviction that this is a profoundly sinful condition. How then would a spiritual father react to the confession of either of these sins? In view of the strength of feeling it was surprising to find that, in fact, confessors reacted with a great deal of understanding and a willingness to work patiently within an unsatisfactory state of affairs until God was able to lead the person into greater knowledge. A priest in a housing estate said of people in irregular sexual relationships:

> I would allow freedom but would not allow
> people in irregular relationships to receive
> communion, except occasionally those who

20. Călin Sămărghiţan, interviewed in Sibiu, 1997.
21. Fr Eugene Jurca, interviewed in Timişoara, 1997.

are clearly going to marry.[21]
A theological student, similarly, was opposed to radical or
rough treatment of those confessing homosexual behaviour:
It is like a disease. You don't do surgery first.
You try treatment and only use surgery if
the treatment fails. Try to persuade.
Strengthen their will. If they come to confession they are seeking the will of God but
they may not yet have the strength to do
it.[22]

This was actually the treatment accorded a young man
whom I met on a train in Moldavia, who told of how he
had confessed homosexual activity to none other than Fr
Cleopa himself and had been amazed to be given absolution and told to go to communion straight away. And the
Metropolitan of Timisoara spoke of his own disappoint-
ment with young Orthodox in Timisoara who had, shortly
before, demonstrated against the European Community's
insistence that Romania's laws against homosexuals should
be relaxed. As he saw it,
Homosexuality is a kind of sickness. A spiritual father should not reject a person who
is ill but should direct him in such a way
that his disease can be healed. I was much
against the position of our young Christian
Orthodox who said publicly that homosexuals should be imprisoned. The Church does
not use police means of control but treats a
person with spiritual means until he is
healed. Confession and the Eucharist are
very effective means of healing someone.
Not prison. I am sure a good confessor who
encounters a homosexual can heal him
from his homosexuality, since homosexu-

22. Dan Săbau, Timişoara, 1997.

ality is a physical disorder but with a spiritual dimension. The main point is to heal him, not to kill him. [23]

In a more general way the chaplain to students in Timisoara showed a similar willingness to be patient and not to be shocked.

> The main problems which I experience in the confessional are problems of faith. Ifind that if people attend church and keep the commandments the problems of faith fade away. With people's sexual problems I prefer to take a gentle approach. Canon 106 of the Sixth Ecumenical Council gives power to the priest to be gentle. Sex is the most frequent problem with students, due largely to a lack of education. [24]

Clearly for him, as for the other priests who spoke with us, sacramental grace and teaching must work together in the formation of the Christian person. Through this grace and teaching Christians will come to know what sin is and be able to turn away from it.

Another priest expressed his understanding of spiritual fatherhood in a way which helps us to understand why the confessor/penitent relationship, which looks as if it could be very directive, is not always so:

> One must not transform a spiritual father into a guru. Gurus can give instructions and commands. A spiritual father helps you make decisions. He relies very much on freedom of choice. I don't want to compel but to

23. Metropolitan Nicolae, interviewed in Timişoara, 1997.
24. Fr Marius Ioana, interviewed in Timişoara, 1997.
25. Fr Eugene Jurca, interviewed 1997.

persuade.[25]

Yet one must not idealise. Many, perhaps most, priests are authoritarian and more inclined to give instructions than to seek to help a person towards full understanding and an honest decision. The young priest quoted above is unusually open to people and also very critical of most of his fellow clergy. Yet it is encouraging to see that even in areas, like sexual morality, where Orthodox teaching is unambiguous some priests recognise that they cannot simply issue *fiats*. People need to be persuaded, and persuasion takes time and patience. The attempt to persuade also shows a respect for the other person, and this is lacking when a priest relies simply on his authority to stop sinful behaviour. Again this willingness to persuade rather than to command is part of the spiritual father's concern that people should accept responsibility for their whole spiritual life. Sins are their responsibility, as are all their actions. They must not be unhealthily dependent on a spiritual father but learn from him to relate confidently to Christ.

CONFESSION IN THE COMMUNITY

In understanding the role of confession within the Romanian Orthodox Church one has to remember that until recently Romania was a largely agricultural country with the largest —and certainly the most devoutly Orthodox—part of its population living in the villages. This pattern is now changing and we hear views from the educated young which are very different from those of the village elders. But much of the understanding of confession has been formed in a rural community where everyone knows everyone else and where there is no such thing as private sin or private virtue. The Patriarch himself came from such a community in Moldavia and his recollections of it help to place this discussion in a larger context.

I now see my native village as a community
of wise people. All of them were good believers—men and women—as were my parents, and I was one of eleven children. . . .
In my village, on the day before a celebration, the priest rang the bell at 5 o'clock. If
we were in the field we stopped work then
as the feast had begun. Thus the feast had a
physical dimension, not just a spiritual one.
At least one member of the family would
then go to church to consecrate the whole
family. Before he went to church he was
supposed to ask forgiveness of the other
members of the family. When he got to
church, after kissing the icons he would
then kiss the hands and ask the forgiveness
of the senior members of the congregation
and of his god-parents if they were there.[26]

Confession traditionally began then with this mutual
acknowledgement of sin, this mutual giving and receiving of
forgiveness. The boundaries between this social awareness
and sacramental confession are not sharply delineated but
merge and blur. In such a village community people generally knew who was in a state of sin, who could not or should
not receive communion. Likewise the village shared in the
sinner's restoration. Confession and absolution had a communal dimension. This is obviously far less true in a city, and
the young people of today who have not grown up in villages
either *have* a far more individual awareness of șin, or (and
this was clearly true in Timisoara) have found within their
student community a common life that provides an adequate
substitute for the village community. Growth in Christian life,
confession and following spiritual fathers' directions were
something that the students in Timișoara shared in a quiet

26. Patriarch Teoctist, interviewed in Bucharest in 1997. Fr Dan Sandu
remembers the same custom in his village, fifty years later!

but impressive fashion.

On the other hand, the emphasis on confession within a village life centred on a particular priest can lead to problems, as the Patriarch himself acknowledged:

> The holy fathers say we shouldn't change our confessors. Sometimes the faithful exaggerate this rule, for when they get married, or move home to another village they think they shouldn't change their confessor so they give up going to confession.

This kind of misunderstanding, which happens in all churches, suggests that people allow their Christian faith to be too deeply identified with a particular community and have not understood that it is primarily concerned with God. Nevertheless, the practice of going to the same confessor—who knows the family, the person, and the circumstances of their lives—is an important principle which, in the clear teaching of the Romanian clergy, should be altered only in special need.

> We recommend that people use the confessor they can reach most easily because the power of confession is not dependent on the experience of the man, but is given to all confessors. Liturgical confession should be done by the faithful with his own priest. The priest is supposed to know the souls of the faithful with whom he lives. In this way he will be able to get in contact with the family, with the circumstances of the family, with the young people.[27]

So strongly did the Patriarch see the role of community in repentance that he was prepared to see that the process of sacramental reconciliation may be found outside the for-

27. Patriarch Teoctist, interviewed in Bucharest, 1997.

mal confessional and beyond the ministry of the priest:

> In the wide sense of the word, confessing includes example, advice and wisdom. All monks in a monastery and even all believers, even faithful women, have this through the fact that they answer questions about faith and practice. A person may tell his troubles to another person and that will be a kind of confession; and he will receive advice which is a form of spiritual advice. I have seen all the brothers in a monastery as confessors and I used to gain wisdom from the words of all of them. [28]

Again, it helps our understanding of confession to see it set with such blurred boundaries; it is a part of the activity of God within his Christian community. Confession must not be limited to the individualised, atomised event, as it is often perceived to be in a secular world where religion is habitually isolated away from 'real life'.

PENANCE

The word 'penance' has gone through a number of meanings in the centuries of its Christian use. It comes from the Latin *paenitere*, meaning 'to be sorry', and has always retained this sense of expressing sorrow. In some centuries the ways in which people were asked, or themselves felt moved, to express sorrow emphasised a degree of pain and suffering. Walking barefoot to Rome, submitting to a savage whipping, fasting in such a rigorous fashion that one's health was permanently impaired, gave penance a sense of unpleasant, perhaps even painful, punishment for wrong

28. Patriarch Teoctist, Bucharest, 1997.

done.[29] It is sometimes used in this sense still in ordinary
conversation. In western Christendom, however, a penance
given at the end of confession tends now to be a largely
token act of thanksgiving, or a psalm or a reading that
may emphasise a part of the counsel given in confession.
In the Romanian Orthodox Church this part of the sacrament of penance has retained a far greater significance than
it has elsewhere, even in the East. In the Russian and Greek
Orthodox Churches, it has now become very unusual to
give a penance at all. In Romania penances after confession appear to be universal. Significantly, though, the term
used to describe them is 'canon', a term referring primarily
to the canons of the Orthodox church on the appropriate
penances to be given for particular sins. There was some
disagreement amongst those interviewed as to whether it
was desirable to modify these canons in modern-day practice. What was clear, however, was that most priests do
modify them. As Professor Cândea said:

> In Orthodoxy we do not modify canons and
> penances, which date from the eleventh Cen-
> tury. But each confessor can adapt them on
> his own responsibility. Our problem in this
> matter of penances is not to satisfy God. I
> cannot offend God because he is too great.
> Our problem is to put ourselves on the good
> way— to erase the sin and feeling of guilt
> and to gain peace.[30]

His statement encapsulates two important principles: First:
a priest has a responsibility in the matter of confession; in a
very real way he must take the consequences on himself if
he gets things wrong. Part of his relationship with his spiritual child lies in sharing the responsibility for sin and the
responsibility for penance. There are several oral traditions

29. Since *paenitet* (according to Lewis and Short's *Latin Dictionary*) is derived from *poena* (Gr. ποινή), 'punishment', this is not surprising.
30. Professor Virgil Cândea, interviewed in Bucharest, 1997.

in Romania relating how great spiritual fathers imposed quite severe penances on people–four hundred prostrations, for instance—but then volunteered to do half of them themselves. Fr Cleopa himself, a notably strict confessor, recognizes different people's capacities:

> A penance must be in accord with each person's strength. One person is healthy and strong in body and can fast and not eat till evening; but another, poor man, if he does not eat two or three times a day collapses.[31]

In a later book he expands a little on this:

> The spiritual father must keep the measure of truth, that is he must keep the middle way between love and sternness, between careful interrogation and laxness. He must temper his advice as the Lord teaches him, from case to case; love with justice and reproof with patience and kindness. Then he must apply the canons according to the measure of the sins, according to the spiritual and physical condition of the believer, and in accordance with the practice and canons of the Church.[32]

On the other hand, the adaptation of traditional penances may be considerable, as we see with an experienced parish priest in Sibiu:

> In general I ask people to say prayers and to be merciful. I don't favour long drawn out penances as people don't do them. I would rather ask them to help a poor family, help poor children. For adultery or abortion I would ask them to dress a poor child

31. *Ne Vorbeşte Părintele Cleopa*, 2:12.
32. *Ne Vorbeşte Părintele Cleopa*, 5:92.

(instead of seven years separation from Holy Communion) and I would insist as strongly as I can that the sin should not be repeated. . . . The purpose of the penance is that the person is waiting for a canon to give him a sense of putting things right, and as a punishment. You give canons to make a religious teaching. . . . The penitent may not know prayers or have read at all from the Bible, so a penance might introduce them to this. I also encourage religious readings from whatever books they have. . . .Occasionally I have stopped people from receiving communion, but not for many years. We can't compare today with the past. I believe that someone like Saint Basil, if he had lived today, would have been more merciful.[33]

In this remark there is the recognition that people do need to feel they have made some kind of reparation for their sins. In that sense the penance may be backward-looking. But the real movement of the penance is towards the future, towards growth in Christian living. The second important point to note here is that the penance is not directed towards God. It is not intended to satisfy the wrath of God. Penances are directed towards the penitent and are intended to establish good behaviour. Fr Mihai continues:

A canon is not done for merit. It is not done to gain healing or to be forgiven. It is more to teach or train you. It is not a juridical act to win virtue. In a way it is punishment— you must feel that you do these canons not to oblige God to make you righteous but to show yourself you were wrong and feel you

33. Fr Mihai Sămărghiţan, interviewed in Sibiu, 1997.

were wrong. It is a tool you work with yourself. A penance is directed not towards God,
but against the sin. It goes with your will
and desire to fight against the sin. It strength-
ens you but doesn't win God's mercy. [34]

That would also be the opinion of a professor from
Bucharest.

In confession the priest gives penances and
counsel which help to establish and secure
for the future the forgiveness given by
God. [35]

Even so, the penance is not simply a helpful recommenda-
tion to be accepted or forgotten. Fr Cleopa says firmly:
You must do your penance. Someone who
receives a penance and does not do it cannot be cleansed of the leprosy of sin and
nor will his spirit be delivered from the service of the devil. [36]

A somewhat more rigorous attitude was shown by the professor of moral theology in Sibiu, but his concern was directed towards ensuring that repentance is real and great
enough to deal with the serious nature of sin:
With regard to penance, all canons are available for the confessor to use. This is not rig-
orism but realism. There is no forgiveness
bigger than repentance. Without canons you
cannot have of repentance. *Duhovnics* now
respond to sins at a low level. A *duhovnic*
must set high sights. If the *duhovnic* has

34. Fr Mihai Sămărghițan, Sibiu, 1997.
35. Buga, *Pastorala*, p. 104.
36. *Ne Vorbește Părintele Cleopa*, 2:11.

mercy for his spiritual son it is not good for him.[37]

Canons, therefore, refer not only to the canons laid down for particular sins, but to the kind of advice given for overcoming persistent sin. A young theological student who admitted to being much given to anger said:

> Canons teach a more realistic approach to spiritual life. They lead to a greater understanding of oneself. Most canons point to concrete things: 'Say a Prayer of Jesus before getting angry'. The teaching is directed towards behaviour. [38]

A young woman saw the canons in a similarly positive light:

> Canons help to solve the problems I have. That is their main purpose. They are not a punishment. My spiritual father gives me things to read and prayers to say.[39]

And a priest underlined the fact that in confession one is dealing with hurt people whose primary need is for healing and restoration to strength and health:

> Canons help a person come back to righteousness. Mostly they are intended for healing, but include teaching and prayer. They also try to make a person accept his responsibility. If you save a person from drowning you don't beat him, but resuscitate him.[40]

It is this therapeutic aspect of penance which Bishop Kallistos Ware emphasises as being the classic understanding of the Christian East:

37. Fr Moldovan, interviewed in Sibiu, 1997.
38. Dan Sabău, interviewed in Timişoara in 1997.
39. Laura Maruşter, interviewed in Timişoara, 1997.
40. Fr Marius Ioana, interviewed in Timişoara, 1997.

A juridical concept of confession would focus on Christ the judge giving absolution
from our guilt. A therapeutic concept fo-
cuses on the sacrament of healing. It would
involve the whole life structure and would
be closely related to the sacrament of healing. . . . Penances are part of the process of
healing. Christ is the surgeon. The priest is
the orderly who wheels the patient into the
surgery. Penance is a tonic to help us recover. Despite being absolved we may not
be immediately ready for communion.[41]

Bishop Kallistos, reflecting the fact that Russian and Greek
churches do not generally give penances, thought that penances may be given *more* often in a monastic than in a parish context. Monks can impose a kind of obedience which
is appropriate only to monasticism. Other people must learn
to follow their own consciences. This would suggest that
confessional practice in Romania is much more influenced
by monastic practice than is generally the case in Orthodox
Churches. Considering the high esteem monasteries are
generally accorded and their central place in Romanian
church and national life, this would not be surprising, but
it provides a useful perspective on the whole tradition of
spiritual fatherhood in Romania—that it has been so deeply
influenced by monastic concepts of obedience.

   The probability that Romanian confessional practice is
influenced by the monastic disciplines raises the spectre of
all kinds of extreme demands made by confessors on monks
being imposed on lay people; one thinks, for instance, of
desert monks watering dry pieces of stick for years on end.
Clearly some of the hesitation we noted earlier about going to monastic spiritual fathers centred on this fear, no
doubt with some justification, but a student with a very

41. Interviewed in Oxford in 1998.

modern outlook on life did not feel that the canons he had
received were directed towards breaking his will.

> The purpose of a canon is to make me feel
> responsible and to clarify my position in
> respect of my problems. It helps me to find
> answers to my problems. I've never received
> a canon which seemed to be a punishment.
> Nor has it ever seemed to me that my spiri-
> tual father was trying to break my will.
> Rather he tries to direct it. My spiritual fa-
> ther sees the will as a kind of energy. It can't
> be stopped; it must be well directed. With-
> out the will a human being is no longer a
> person.[42]

In this acceptance of penances as a normal part of confessional life we see the importance of the doctrine of synergy
in Orthodox theology. All salvation comes from God, yet
God asks for human cooperation. Men and women work
together with God in the task of perfecting their souls. It is
not enough to accept forgiveness of sin and go happily on
one's way. The sacramental grace of absolution is forward
looking, not just backward looking. It demands appropriate human response:

> To receive forgiveness it is not enough to
> have just the grace of God; the contribution
> of the penitent is needed. This is what is
> meant by *synergeia*—grace, deeds, and faith.
> Faith and deeds depend on human effort
> With these the person becomes a new be-
> ing and through communion he or she re-
> ceives special strength not to commit sins
> any longer.[43]

42. Constantine Jinga, interviewed in Timişoara in 1997.
43. Patriarch Teoctist, interviewed in Bucharest, in 1997.

WHY GO TO CONFESSION?

When trying to understand confession in the life of faithful Christians, one can easily get stuck on immediate problems of sin, and the practical questions of individual confessions. Yet it is important to see the role that this sacrament plays in the journey each Christian is seeking to make with God. Penance is more than simply being forgiven from time to time, rather like taking a shower from time to time in order to wash off the accumulated dirt. Repentance is a movement in the Christian life which must be constantly explored, constantly repeated, constantly deepened. It is also one of the most fruitful aspects of christian life, and so it was in terms of repentance that the Patriarch attempted to set the importance of confession:

> A real Christian spiritual life cannot be continued and cannot progress without repentance. The confessor is the one who can test and observe the level of repentance in each of us. The spiritual father has a supreme right over the person confessing to him. The confessor is bigger than I am even as Patriarch. The role of the confessor in the Orthodox church is to build the image of Christ within the human being. . . . Only when believers repent and receive the forgiveness of God through confession do they take a step forward towards God.[44]

Bishop Streza made the same point independently:
> The aim of confession is not only to be absolved, but to progress, to travel hand in hand with Christ. For when you take communion you have to take Christ in yourself.

---

44. Patriarch Teoctist, interviewed in Bucharest, in 1997.

You become Christophor—the bearer of
Christ.[45]

It is the realisation that he bears Christ within him that
encourages the devout Orthodox to take confession seriously. Likewise, it is the importance of the whole journey
of christian life which brings him to a spiritual father for
counsel that goes beyond the absolving of past sins. We
may, therefore, close this section by considering some of
the teaching of Fr Cleopa Ilie on confession to see how it
compares with what has been said above.

FR CLEOPA ON CONFESSION

Fr Cleopa saw a great urgency about confession. Sin is not
to be taken lightly, not to be left until time and opportunity
make it convenient to deal with. Speaking largely to peasant people he tells them,

> If you are mortally sick, do not run to the
> doctor, for you could die, and you would
> die unconfessed. First confess and then go
> to the doctor. If you die you will have light-
> ened yourself.[46]

Such practical yet uncompromising advice underlines his
conviction that confession is not simply a means of living
better in this world. It is a matter of heaven and hell, life
and death, more important than physical health because it
concerns eternal and not just earthly life. Yet Fr Cleopa did
not see confession simply in terms of preparation for death.
In common with much that we have seen above he encouraged frequent confession and listed five advantages of
the discipline.

45. Interviewed in Caransebeş in 1997.
46. *Ne Vorbeşte Părintele Cleopa*, 2:9.

☐ First, sin does not take root in us and
Satan's nest is ripped out. We sin so much,
constantly, every hour, we need to be constantly taking out these sins.

☐ Secondly, a man remembers more easily
the sins he has committed since his last confession and frequent confessions are more
likely to be sincere.

☐ Thirdly, a person who commits a mortal
sin can quickly get rid of it.

☐ Fourthly, he approaches death with a pure
spirit in hope and grace.

☐ Fifthly, the knowledge that he will soon
go to confession helps to keep him free from
sin.[47]

Such stark well-ordered teaching is typical of Fr Cleopa,
who had a lifetime of experience preaching to the devout
and simple people of Moldavia. As to what the person
should confess, apart from obvious mortal sins, Fr Cleopa
reiterated the teaching of all priests—leave nothing out.

Do not think that small sins are not serious.
You must confess them, as you hear in the
Gospel, 'Nothing unclean will enter the
Kingdom of Heaven'.[48]

Fr Cleopa wanted people to take responsibility for their sins.
This shows itself in two ways. First, there is the need not to
try to blame others, not only because this avoids responsibility but also because it actually introduces sin into the
confessional. 'Confession must be pure and must not speak
evil of anyone else, not even of the devil.'[49]

47. *Ne Vorbeşte Părintele Cleopa*, 2:18-19.
48. *Ne Vorbeşte Părintele Cleopa*, 2:22, citing Ephesians 5:5 a little freely.
49. *Ne Vorbeşte Părintele Cleopa*, 2:9.

Secondly, he insisted (as we have seen more than once above) that people can avoid sin if they really want.

> A man has as much power against sin as do all the devils of hell if he does not wish to sin; for God gives him the great power, from Baptism, to overcome the temptations of the devils.[50]

This may seem unduly optimistic to Western Christian who identify with Saint Paul in Romans 7, when he admits his own inability always to do what is right or to refrain from doing what is wrong. Men do not have it in their unredeemed nature to follow the ways of God, and though in baptism that nature is restored in us, like all things in the Christian life, its right working cannot simply be assumed. Christian life has to be worked at. Learning to use the power God has given us is one of the main reasons for going to confession and taking the advice of a spiritual father. Fr Cleopa would probably have considered the nub of the problem to be contained in the phrase 'wish to sin'. The reality is that people do wish to sin, whatever they say, and often whatever they think they feel. The purpose of the ascetical life within and outside monasticism is to purify the will, to allow God's grace to enter into its very depths and change the will into one that always wishes to do the will of God. This may sound like an exhausting task, one which is hopelessly beyond our strength. But Fr Cleopa counters this sense of despair by reminding us that God is here, understanding and enabling us even in our sin:

> In God's goodness there are no boundaries. He knows our weakness, that we sin willfully and unintentionally, knowingly and unknowingly. There is not a moment when we do not sin before God. But no one knows

50. *Ne Vorbeşte Părintele Cleopa*, 2:20.

the nature of man better than God, for he
made us from nothing. Therefore when we
return to him with tears, renouncing evil,
with a good confession, he forgives us.[51]

In the end it is God who saves us. We do not save ourselves. For all the deeply personal and costly nature of confession the sacrament remains in God's hands, not our own.
Every spiritual father must be aware that it is not his action, nor his advice, but God's action and God's grace working through him that restores a penitent to life and helps
him along the way to God. The reason people come to a
confessor like Fr Cleopa is because they sense his closeness to God. This closeness makes confession not more
frightening, but more reassuring, because it is through the
presence of God manifested in the confessor that the penitent discovers the love, the mercy, the compassion, and the
understanding which transforms confession into an act of
love gratefully entered into and life-givingly enjoyed.

51. *Ne Vorbeşte Părintele Cleopa*, 2:14.

Top left: Fr Cleopa Ilie. *Top right:* Bishop Laurentius Streza. *Bottom:* Agapia. Staretsa Eustochie *(left)*; Fr George Guiver CR and author *(right)*.

Top left: Metropolitan Nicolae of Timişoara. *Top right:* Fr Eugene Sturca. *Bottom:* Metropolitan Serafim Joantă with Sr Christine SLG at St Andre's Abbey, Bruges.

Top: Bishop Laurentius with the author near Caransebeş.
Bottom: Mirfield brethren with monks of Secu Monastery.
Fr Daniel *(second from right)* was imprisoned for many years.

Top: Agapia monastery.
Bottom: Brâncoveanu monastery, Simbăta de Sus.

Top left: Călin Sămărghiţan. *Top right:* Christian Pavel.
Bottom left: Constantine Fageţan. *Bottom right:* Constantine Jinga.

Top left: Daniel Sabău. *Mid-left:* Florin Doboş.
Bottom left: Laura Maruşter. *Top right:* Mircea Szilagyi.
Bottom right: Anişoara Carol with orphans.

Sibiu, showing its German architecture.

Neamț monastery, Moldavia.

Chapter 7

The Way to God

'Only in freedom can a person choose his own way.'[1]

THE PRACTICE OF CONFESSION and spiritual direction can seem constraining to modern Christian people, used to making their own decisions in life and convinced that they alone know how their relationship with God should develop. A spiritual father may seem a tyrannical, dominating figure depriving the sensitive Christian of the kind of freedom he or she needs to grow in confident love for God. We have already seen that the tradition of spiritual fatherhood as it is found in Romania has the sensitivity and gentleness which is characteristic of good fathers. In this chapter we shall look first at the importance of freedom in the Christian person's growth towards God and then look at some of the goals of this journey, divinisation (*theosis*) and dispassion (*apatheia*)—two of the most often misunderstood characteristics of the Orthodox teaching on the spiritual life. This will lead into a discussion of *ascesis*, ascetical labour being the means by which dispassion and divinisation are achieved.

One of the charming pictures which has come down to us from the time of the Desert Fathers is that of the young monk or the earnest enquirer asking an older monk, 'Father, give me a word'. The request has been repeated down the centuries and remains basic to the Orthodox tradition of spiritual fatherhood. Disciples—male and female, lay

---

1. Plămădeală, (1995) p. 146.

and monastic—have gathered at the feet of well-known spiritual fathers, sometimes with specific questions, more often with the simple request, 'Father, give me a word'. The request makes a number of assumptions. One, that the answer when it comes will be worth hearing. It is not sheer inquisitiveness that has caused the disciple to ask it. The motive is not a kind of spiritual dilettantism, but assumes that the spiritual father speaks words that come from God, words which will have a particular and unique significance in the enquirer's life. It has, too, a kind of personal quality about it. The questioner is not asking for a generalised sermon or a universal statement of theological truth. He wants a word that speaks to him, some short, simple piece of advice that will direct his way towards God. A second and possibly more important assumption is that when he receives the word, he will be able to follow it. There would be no point in asking for advice or direction if he had neither intention, nor desire, nor ability to take up what was offered. Orthodoxy, in common with most christian theological traditions, sees the human will as damaged and constrained by the Fall, but not utterly corrupted. As persons, we enter on existence with a weakened will and a nature which will tend to seek out the easy way. We are surrounded by temptation and by examples of evil and will easily acquire habits which are bad, even sinful. But we can still choose otherwise, and having chosen, we can act otherwise. Of all the advice given in the spiritual life the most common admonition is to choose rightly. The will must be educated, it must be taught to choose well. The will must be strengthened so that it may hold to what it has chosen. It is true, of course, that it cannot do this alone. Orthodoxy has often been accused of Pelagianism, that is the teaching of the monk Pelagius 'that man can take the initial and fundamental steps towards salvation by his own efforts, apart from divine grace.'[2] The accusation is unfair,

2. Cross & Livingstone p. 1248

as the teaching of Pelagius never found its way to the East and so his heretical views did not trigger off the extensive discussion of the human responsibility for salvation that took place in the West under the great Augustine. Nor has Orthodoxy had to respond to the justification by faith or works controversy which has moulded much of the Western understanding of the human response to God since the sixteenth century. Indeed it would seem that Plato rather than Pelagius is the source of the emphasis on personal effort in the spiritual life. As Anthony Meredith writes:

> Christians learned from Plato not only the importance of strenuousness in the service of God, and of the realization of the ideal, but also something of great importance about the nature of the end to be pursued.[3]

Plato himself shows how demanding and life changing this pursuit must be:

> ...there resides in each man's soul this faculty [to see light] and the instrument wherewith he learns, and that it is just as if the eye could not turn from darkness to light unless the whole body turned with it; so this faculty and instrument must be wheeled round together with the whole soul away from that which is becoming, until it is able to look upon and to endure being and the brightest blaze of being.[4]

God is worth any amount of ascetical struggle. Yet Orthodox Christianity has its own ways of insisting that christian life needs the constant support and intervention of God and that, however much responsibility men and women have for their christian life, they cannot work alone. A large

3. Meredith, p. 12.
4. *The Republic,* VII. 518C; translated by A. D. Lindsay (London: Everyman, 1906) 1948.

part of the centuries of battle to establish a sound doctrine of the Trinity was taken up with the need to ensure that the active role of both Son and Spirit in human life was established. Throughout the *Philokalia* the most constantly repeated text is, 'Without me, you can do nothing'. But it is equally true that without our willing cooperation God cannot save us. If we are to choose what is good we must be free. God does not want to compel good behaviour because he wants our love. Love, of its nature, cannot be compelled, but must be freely given. One of the first aims of the spiritual life is to acquire that freedom.

This is a freedom of liberty, not a freedom of licence. A Christian understanding of liberty is rooted in the biblical belief that each person is made in the image of God and must be trusted to act as a child of God. The trust will not always be fulfilled, but trust must be given if freedom is to be learned. A spiritual father must trust his disciple just as the disciple trusts his father. Determining how far to trust is a crucial characteristic of the discernment which a spiritual father must exercise in the counsel and direction he gives to those who come to him. It is the trust which transforms the relationship from one that could be dictatorial, autocratic or oppressive into one that is life-giving, for trust is an aspect of love and love is fundamental to growth in the christian life. As one Romanian spiritual writer sums it up: 'Only in the perspective and climate of love does authority not mean tyranny and liberty not mean just anarchy.'[5]

Whatever the demands made on a person in the course of the journey to God it must never be forgotten that love undergirds it all and that love is its goal. This is most simply and beautifully expressed by one of Romania's great spiritual fathers:

> Let us love each other truly. Let us try to
> love the whole world, regardless of whether

5. *Plămădeală* (1995), p. 78.

they are called to good or evil. Let us love
much and let us love well. Let us love
wounds and let us love those who wound
us. Christ is hidden in those whom we love.[6]

The last two sentences make it clear that Fr Arsenie is not
indulging in mere sentimentality about loving feelings towards the world. We must aim to love the whole world
because God does that and we wish to enter into the nature
of God. But very many people in the world are very wicked
indeed and not immediately lovable to those who have not
learned to see them as God sees them. They will wound us
as they wounded Christ. The wounds will test our love and
if we respond aright they will teach us to love. As one monk
said who had spent ten years in Romanian communist prisons: 'It was not the beatings that hurt me. It was the sense
of evil in those who were beating me that really upset me.'[7]
He was distressed that men who were created by God in
the divine image and likeness should have such evil in them.
That is a common experience of those who have suffered
torture and cruelty in the name of Christ. They discover in
themselves a deep concern for their torturers who are still
children of God and need to be loved out of the evil into
which they have fallen.

DIVINISATION

Love of this magnitude is clearly beyond nature. It comes
from God and is a sign of participation in the nature of
God. Our participation in the nature of God begins at baptism, otherwise the concept of being baptised into Christ
has no meaning at all. But growing into Christ, letting
Christ be formed in us, and so coming to share in the

6. Fr Arsenie Papacioc, cited by Bălăn, *Convorbiri Duhovniceşti,* p. 461.
7. Fr Pantilimon, interviewed at Ghighiu monastery, 1997.

divine nature is a life-long task; indeed it is the great task of Christian life which continues beyond death. And if Gregory of Nyssa's teaching on *epictasis*, 'the restless upward movement of the created spirt towards the uncreated infinite spirit of God',[8] is accepted, the task never really ends. This is the process of divinisation, of *theosis*, of *indumnezeire*. It is so central to Orthodox spirituality that a young priest in Ploieşti[9] was able to give a good description of it without any thought at all:

> Man is called to be like God. He is made in the image of God and must aspire to a likeness with God, to become himself God. Deification of human nature is made by Jesus Christ through his teaching and through communion with Christ and through the links between Christ and his Church. The divinised man is the man who finds heaven here on earth. After the fall of the first parents a nostalgia for heaven remains in the soul of man and in all history man yearns after this. Now in the twentieth century it is difficult to understand the relationship with God. Today we must choose quickly because all things happen so fast. Man must choose between what seems true and what is real indeed but is placed somewhere secret. A man can't make a real link with God just by returning to God. To find the treasure in his heart man must look in his own heart and discover God. He will himself become, through his own effort, like God. Deification of man means his liberation from what belongs to evil. It means also

8. Gregory of Nyssa, *The Life of Moses*, 2.242-246, translation by Meredith, pp. 108f.
9. Ioanin Chilan, interviewed in 1997.

> the ontological union with God. Deification
> means the spiritual ascent of man. The man
> becomes divinised not by standing in one
> place, but by moving to God.[10]

For this young priest to say that a man achieves divinisation 'through his own effort' is, of course, overstating the case, though in preaching and in conversation many priests and monks would say the same. The stress on individual responsibility and the anxiety to push people on to keep trying ever harder does lead preachers to suggest that we can do it alone. This way of speaking needs to be seen, however, in the context of a life lived within the Church and within a liturgy which makes very clear the all-pervasive presence of God. The very serious way in which we have seen people enter into the sacraments of confession and communion is part of the acceptance of this personal responsibility for salvation. But these very sacraments make it clear that all movements of sanctification actually come from God. Perhaps this relationship between personal effort and sacrament provides a fitting expression of the synergistic process of sanctification. Behind the oft repeated assertion expressed by this young priest lies a long patristic tradition at which we must look now.

One of the first problems we modern men and women have with the concept of divinisation arises from a misapprehension about Christian teaching concerning the nature of the material world. Our neo-platonic inheritance has left us with a feeling that all matter is evil and in total contrast to the spiritual nature of God, which is the spiritual state to which we aspire. This understanding would seem to rule out any possibility of human nature being actually transformed into the nature of God. All one may hope for is that the soul will eventually leave behind the material and ascend to God. While it is true that Christian

10. Cp. Gregory of Nyssa, *The Life of Moses*, 2.242.

spirituality tends to emphasise very strongly the sinfulness of humankind and the need we have to be saved from sin and delivered into the hands of God, yet in fact Christianity has always insisted that this is *not* what we expect, because the world which God has created is not inherently evil. In the Christian ascetic tradition, great attention is given to the control of the body and of the fleshly passions, and to the cultivation of the spirit. From this it is easy to get the impression that Christianity is deeply opposed to the body and to its material nature. Many Christians have fallen into the kind of platonic dualism which accepts that matter is completely different from spirit and cannot be part of a truly spiritual life. This rejection of the material world is not the teaching of the Church, either in East or West. However strongly theology emphasises the catastrophe of sin and the disastrous consequences on human nature of the original fall of man, Christians can ever forget that, in the biblical story and in the theology founded upon it, man was created by God. God who is utter goodness cannot create what is evil, but 'God created man in his own image, in the image of God he created him; male and female he created them'[11]. As John of Damascus, amongst many others, insisted, matter itself is not evil. 'Do not despise matter', he tells us, 'for it is not despicable. God has made nothing despicable'.[12]

Not only did God create man good, as he created all things good; 'God created man in his own image, in the image of God he created him; male and female he created them'.[13] What then is the image? For Paul, the image is Christ. (I Cor 4:4-6, and 15:49; Col 1:15) 'Christ is the image of the unseen God' and this is the image which is ours as we seek to attain 'to the measure of the stature of the fullness of Christ'. (Eph 4:13) The Fathers follow Paul in teaching that

---

11. Genesis 1:31.
12. John of Damascus, *On the Divine Images, First Apology*, 16. Translated by David Anderson (New York: Saint Vladimir's Seminary Press, 1980) 24.
13. Genesis 1:27.

Christ is the image of God and man is made in the image of God, that is, in the image of Christ.[14] Yet, human beings must not presume that because they are made in the image of God their salvation is assured. Although created in the image of the Second Person of the Trinity we are not of divine nature. Between human and divine nature remains a gulf. 'All things are distant from God not by place but by nature.'[15] Only through the incarnation and the loving condescension of God in taking human flesh into the Godhead can this gulf be bridged.

The importance of the image of God in man is not only that we have a foundation which we can recover and build on. Gregory Palamas sees this image of God within man as a kind of mirror in which we can discern God more clearly than in the natural world. To discern God we must, however, rid ourselves of the sin which darkens the image and so begin the process of being restored to the likeness of God which belonged to Adam and Eve before the Fall.[16]

Restoration does not come easily nor is it accomplished in a moment. The fall of man into disobedience brought disintegration of the unity of body, soul, and character which God intended. It was to re-establish this unity that God became man. In the words of one Orthodox theologian:

> The Redemption of human nature accomplished by Christ the New Adam consisted essentially in the fact that a sinless *hypostasis*, even that of the Logos, freely took over human nature in the very state of corrup-

14. Origen, *Contra Celsum* 6.63; translated by Henry Chadwick (Cambridge: Cambridge University Press, 1953). See also Irenaeus, *Adversus Haereses* 5.16.2; Clement of Alexandria *Protreptikos* 12, Cyril of Jerusalem *Catecheses* 14.10, Athanasius *Contra Gentes* 34, *De Incarnatione* 13, John Chrysostom *Homelia in Genesis* 8.3-4.
15. John of Damascus, *On the Orthodox Faith*, 1.13.61; translated by Frederick H. Chase, *John of Damascus: Writings*, Fathers of the Church, 37 (Washington, D.C.: The Catholic University of America Press, 1958, rpt. 1981) 199.
16. Meyendorff (1964) pp. 120f.

tion in which it was... and by the resurrection re-established its original relationship
with God. In Christ man participated again
in the eternal life destined for him by God.[17]

That deification is achieved through the incarnate Christ
cannot be stressed too strongly. As one Romanian priest
put it quite simply, 'The purpose of the incarnation was to
bring the possibility of deification to man'.[18]
The real anthropological meaning of deification is
Christification. The way of deification is by union with
Christ, because it is precisely union with him who is the
true (as opposed to the platonic) Archetype which leads man
to fulfilment.[19] In fact, Nicolas Cabasilas, writing in the fourteenth century, liked to stress that the Archetype on which
we were created exists not only in the past but also in the
future: 'The essence of man is not found in the matter from
which he was created, but in the archetype on the basis of
which he was formed and to which he tends.'[20] Christ has
overcome the three things that separate us from God: fallen
nature, sin, and death. By his incarnation and hypostatic
union he has made it possible for us to enter the nature of
God, but only through him. Through his passion and death
on the cross he liberated humankind from sin. Through
his resurrection he has set aside mortality.[21] Deification is
rooted in the nature of the incarnate Christ. It is in his
image that we are formed, and to this image, through him,
that we are restored. 'God came forth with the humanity
he had assumed, a unity from two opposites, flesh and spirit:
the second of these conferred deification. The first was
deified.'[22]

17. Meyendorff (1974) p. 117.
18. Fr Mihai Sămărghiţan interviewed in Sibiu 1997.
19. Nellas, p. 39f.
20. Nellas, p. 33.
21. Nellas, pp. 111ff.
22. Gregory Nazianzus, *Oration* 45.9: *On Easter;* PG 36:633D; trans. Nicene
and Post Nicene Fathers, series 2, volume 7:426.

From this we understand that deification, even though it restores the likeness to the image of God within us, is not backward looking to a mythical past, but forward looking to eternity. 'Man, having been created in the image of the infinite God, is called by his own nature . . . to transcend the limited boundaries of creation and to become infinite.'[23] The movement, however, is not automatic and nor is it impersonal. The way to deification lies always through Christ; and it is through humankind's entry into Christ that the Trinity again becomes accessible in an immediate and intimate fashion.[24] Christ has brought humanity into the Godhead, thereby enabling human beings to enter by grace into that Godhead. Christ also comes to us, most particularly in the sacraments which are gifts of himself to us in our human need. Deification is made available to us through baptism and the Eucharist, of which Palamas says, 'From these two acts depends our entire salvation, for in them is recapitulated the whole of the divine-human economy'.[25] This perception has a number of important consequences for our study.

In the first place, it makes clear the deeply personal Orthodox understanding of the sacraments and of sacramental grace. 'In the East the notion of grace is identified with that of participation; grace is never a created gift but is a communion with divine life.'[26] In the sacraments Christ acts. Baptism takes us into the body of Christ so that, when we pray, we pray in Christ. Indeed our whole life is lived in Christ. Prayer in the name of Jesus is, as we shall see, intimately affected by this perception that as Christians we live in Christ.

Secondly, the Eucharist may be seen, not just as a sacramental help to growth in christian holiness, but as the context and the means of all such growth. The Eucharist is

23. Nellas, p. 28.
24. Meyendorff (1964) p. 159.
25. Palamas, *Homily 62*.
26. Meyendorff, *Christ in Eastern Thought*, p. 115.

central to the process of deification. As one young Romanian said:

> The significance of deification is to make
> yourself God, through communion with
> Christ only in the Church. It is our life in-
> side the Holy Trinity.[27]

The Eucharist is the meeting place of heaven and earth.
There the life of the Holy Trinity becomes our life. There
Christian worshippers mingle with the saints. It is a liturgical space and time in which Christ is present, Mary is
present, the saints are present. By being present at this liturgy we move into a world of heaven and are a little transformed by it.[28]   If this happens when we simply attend the
Eucharist, then how much more true it is when we receive
Holy Communion. Then our natures mingle more intensely with that of Christ. Gregory of Nyssa describes this
experience in uncompromising language:

> The immortal body [of God], by entering
> the one who receives it, transforms his en-
> tire being into its own nature. . . . He [Christ]
> in the Eucharist unites our bodies with him-
> self, so that mankind too, by its union with
> what is immortal, may share in incorrupt-
> ibility.[29]

There may appear here to be a confusion between the immortal state which we will finally enter with God and the
material state in which we exist now, and as a result of
which our bodies will certainly corrupt, regardless of how
often we receive the sacramental body of Christ. Yet the
eastern fathers love to stress this paradox of corruptible
bodies taking on incorruptibility, though they work out the

27. Calin Sămărghiţan, interview in Sibiu, 1997.
28. Nellas, 1987, pp. 166ff.
29. *Catechetical Oration* 37; PG. 45:93C; Nicene and Post Nicene Fathers,
series 2, volume 5:504f.

practical consequences no more than Paul did. Yet when one sees how strong is their belief that in communion one is taken physically into the nature of God, one is able more easily to appreciate the importance to spiritual growth of a spiritual father, for in the eastern tradition (and very much in the Romanian) he it is who guards the path to communion and gives permission for a person to receive communion. Humanly speaking, he takes responsibility for the process of deification in a person.

Thirdly, communion cannot be seen in isolation from the whole life of grace, since it is this which the spiritual father must assess and guide. Prayer, fasting, and the realities of loving one's neighbour are the areas the *duhovnic* must constantly watch in the life of the spiritual child because these are the immediate ways by which the Holy Spirit works the deification of man. Nicolas Cabasilas describes the all-embracing nature of our life in Christ when he writes:

> He who seeks to be united with [Christ] must share with Him in His flesh, partake of deification, and share in His death and resurrection. So we are baptised in order that we may die that death and rise again in that resurrection. We are chrismated in order that we may become partakers of the royal anointing of his deification. By feeding on the most sacred bread and drinking the most divine cup we share in the very Flesh and Blood which the Saviour assumed.[30]

Once again the very close identification of the Body and Blood received in communion with the Flesh and Blood assumed by Christ explains the great care which needs to

30. *The Life in Christ*. Bk 2 paragraph 1 p. 65. PG 150:521A; deCatanzaro translation, p. 65.

be taken to ensure that people are worthy to receive communion, and also makes clear the largeness of the claim which is made for the efficacy of the sacraments. Through them life is changed. Deification is not simply a reward given after death as a consequence of good behaviour. It is an anticipation here on earth of that life which we shall experience forever hereafter. Participation in the divine nature has exciting consequences *now*. One of those is the gift of seeing the light which emanates from God himself.

> 'In him was life and the life was the light
> of men. . . the true light which enlightens
> every man was coming into the world'
> (Jn 1:4f.).

Plato, as we saw above, thought that the achievement of this vision of light was the aim of the good life. When a Romanian laywoman was asked about divinisation, she saw it immediately in terms of light:

> Our life should be a constant longing after
> God and after a sacramental union with him
> in unfailing light, a permanent ascent to-
> wards resurrection.[31]

The terminology of light is not merely a figure of speech. Saint Gregory of Palamas achieved particular fame for his insistence that men and women could see and experience the true light of God through their prayer. He was by no means the first. Saint Irenaeus, in the second century, was the first we know of to make the astonishing assertion: 'Jesus Christ on account of his great love for us became what we are so that we might become what he is'.[32] This,

31. Anişoara Carol interviewed in Bucharest, 1997.
32. *Against Heresies*, V. Preface; PG 7:1120B; Ante-Nicene Fathers 1:526. Athanasius puts this still more strongly: 'he became man that we might become divine' (*De Incarnatione*, 54.11; PG 25:192B; translated by R.W. Thompson, *Contra Gentes and De Incarnatione* [Oxford: Oxford University Press, 1971]).

he says, is achieved through participation in the God who is light.[33]

> To see light is to be in the light and to par-
> ticipate in its clarity; in the same way, to see
> God is to be in him and to participate in his
> life giving splendour. Therefore...those who
> see God participate in life.[34]

Nicolas Cabasilas, whose understanding of sacramental life we have already appreciated, sees those sacraments also in terms of light:

> Through the intermediary of the sacra-
> ments as through a great opening the Sun
> of Righteousness shines into this dark world
> . . . . And the Light of the world conquers
> this world ... When the rays of the sun pen-
> etrate a room, a burning candle no longer
> attracts the eyes of those who are watching:
> so likewise the glory of the life to come,
> entering this world by the sacraments, tri-
> umphs in those souls over the earthly life
> and blots out the beauty and brilliance of
> this world.[35]

Light and life are clearly as closely related for Cabasilas as they were for the writer of the fourth gospel[36] and the glory of the life to come is Christ; as Macarius describes it:

> . . . the soul which has been fully illumi-
> nated by the ineffable beauty of the glory of
> the light of the face of Christ and filled with
> the Holy Spirit, worthy of becoming the

33. 1 Jn 1:5.
34. *Against Heresies.* IV. 20.5.PG 7:1035B; Ante-Nicene Fathers 1:489.
35. Cabasilas, *Life in Christ* PG 150: 504 BC (my translation). In deCatanzaro's translation, p. 50.
36. Jn 1:9.

dwelling and the temple of God is all eye,
all light, all face, all glory and all spirit, . . .
Christ adorning it in this way, carrying it,
directing it, supporting it and decorating it
with the spiritual beauty.[37]

A person who has experienced this transformation of his
being will, of course, make the perfect spiritual father. As
Palamas again describes this experience:

Someone who participates in divine energy
becomes in some way light in himself; he is
united to the light and with the light he be-
holds with all his faculties all that remains
hidden to those who do not have this grace;
thus he surpasses not only the corporal
senses but also all that can be known (by
the intellect) . . . for the pure in heart see
God . . . who as light dwells in them and
reveals himself to those who love him.[38]

The understanding of light in this context includes also the
quality of warmth. Fire gives light and warmth and is a
favourite image for the working of God in human nature.[39]
So Father Teofil of Sâmbăta de Sus describes deification in
terms of heating and uses a common image from the Fathers:

Deification means to make from a man a
unity with God such that God might be more
evident than the man. In the person of the
Son of God human nature and divine nature remain the same, even though united
and made one. This means that human nature is deified in the person of the Son of

37. *Homily* I; PG 34:452AB.
38. Palamas, *Homily on the Presentation of the Virgin in the Temple*; ed.
Sophocles, pp. 176-177 – cited and translated by Lossky (1963) 133.
39. Cp. Heb 12:29: 'Our God is a consuming fire.'

God. . . . What deification means is shown
by the Holy Fathers as iron which is heated
in fire. If you put iron in fire it receives the
quality of fire. It burns and grows red having something of the quality of fire.[40]

Fr Teofil also makes the point that in christian belief not
only are we sons through adoption, but through our incorporation into the Son of Man we take on the uncorrupted
human nature of the Son of God. Divinisation is founded
on our participation in the mystical body of Christ and on
our eventual entry in Christ into the life of the Trinity. As
we have seen, this is a process which looks forward and
not back. In Cabasilas' words:

It was for the new man that human nature
was created at the beginning. It was for Him
that our intellect and appetitive aspect were
prepared. We have received our reason that
we might know Christ, our desire that we
might run towards Him; we have memory
that we might bear Him within us. He is
the Archetype for all who have been created. It was not the old Adam who was the
model for the new, but the new who was
the model for the old.[41]

Clearly, despite the tendency of some priests to speak as if
all the work is ours, deification is not something we achieve
for ourselves. It is given to us by God. We do not possess it
of our own. We do not lose our human nature, which is
always separate from the divine nature. But, as Saint
Symeon the New Theologian says, 'I am a man by nature
and God through grace'. In the end it is not simply we who

40. In an interview with me at Sâmbăta de Sus, 1996.
41. Cabasilas, *The Life in Christ* 6; PG 150:680A; deCatanzaro, p. 190.

come to God, but Christ who brings us. Christ takes humanity to himself, purifying it and redeeming it, making it what God intended it to be. Then,

> last of all, he came to God Himself, bringing the true revelation of humanity with Him. On our behalf . . . he appeared as man in the sight of God the Father.[42]

It is this sense of promise for the future already experienced now which gives the christian Gospel its exciting sense of expectation. In expressing this hope, the Orthodox claim to do better than the Western Christian whose theology is centred on salvation, a doctrine which until recently at least tended to be focused on salvation from the consequences of sin, rather than salvation into life: 'Deification,' one Orthodox points out,

> is better than salvation. Salvation means healing, restoration of man to the stage from which he fell. Deification is more. It is what Jesus brought, grace upon grace, not just our entrance into grace. We want the Kingdom of God which is not just from the earth, but on the earth.[43]

Deification, then, is the goal which draws us 'to know the love of Christ which surpasses knowledge, that you may be filled with all the fulness of God'.[44]

Divinisation does not stop with humankind. We are part of the created universe and if we share in heaven and the nature of God we do not cease to be part of this world which feeds us and whose material nature makes up the flesh and bones which are part of the whole man whom Christ has saved. As we become 'partakers of the divine nature in Him', so too is the material world taken up into God. We

42. Maximus the Confessor, *Ambiguo*; PG 91:1309C.
43. Fr Moldovan, interviewed in Sibiu 1997.
44. Ephesians 3:19.

become the means of its salvation, of the transformation of its nature into the nature of God. Fr Moldovan expresses this in an earthy but telling way:

> All material has the possibility of being divinised into God. Even beans and potatoes become part of us and receive the capacity to think. So us with God.[45]

This is part of the graciousness of God: that we should not only be the recipients of salvation but ourselves be co-workers with God, sharing in his task of saving a world. To some extent the world is saved by our absorption of food and its transformation into our flesh. God uses such humble means as this to achieve his recreation of the world. But equally, through our minds and our ability to make good choices, that is, choices which lead us to God, the fundamental disobedience of humankind in this world is changed and re-centred on God:

> The importance of the human being for all creation, for the salvation of the world, is that only the human being can think and become a means of sanctifying the world.[46]

Responsibility for the world's sanctification belongs to every Christian. As we seek to grow into Christ, being transformed into his likeness,[47] we are participating in that 'taking of the manhood into God'[48] which is one of the more amazing consequences of the Incarnation of Christ; through this comes also the recreation of a damaged but God-created world. Particularly is this the responsibility of the monk and of the spiritual father who has been called to

45. Fr Moldovan. Interviewed in Sibiu in 1997.
46. Fr Negruţiu. Interviewed Timişeni monastery, 1997.
47. Rom 12:2, Gal 4:19.
48. Athanasian Creed (*Quicunque vult*), cited from *The Book of Common Prayer* of the Church of England.

guide others in this way. How is it done? We have seen the importance of free choice and the responsibility to live constantly out of those choices. That means that divinisation cannot be achieved automatically by a reception of the sacraments or by a formal, even if very frequent, participation in the liturgy of the Church. We start a long way from God. Our souls are in confusion and ignorance. Yet we can choose between good and evil and, as we do that we begin to make the choices that will bring us to that state in which deification becomes a real possibility. As Fr Cleopa describes it:

> The soul is like a ship tossed around on the waves, but the mind directed by God is the eye of the soul acting as a helmsman.[49]

APATHEIA[50]

The state we seek is that of *apatheia,* in Romanian *despatimire,* or in English 'dispassion' (or passionlessness – the term is difficult to translate). At first sight (and, to be fair, in not a few of the books written about it) dispassion appears to mean a total lack of feeling, an insensibility. This is due in part to the fact that a stoic term has been taken over and effectively redefined. To understand what the term now means within its christian context is essential.

As a characteristic of the spiritual life, *apatheia* is extremely unattractive to a modern Westerner. This aversion is not simply due to the unattractiveness of virtue to those who are deep in sin; nor is it simply a result of the materialist, secular nature of western civilization which causes us to

---

49. *Despre Vise și Vedenii,* p. 15.
50. This section, though far from exhaustive, shows something of the range of writing which exists on both deification and *apatheia* and indicates their enormous importance in the spiritual life. However, I found in interviews that most of those who had not formally learned theology had no real idea about what *apatheia* and deification were. This limited the opportunities I had to discuss the problems which *apatheia* raises.

recoil from this virtue of a past which appears to be world-rejecting and obscurantist in its apparent withdrawal from involvement in human, social and political affairs, and destructive of all human joys. Quite serious objections to *apatheia* are sometimes made—some of which are characteristic of our age. The first objection may be considered theological.

God created the world and made it good. He created humankind to live in the world and to enjoy it. He created individual human beings, men and women, to love and be loved. He intends us to be taken up in the joy of this creation, to enjoy the pleasures of sex in its right context, the delights of children, the enrichment of friends. Christianity teaches that man fell into sin and that this sin has deeply distorted the human character. But the incarnation, redemption, and resurrection has made it possible for us to recover from this distortion, to enjoy again the pleasures which God intended for us and to achieve that fullness of life which is both bodily and psychological, which includes physical well-being and the capacity to love without which we cannot be truly human. *Apatheia* appears at first glance to deny all this, to deny the goodness of God's creation—and so to blaspheme. It is not enough to insist that Orthodox theology accepts that this is a beautiful and God-created world, if we are convinced that we are not allowed to enjoy or desire the good things that God has placed before us.

A second criticism of *apatheia* centres on particular human emotions which are not comfortably expressed in society, but which are still thought to be good—particularly perhaps the passionate anger against injustice. Too often the Church has contemplated heaven while men (often men of the Church) have done unspeakable things against people on earth. Is it because Orthodox spirituality centres itself on that freedom from all passions that believers have been encouraged simply to put up with their suffering, to endure injustice, to ignore the pain suffered by others? Is it because of that holy indifference to the wickedness in the world that the East has made such slow progress in the technological advances which have made life so much less laborious in the West; made equally slow progress in the growth of political institutions which allowed real freedom and human dignity to all people; made such slow progress indeed that an ideal breeding ground for communism was created? If so the suffering of the major part of the Orthodox world under communist systems of government might be seen as no more than her due reward.

Perhaps the strongest argument against dispassion, as we tend to understand it, is that Christ himself, whom in all things we seek to be like, certainly had feelings and showed them. He spoke of the beauty of the fields; he cared passionately about the people who came to him in great numbers 'as sheep without a shepherd'.[51] His heart was moved to compassion for them. He was angry with the pharisees, angry sometimes with his own disciples, and notoriously angry with the money changers in the temple. It is easy to read off a Jesus who was filled with a passionate social concern and whose love roused him to an anger which drove him to act for the weak and against the powerful. Is his an anger and compassion that we can imitate if we seek *apatheia*? Saint John Chrysostom certainly knew a compassionate anger on behalf of the poor.[52]

Clearly the meaning of *apatheia* and an adequate translation of it is crucial to the understanding of Orthodox spirituality by Western Christians This is doubly necessary to this study since *despătimire* features strongly in the writings of Fr Cleopa and other Romanian spiritual fathers, as it does in all the writings of the Greek holy fathers.

---

51. Mark 6:34.
52. Cp. *In Col. hom.* 7, 4-5 (PG 62 349-352); *In I Thess. hom.* 1.4 (PG 62: 466-467), and *In Heb: hom.* 11. 3; (PG 63:94; translated in the Nicene and Post-Nicene Fathers series, volumes 12 and 14. See J. N. D. Kelly *Goldenmouth*, pp. 134, 136.

The first point that needs to be made has been suggested above. Eastern Christianity, like Western, takes very seriously the implications of a world created good by God and redeemed by Christ. In the early centuries neoplatonic heresies which attempted to drive a wedge between spiritual man and the material world were firmly disposed of. Monks and other ascetics embraced ascetical practices that leave us amazed, but the writings and sayings of even the most severe of them, the Palestinian and Egyptian desert fathers, witness to a wholeness of life which aimed at a purification of the flesh rather than at its destruction.[53] Moreover, as Alexander Schmemann, amongst others, loves to point out,[54] the sacraments that are at the heart of all Christian life, East and West, are not simply isolated dispensers of individualized grace. Rather they act through us on a world which is itself being renewed by Christ. Patristic teaching has always taken seriously Saint Paul's insight that 'Creation waits with eager longing for the revealing of the sons of God'.[55] Our salvation through the sacraments also brings about the renewal of the world we live in. Above all, the Holy Liturgy of the Eucharist through its prayer and action draws the whole world into new eschatological time. This world-renewing theology cannot be the background to a world-rejecting spirituality.

Secondly, we might look at the very comprehensive list of 'passions' which Fr Cleopa provides.[56] It is clear that these refer, not to feelings or emotions, but specifically to sin. We

---

53. See, for example, *Dorotheos of Gaza: Discourses and Sayings,* trans. Eric Wheeler (Kalamazoo: Cistercian Publications, 1977); *The Sayings of the Desert Fathers,* trans. Benedicta Ward (Kalamazoo 1975); *The Syriac Fathers on Prayer and the Spiritual Life,* ed. trans. Sebastian Brock (Kalamazoo 1987).

54. For example, Schmemann (1976) p. 119: 'The offering of bread and wine: life itself restored as sacrificial movement to God, a movement that unites us to Christ's perfect Sacrifice and Self-Offering, that includes in it our whole life and the life of the whole world.'

55. Romans 8.19ff.

56. See above, Chapter 3.

may question his identification of a few of these—laughter, irony, using make up—as sin, though each of them can be explained in a context that would identify their sinful character. But everything else, from abortion, murder, and quarrelling to self-advertisement, deceit, and flattery, are quite clearly sinful. Why then does he not simply call them sin (*păcătos*) instead of calling them passions?

It is because, as a spiritual father, he is concerned more with the cause of sin than with the deeds themselves. Sins do not simply exist. They are a result of movements of the spirit, of deep desires, of wrong and distorted attitudes. To sin, one must in some sense consent to wrongdoing, either by actively wanting something wrong, or by passively allowing oneself to be led into evil. The person who has watched carefully over his mind, identifying its movements, keeping guard against demons, knows only too well how many and how varied are the thoughts and feelings which lead to a relatively small number of sinful actions. Trouble starts in the mind, and this is where the vigilance must be maintained and the battles must be fought. *Apatheia* is then the destruction not of all feelings and movements of the heart, but of those which are sinful in character.

Behind the struggle for dispassion is an awareness of the subtle process by which the smallest thought can lead the mind to assent to sin. Saint Theodosius describes this progress:

> Every assent in thought to some forbidden desire, that is, every submission to self-indulgence, is a sin for a monk. For first the thought begins to darken the intellect through the possible aspect of the soul and then the soul submits to the pleasure, not holding out in the fight. This is what is called assent...when assent persists it stimulates the passion in question. Then little by little it leads to the actual committing of the sin.[57]

Apatheia is, in fact, not a negative, destructive movement at all, but corresponds to the western term, 'the ordering of the affections'. In a world where all kinds of things are constantly clamouring for our attention we need to be turned towards God, desiring him above all else. Then other things will be revealed in their true character, evil for what is evil and good for what is good. Evil attractions can then be disowned and good things can be seen in relation to God. Then we shall be able to enjoy them as God means them to be enjoyed— not apart from God, but as gifts from God, each more precious because it is a gift from God and each thereby enhancing the goodness of the giver. Saint Gregory of Palamas sums this up well when he says

> Our passionate life must be offered to God, living and active, so that it may be a living sacrifice...When our glance is meek . . . when we draw down and pass to others the mercy from on high, when our ears are attentive to the divine teaching, when our tongue, our hands and our feet all serve the divine world. Is not this observance of God's commandments an activity common to soul and body?[58]

Here we see a soul which is not deprived of passion, but which is wholly directed towards God. In offering the passionate life to God the Palamite does not mean that the passions are taken away. Aspects of our nature which are not sinful, when offered to God, are generally returned purified, enhanced, or transformed. This is one of the great

57. *Philokalia* (English translation) vol 2:18.
58. *Triads* II.2.20, cited by Meyendorff, *St Gregory Palamas and Orthodox Spirituality*, p. 114; trans. Robin Amis, *The Triads*. (South Brent [UK] – Chicago [USA]: Praxis Institute Press, 2002).

aims of the spiritual life in Orthodoxy—not to escape from our humanity but to transform our human nature into what God always intended it to be. This transformation includes our feelings and even our flesh.

We may now see the importance of the defence system which Fr Cleopa describes. First there is the watchfulness, that unresting attention to the state of one's mind which ensures that any wrong movement is immediately spotted and dealt with. As a background to watchfulness is the faith, the belief in God, the confidence that he is stronger than anything that can invade us. Without that confidence we would soon despair. Moreover, when the Orthodox speak of belief, they do not simply mean a conviction that certain things concerning God are so—that could be a purely subjective state of mind. Belief must be right belief, and right belief is established by the Church and the Holy Tradition. Wrong belief leads very quickly to distorted action. Heresy very quickly leads to sin. Then, too, although the vigil must be unremitting, it is conducted not in anxious fear but in loving gratitude for the goodness of God and the state of love and light to which he is bringing us. This heartfelt thankfulness keeps us truly centred on God and our motive for searching the heart and mind is not self-centred desire for self-preservation but love for him to whom we owe everything. And finally there is the necessary quality of discernment. This is both a gift from God, and an insight gained by the use of our own well trained reason. Demons are seldom immediately spotted, and Fr Cleopa himself—like ascetics through the ages—describes how the devil can appear as an angel of light. Discernment is one of the many gifts through which God and man cooperate in the salvation of the soul.

Another modern spiritual father may help us to see the significance of the struggle against the passions. Archimandrite Sophrony[59] says, 'Sin does not reside in any

59. Formerly spiritual father of the Monastery of Saint John the Baptist, Tolleshunt Knights, Essex, and biographer of Father Silouan of Mount Athos.

natural function of man, but in the passions'.[60] Sin does not belong in man by nature. It is part of the disorder which has entered the human existence and is particularly identified with the turbulent state of a soul which is resisting God. The point Father Sophrony wants to make is that the soul, particularly the monastic soul, must aim to be wholly and undistractedly centred on God. 'Purity of mind is a special gift of monasticism unknown on other paths, and the monk can only reach this state through obedience.'[61] Obedience to the spiritual father, as to God, involves setting aside all the self-centred, self-indulgent feelings which turn us away from God. Even good emotions can turn us away from God, and we need to recognise that there is a hierarchy of goods in which the lesser must sometimes give place to the greater. Indeed the renunciation of the lesser goods may be the very means by which the greater good is achieved. 'The call to the monk to renounce love for his kin and for the world in general in order to live in the likeness of Christ, causes a deep rupture in the soul. The soul is swept by great storms. . . .'[62] These agonizing storms are necessary, says John Climacus, since they are needed to sweep away the passions. There is a 'necessity of pushing this inner conflict to its utmost limits, in order that the depths of the soul may be revealed. . . it is necessary for our souls to dwell both in hell and in God'.[63] The pearl of great price[64] needs sometimes to be paid for with all the other pearls in our possession.

Dispassion, then, is a state which comes about when emotional storms have subsided and when the soul has truly submitted to God. In that respect, *apatheia* is not like

60. Archimandrite Sophrony, 'Principles of Orthodox Ascetism', translated from the Russian by R. Edmonds, in Philippou, ed., *The Orthodox Ethos*, p. 281.
61. *Ibid.*, p. 271. 'Purity of mind' is Cassian's way of talking about, while avoiding the term, *apatheia*.
62. *Ibid.*, p. 269–citing PG 88:708C.
63. *Ibid.*
64. Mt 13:46.

the stoic virtue of the same name—a state which must be sought *for its own sake*. Rather it is a state in which all one's feelings and desires have been taken up into God so that nothing can then distract them from God.

Although the terms in which Fr Cleopa has described *apatheia* suggest that the passions are simply the disturbances created by sin and the struggle for dispassion is a struggle to escape from sin, we must see that there is more to it than this. *Apatheia* is also more positive than this. The aim of *apatheia* is not merely the eradication of sin; it is the regeneration of the whole person in his orientation on God.

John of Damascus, among others, consistently taught that matter is not evil, nor is the body ultimately corrupt. The Damascene insists that matter is fundamentally good because it was created by God.[65] Moreover, since the Son took on flesh matter has become the very means through which we are saved.[66] Christianity does not seek to destroy matter, nor does it seek to destroy the feeling, affective capacity in man. It recognizes that sin does not elevate these aspects of human existence (as sinful people often claim it does). It corrupts and destroys them. Through radical and often painful *ascesis* matter and human feelings are taken out of the domain of evil and are placed once again firmly in the domain of God. It is then possible for God to work the salvation of the world through the person of the passionless monk. We have already seen (above p.217) how Gregory of Palamas expresses very movingly the way in which the passionate life is directed to the service of God.

---

65. *On the Divine Images* 1.16; PG 94:1245C; Anderson translation, p. 24: 'Do not blame matter, for it is not dishonourable. Nothing is dishonourable which was brought into being by God . . . The only thing that is dishonourable is that which did not have its origin from God, but is our own invention through a movement of the will and voluntary decline from what is according to nature to what is contrary to nature, that is to say through sin.' In any programme of salvation, it is important to recognise that the body will participate in some way that does not presume the total destruction of its material nature.

66. *On the Divine Images* 3.34.

This direction can only be set by obedience to God. The spiritual fathers teach that obedience is the key to dispassion, because as disobedience disorientates, disorders and destroys the soul's relation to God, obedience restores the world made new in Christ.[67] Thus our bodies themselves become the place where we meet Christ. For 'since the Incarnation, our bodies have become 'temples of the Holy Spirit who dwells in us' (1 Cor 6:19); it is there, within our own bodies, that we must seek the Spirit, within our bodies sanctified by the sacraments and engrafted by the Eucharist into the Body of Christ . . . we find the Light of Mount Tabor within ourselves'.[68]

Dispassion is not an end in itself (as it was with the Stoics) nor is it simply an aim for the great mystics. Here a priest describes it in an ordinary diocesan newspaper as appropriate for all his readers.

> The aim of dispassion is to gain self control and place yourself at the disposal of God, to offer yourself freely to him; it is a position through which you will obtain another perspective on things.[69]

We may see the value of dispassion when we consider its opposite:

> Why do the demons wish to excite in us gluttony, fornication, greed, anger, rancour and other passions? So that the mind under their weight should be unable to pray as it ought; for when the passions of our irrational part begin to act, they prevent the mind from acting rationally.[70]

67. On one visit to Romania I asked each spiritual father, and one abbess, what was the first teaching a novice must learn. 'Obedience', they all replied.
68. Meyendorff, *Gregory of Palamas*, p. 113.
69. Nicolae Stoica, *Telegraful Român*, Nr. 43-44. (1996).
70. Saint Nilus of Sinai, *153 Texts on Prayer*, 51; translated by E. Kadloubovsky

A person who is controlled by passions clearly is not free. He cannot use his God-given faculty of reason. He cannot pray. He cannot love, and that deprives him of the greatest happiness known to humankind. By way of complete contrast we see the result of dispassion in what is actually its cause:

> When love arises in souls fascinated by God the day of dispassion occurs at once, O my God, dissipating the darkness of passion and lust.[71]

Another way of seeing dispassion is as a consequence of true humility, that virtue of the Christian life which is constantly spoken of by Romanian spiritual fathers, both to monks and to lay people. Saint Dorotheus of Gaza gives us an example of this. Most people, when they hear themselves criticised, get upset and angry. Pride is the cause of this anger. If, however, they recognise that the criticism is just, or if not just, at least worth hearing, they will not be upset or angry, but contrite or even grateful. Even if the criticism is completely unjust, they will not be upset since they have no pride to be upset.[72]

Dispassion and humility, being closely identified, are difficult to describe in words because they are divine characteristics truly experienced only by those who have entered into the divine nature. They are understood best through meeting the spiritual fathers in whom these virtues have become real. The fathers' amazing, personal attractiveness makes virtue itself attractive. They show that humility is

---

and G.E.H. Palmer, *Early Fathers from the Philokalia*, p. 133.

71. Symeon the New Theologian, *Hymn* 39.15; ed. Koder, Sources Chrétiennes, 174 (Paris: Cerf, 1971) 478.

72. See Saint Dorotheus, This translation is taken from *The Divine Office of the Roman Rite*, Vol. 3: 143. (London: Collins, 1974). See also *Dorotheos of Gaza: Discourses and Sayings*, Chapter 7: On Self Accusation, translated by Eric P. Wheeler (Kalamazoo: Cistercian Publications 1977) pp.141f. See also Sources Chrétiennes 7:82 (Paris: Cerf, 1963).

not a depressing grovelling in the dust, but an utter lack of
concern for oneself, a delight and interest in others, an
overwhelming gratitude for the sheer goodness of God. In
them, too, dispassion does not seem to be a lack of feeling
because love is so clearly present. So, often, is enthusiasm
and joy. Above all they appear to be free. In the imagery of
ships sailing on water so beloved to the spiritual fathers,[73]
they appear to float lightly on the world, totally free, moving with grace and swiftness, travelling unhesitatingly to
God. A description of such a person as Archimandrite
Chrysostom Postolache at the Bucium Skete near Iaşi helps
one to appreciate the sheer attractiveness of these often misunderstood virtues:

> A shining face, a penetrating confessor, a
> devout priest not worn out by six decades of
> priesthood, a gentle spirit, peaceful and filled
> with right discernment...To this we may add
> his natural qualities: calm and measured
> speech, gentle and balanced words, going
> without haste, a warm reception, fatherly, a
> bright and clear appearance, modest clothes,
> hair white as snow gathered together de-
> cently under his cassock. Any speech with
> Father Chrysostom is always blessed and
> creative for the soul. The words of his holi-
> ness strengthen you in faith, encourage you
> to good works, increase your patience, com-
> fort you in temptation, anoint you with joy
> and hope on the way of salvation and raise
> you up with your soul towards Christ.[74]

That a well known ascetic can be so filled with joy comes as
a surprise to all who have not met true asceticism before.
Joy is a characteristic of the ascetical life, and consideration

73. Cp. John Climacus. *Ladder* 26.52.
74. Bălan, *Convorbiri Duhovniceşti*, p. 243.

of this joy provides us with a healthy point at which to begin our exploration of the significance of ascetical labours
(voinţe). This may be best illustrated by an account of a
meeting with one of the great ascetics of today.

There are times in Romania when you wonder whether
you have slipped into an earlier age. The margins of time
shift and reality seems other than it was. Such an occasion
for me was a visit to Fr Iustin of the monastery at Petre
Voda. I had been staying at the nearby monastery of Durau
and the Mother Abbess asked me if I had met Fr Iustin.
No, I replied, but I had heard of him and would like to
meet him. Well, she said, Fr Clement would take me. It
was snowing heavily and Fr Iustin lives up in the mountains, but Fr Clement is an expert driver. Fr Iustin's story is
remarkable. During the communist time he spent some
years in prison. In 1991 he had a vision of heaven descend-
ing to earth, a sign that he must start a new monastery in
the mountains. So he went, on his own, to live in the forest. Today, six years later, he has about fifty monks around
him, many well-educated men who have left all to follow
him in this life. We drove up the slippery snow-covered
road through the trees and came into a clearing where some
rather battered wooden houses stood. Monks scurried
through the falling snow. I was taken to a wooden house
and shown into a passageway where two peasant women
sat waiting to see Fr Iustin. After a few minutes he came
out of his room. He was tall, looking a bit like Saint Serafim
of Sarov. He moved quickly but with grace and had about
him no sign of the pomposity or self-consciousness which
can afflict even great spiritual fathers. He was entirely relaxed and light-hearted and invited me into his cell. It was a
small room, unheated, somewhat dirty, with a pile of loaves
of bread (gifts from the faithful) in a corner. All this was
unimportant when Fr Iustin began to speak. I had a sense
of closeness to Christ. He spoke quite simply the words of
Christ. I felt I could trust his discernment. Nothing he said
was original or even memorable. What counted was sim-

ply his presence, challenging me to ask serious questions
about myself, my own following of Christ. He was free, he
was happy. He was relaxed and calm and gave a feeling of
peace. Here, it seemed to me, was a person in whom one
saw manifest the Beatitudes—the poor in spirit, the peacemaker, the one who mourns and is comforted, the meek
who inherits the earth. He was an ascetic who had fasted
and prayed and endured much at other men's hands. He
had set aside all power, all ambition, and so he was free to
attend to the words of Christ and to speak these words to
the hundreds of people who come to see him and to the
monks who have stayed with him.

It is with Fr Iustin in mind that I reflect on the nature of
ascetical joy. At first sight it may seem a contradiction in
terms to speak of ascetical joy, since to the modern western
mind asceticism is suffering, deprivation, and hardship. To
most Westerners, even Christians, asceticism seems unnatu-
ral, even pathological and carries with it the suggestion of
masochism or fanaticism. While it is, of course, undeniable that ascetical practices are, of their very nature, often
uncomfortable, it is important to see that for the Orthodox
who practise them they are exhilarating and lead to inexpressible joy. So the present Metropolitan Daniel Ciobotea
spoke of the monastic lenten disicipline:

> The first week of the Great Fast is hard since
> we don't eat until the evening. But it is ex-
> hilarating to feel you are fighting a battle
> and when we get used to the fast we find a
> real regret that the battle is now past. . . .
> Orthodox life is tough but one receives great
> joy, an intense experience of the presence
> of God. When fasting, for instance, we in-
> crease the spiritual food. We read more, we
> have a richer Office and better music, more
> alleluias, so that we are not left empty.[75]

75. Interview in Iaşi, April, 1998.

Metropolitan Daniel explains here that fasting is essentially a work of preparation, clearing the space in which spiritual work can take place, heightening the awareness and sensitizing the spirit. The Orthodox theologian Olivier Clément provides a good description of the fruits of fasting:

> Fasting lightens the body, prepares it for resurrection and opens it to healing grace. It makes the soul more readily transparent and predisposes it to the study of Wisdom, to listening to the Word. It makes sharing and mutual help possible.[76]

Many great Church teachers, amongst whom Saint John Chrysostom and Saint Ignatius of Loyola are two of the best known, fasted immoderately in their youth and came to regret it. Saint Diadochus of Photike warned his disciples against excessive fasting and showed how necessary it is to seek a balance in this practice:

> When heavy with over-eating, the body makes the intellect spiritless and sluggish; likewise, when weakened by excessive abstinence , the body makes the contemplative faculty of the soul dejected and disinclined to concentrate.[77]

Finding the middle way between these two equally harmful extremes takes a great deal of sensitivity and experience. Until the earnest young Christian has acquired the grace of discretion (itself one of the main aims of the ascetic life) he must turn constantly to his spiritual father for guidance. A good spiritual father will as often restrain his enthusiasm as urge him on to greater deeds. There is always the danger in fasting that a person begins to believe that his fasting will earn him particular graces, instead of

---

76. *The Roots of Christian Mysticism*, p. 141.
77. *On Spiritual Knowledge and Discrimination*, 45; *Philokalia*, 1:266.

seeing it as a way of preparing himself to receive gifts from God. Fasting clears a space in a person's life, a space which God can enter; and the restraint on food or other material distractions tends to sharpen up the senses and make one more receptive towards the experience of the spirit. Although fasting has a penitential aspect it is undertaken not as punishment but as purification. Indeed the aim of asceticism itself is purity, not purity in an aseptic, colourless sense, but a purity in which the sickening, burdensome chains of sin have been discarded and the spirit is able to rise freely and joyfully to God. Maximus the Confessor writes of this, 'A pure soul is one freed from the passions and constantly delighted by divine love'.[78]

Such purification encompasses the whole person, including, it is important to note, our rational powers. Monastic spirituality is not opposed to reason but is aimed at directing reason towards God, since it is only when it is thus rightly directed that it can function properly. Again it is Maximus, one of the most used and best loved of the Eastern fathers, who tells us:

> For reason, instead of being ignorant, ought to be moved through knowledge to seek solely after God; and desire, pure of the passion of self love, ought to be driven by yearning for God alone. And the divine and blessed love, which is fashioned from these and through which these come to be, will embrace God and manifest the one who loves God to be God himself.[79]

It is in the process of this purification that reason becomes a tool of discernment. Our growth towards sanctity, or in the eastern terms, towards divinisation, does not take place automatically and without our cooperation. We work with

78. Maximus. *Centuries* 1.34; *Philokalia*, 2: 56.
79. Letter 2; PG 91:397B.

God. We make choices and hold to these choices. Our
choices must be made in the light of our experience of
where God is and of how we have found him in the past.
Through right discernment we are able to break through
the chains of habit and establish new patterns of God-centred
behaviour. Diadochus of Photike, a writer often referred to
by the Romanian spiritual fathers, adds to this the importance of free will, which is, of course, the free direction of
the reason: 'Free will is the power of a deiform soul to
direct itself by deliberate choice towards whatever it decides.
Let us make sure our soul directs itself only towards what
is good, so that we always consume our remembrance of
evil with good thoughts.'[80]

Such self-determination is never complete. Of its nature
it is a movement towards God and human movement towards God never fully reaches its goal. The ascetic can never
relax in the assumption that he has finished his journey.
He is always conscious, one might say ever increasingly
conscious, of how far he has still to go. Yet he experiences
the delights of the *knowledge* of God on the way, because
his journey is motivated by love. In a simple kind of way Fr
Cleopa encapsulates this attitude of love in what he quotes
from another:

> We read in *The Salvation of Sinners* that we
> must have the heart of a judge towards our-
> selves, the heart of a mother towards our
> neighbours and the heart of a son towards
> God.[81]

In many ways that one sentence sums up the ascetical process, describing the way that *ascesis* will involve a tough
treatment of our own bodies as we seek to detach them
from their dependence on evil passions. Yet love of our
neighbour is itself part of the *ascesis* since such love causes

80. *Century on Spiritual Knowledge* 5; *Philokalia* 1:254.
81. *Ne Vorbeşte Părintele Cleopa*, 5:58.

us to choose others' good rather than our own; and all is motivated by the love we feel as sons and daughters of a God whose own love is so utterly steadfast and dependable we know he will never let us go.

As we begin to see that this really is the nature of God we see that much needs to be done to clear away the dross that is preventing us from seeing God more clearly and becoming the persons God has made us to be. Olivier Clément describes *ascesis* as,

> an awakening from the sleep-walking of daily life. It enables the word to clear the silt away in the depth of the soul, freeing the spring of living water. The word can restore to its original brightness the tarnished image of God in us, the silver coin that has rolled in the dust but remains stamped with the King's likeness. . . . It is the Word who acts, but we have to cooperate with him, not so much by exertion of will power as by loving attentiveness.[82]

So we see that *ascesis* is no negative punishment of the flesh. It is not punishing of the flesh at all, except in the sense that athletes—a favourite simile with *ascetics* since at least the time of Saint Paul—subject their bodies to great pain and discipline in order to bring out what is best in them. The purpose of fasting, watchfulness, and long prayer must be kept constantly in mind. If, as seems likely, it was Clement of Alexandria who first took the term *apatheia* from the Stoics and christianised it by making *agape*, (rather than dispassion for its own sake) its goal[83] it is not surprising to read how he describes asceticism in terms of privilege or reward:

82. *The Roots of Mysticism*, p. 130.
83. *Stromateis* 6.9; Ante Nicene Christian Library, Volume 2:497 (Edinburgh, 1869).

> In the end *gnosis* is granted only to those fit
> and chosen for it, on account of the great
> preparation and prior training necessary to
> hear what is being said to us, to compose
> our lives and to advance wisely to a point
> beyond the righteousness of the Law.[84]

Particularly at the early stages ascetical progress is made
through constant attention to our thoughts. We have already seen how important a place watchfulness over one's
thought has in Fr Cleopa's teaching to his disciples. We see
this as well in the fourth-century teacher Evagrius, from
whom much of monastic teaching is derived. He writes:

> If any monk...wishes to take the measure
> of some of the more fierce demons so as to
> gain experience in his monastic art, then let
> him keep careful watch over his thoughts
> ....Let him note well the complexity of his
> thoughts, their periodicity, the demons
> which cause them, with the order of their
> succession and the nature of their associa-
> tion. Then let him ask from Christ the ex-
> planations of these data he has observed.[85]

It is, of course, the 'asking from Christ' which saves this
exercise from being a pelagian exercise in self-improvement.
Christ teaches us. We do not learn by our own cleverness.
Christ shows us what is happening. Christ shares with us
the labour of expelling evil thoughts and controlling disturbing passions. But passions in themselves, as we saw
above, are not always bad. They can be very good. Saint
Theodoret goes so far as to say that passions are a necessary and useful part of human nature since it is the strength

84. *Stromateis* 7.10; Ante Nicene Christian Library, Volume 2:539
(Edinburgh, 1869)
85. Evagrius, *Praktikos*, 50; Bamberger translation, p. 29.

of desire which impels us to seek after the divine.[86] And
Saint Diadochus, in an interesting passage, describes fear
of God as 'a life giving medicine, which through the re-
proaches it arouses in the conscience, burns the soul in the
fire of dispassion'[87].

Gregory of Nyssa goes still further in his *Commentary on
the Song of Songs*. In a beautiful passage he points out how
Solomon 'has inflamed the desire of the one still young
according to the inner man. . . for the hope of being loved
in return disposes the lover to a more intense desire. . . .
Solomon [then] elevates above everything grasped by the
sense the loving movement of our soul towards invisible
beauty.'[88] Then, as the soul cleaves in union with the beloved, Gregory urges, ' . . . love as much as you can with
your whole heart and strength. Desire as much as you can.
I boldly add these words, "Be passionate about it". This
affection for incorporeal things is beyond reproach and free
from lust.'[89] For him the passions are clearly intended to
move the soul on to union with God. It is only when they
drag the soul away from God that they are wrong.

When we find ourselves made uncomfortable by the un-
relenting way in which a spiritual father like Fr Cleopa attacks the passions, we need to remember that at the heart
of the ascetic life is an insatiable longing for divine things,
or, more simply, for God. This longing will often be painful:

> In my earthly nature I am attached to life
> here below, while I also have in me a por-
> tion of the godhead; therefore my heart is
> tormented by the desire for the world to
> come.[90]

86. *Graecarum Affectionum Curatio*, Sermon V *De Natura Hominis;* PG
83:952B.
87. *On Spiritual Knowledge* 17, in *Philokalia* 1:258.
88. The First Homily; translated by McCambly, p. 46f.
89. The First Homily; translated by McCambly, p. 47.
90. Gregory Nazianzen, *Dogmatic Poem* 8; PG 37:452.

Yet the rewards of striving for union with God are so great that they sweep aside any notion that a Christian is condemned to a life without pleasure or joy. In fact divine sweetness pours into the heart. The monks Callistus and Ignatius are not alone in describing this with a great richness—though of its nature the experience is ineffable: 'who will explain the sweetness of honey to those who have not tasted it? It is incomparably harder to explain to those who have not tasted it, that sweetness which is Divine and that transubstantial spring of living joy which ever flows from true and pure prayer of the heart'.[91] And, they continue, 'This spiritual sweetness, this transubstantial spring of life, is at the same time essential radiance and light, inconceivable beauty, the last desire of desires, knowledge of God and mysterious deification, which remains inexpressible even after some expression of it, unknowable in part even after some knowledge of it, incomprehensible in part even after some comprehension of it.'[92]

Gregory of Nyssa had a very high doctrine of man, and this awareness of the nature of man has provided the Christian tradition with the theological justification for the extraordinary impertinence of desiring to be one with God:

> Realise how much more than the rest of
> creation you are honoured by the Creator.
> He did not make the heavens in his image
> nor the moon, sun, the stars' beauty, nor
> anything else you see in creation. You alone
> are made in the likeness of that nature
> which surpasses all understanding, the image of imcorruptible beauty, the impression
> of true divinity, the receptacle of blessed life,
> seal of true light. You will become what he
> is by looking at him.[93]

91. Directions to Hesychasts in *Writings from the Philokalia on the Prayer of the Heart*, p. 243.
92. *Ibid.*
93. Gregory of Nyssa, *Second Homily on the Songs of Songs;* PG 44:806CD; McCambley translation, p. 70.

And in a more sober strain he examines the anthropology of this likeness with God:

> If humanity is called to life in order to share in the divine nature it must have been suitably constituted for the purpose. . . . It was essential that a certain kinship with the divine should have been mixed in human nature, so that this affinity should predispose it to seek what is related to it . . . .Since eternity is inherent in the godhead it was absolutely imperative that our nature should not lack it but should have in itself the principle of immortality. By virtue of this inborn faculty it could always be drawn towards what is superior to it and retain the desire for eternity.[94]

Clearly Gregory is speaking of all humanity, not just of that small part of humanity which enters monastic life. All human nature is made in the image of God and all human nature has within it the longing to be with God. Since asceticism is the means by which this longing begins to achieve fulfilment it is clear that asceticism is not the province of monks only, but that all christian people are called to an ascetical life. Asceticism is inherent in the baptismal vocation, as Maximus the Confessor once declared:

> Baptised in Christ through the Spirit, we receive the first incorruption according to the flesh. Keeping this original incorruption spotless by giving ourselves to good works and by dying to our own will, we await the final incorruption bestowed by Christ in the Spirit.[95]

---

94. Gregory of Nyssa, *Catechetical Orations*, 5; PG 45:21C.
95. *First Century on Theology and the Incarnation*, 87; *Philokalia* 2:133.

All spiritual fathers recognise that the ascetical disciplines of lay persons will be different from those of monks. What is impressive is the extent to which monks and lay Christians do actually share the same devotions, rather than the extent to which their very different circumstances of life might make for differences. To stay with a devout Orthodox family during the fasting seasons and to see how strictly the fast is observed—abstaining from meat and animal products, and sometimes on Fridays from all food (though the guest is still fed, often to his intense embarrassment!)–is an impressive experience for a Western Christian, even one who realizes that life in a rural economy has a natural degree of fasting inherent in it. The Easter Fast comes at the end of winter when there is not much variety of food anyway and when food itself may be in short supply. Families are often poor and their fasting is necessary to eke out small incomes. In this way necessity may be clothed with a spiritual significance that gives it value in the movement towards God. Then, too, the purpose of ascetical labour is to increase charity. The spiritual fathers teach that people living in villages must have an immediate awareness of the demands on their love which their neighbours make, through their sickness, their increasing age, their difficulties, and the many strains of family life. Responding to these needs will be their ascetical way to love. Life in a poor country like Romania is tough for almost everyone. A spirituality which accepts hardship as natural to the sinful human condition is able to use that hardship as a way of controlling the passions and discovering God. Amongst the desert fathers of late antiquity there are many tales of monks who discovered that ordinary lay people were far closer to God than they themselves were, simply because of their loving and generous acceptance of the constraints of daily life.[96] Anyone who has travelled through the monasteries and

---

96. Cp. Kallistos Ware. 'The Monk and the Married Christian,' unpublished essay, pp. 75ff.

christian homes of Romania will be able to give numerous modern examples of the same phenomenon. Fr Cleopa gives touching testimony to his own respect for the lay people who come to Sihăstria in such numbers:

> The faithful do not come to the monastery because of us, but because of their own pure belief that there is more faith in a monastery and that the life of the monks is more chosen. I believe that God does not maintain the monastery for the sake of us monks, for we are sinners; but because of the faithful lovers of Christ. The Romanian people are a people of gold. The faithful from the world are better than we are.[97]

In the end, the measure of asceticism is not how many fasts, how many prostrations, how many hours of prayer. It is the quality of love. 'Love', Maximus reminds us, 'is the goal of every good, being the highest of goods with God and source of every good. It leads forward those who walk in it, being faithful, infallible and abiding.'[98] And Maximus also makes clear the area in which this love must show itself:

> The activity and clear proof of perfect love towards God is a genuine disposition of voluntary goodwill towards one's neighbour.[99]

This is not just some sentimental maxim to encourage good neighbourliness. It is a profound theological truth found explicitly in the Gospels (for example, Luke 10:30-37) and in the Epistles (I John 3:14-18). It is also a fact of long human experience that as we enter into the love of God we find ourselves entering into his love for people. It is completely impossible to love God in any real sense and not

97. *Ne Vorbeşte Părintele Cleopa*, 5:84.
98. Letter 2; PG 91: 396B.
99. Letter 2; PG 91: 404A.

love one's neighbour[100]. What Maximus makes clear is
that such love is not simply a movement of the affections
but is deeper than that; it is a choice of the will, where true
love must always have its base if it is not to be ephemeral.
This love does not depend on our neighbour being nice to
us; it derives from our knowledge of God's love and our
own desire to share in the love of God. Knowledge of God
itself leads to love, as Maximus again points out:

> Love is a holy state of the soul, disposing it
> to value knowledge of God above all cre-
> ated things. We cannot attain lasting pos-
> session of such love while we are still at-
> tached to anything worldly.[101]

Detachment comes at the end of a long process which cul-
minates in the dispassion which itself brings about love.
Further along in the same passage Maximus outlines this
process:

> Dispassion engenders love, hope in God
> engenders dispassion, and patience and for-
> bearance engender hope in God; these in
> turn are the product of complete self-con-
> trol, which itself springs from fear of God.
> Fear of God is the result of faith in God.[102]

To follow Maximus' line of reasoning backwards is instructive here. Fear of God probably refers more to respect for
or awe of God, rather than terror, since such respect is more
commensurate with the faith that must include an awareness of God's goodness and love. This awareness is the
best motive for the effort to control the sinful passions and
desires, and indeed it is only with such a motive —as experience has taught countless generations of Christians—that
passions and desires can be rightly turned to God. As self

100. 1 Jn 2:9ff.
101. *First Century on Love* 1; *Philokalia* 2:53.
102. *Ibid.*, 2.

control is achieved, sufficient calmness and a new ability for discernment enters into a person; a new patience which sees beyond the frustrations and distractions of temporal existence makes it possible to see the goodness which God is storing up for those who love him[103]. That is the surest basis for hope. Once that hope in God is achieved, attachments to anything that is not of God fall away and a person is free to love. Love must be free and freedom is both the prerequisite for love and the surest sign that true love has been achieved.

The word 'love' has been so much used and so often misused in religious and secular concepts that it easily carries a sentimental, purely affective, connotation far removed from the kind of love which is theologically grounded in God. As a corrective to this pervasive popular use, the late Austin Farrer, in speaking of love under its equally debased synonym 'charity', once reminded retreatants that:

> The principle of charity is that rectitude of
> the will which cares for all that is simply
> because it is.[104]

Love is not mere affection, though it may include affection. Human love is derived from God and directed towards God. Love sees all humanity, all creation, all people and things as truly deserving love simply because they are created by God. Love is limitless and, though few of us ever achieve it, the aim of the ascetic is to become so identified with the loving action of God that he shares in the limitless, unbounded and undiscriminating love of God. One result of this plunging into love is a constant and deepening awareness of our sin, of our failure to love as God loves, of our participation in the self-centredness, the sin of all the world from which we cannot exclude ourselves. Indeed, our love for the world makes us want to identify with the world's

103. 1 Cor 2:9.
104. In a retreat address at Mirfield, 1968.

sin in order to repent of it and bring that sin into the realm
of redemption. An ascetic is therefore a constant penitent.
This helps to explain why ascetics make such sought-after
spiritual fathers. As Metropolitan Daniel explains:

> A spiritual father needs to be a penitent.
> People are more encouraged to repent in
> front of a penitent. If a priest is not a peni-
> tent he cannot understand the power of the
> Holy Spirit working in a penitent.[105]

So, for instance, Fr Cleopa often describes himself as a 'rotten one'. To some this may seem an affectation, but it is in
fact a genuine expression of his sense of utter unworthi-
ness before the God whom he sees more clearly than the
rest of us. Modern Western Christians tend to regard penitence as a negative emotion, or as a pathological reluctance
to accept forgiveness from God. Metropolitan Daniel sees
it quite differently:

> Penitence is a theology and a work of lib-
> eration. Fr Cleopa is very free because he is
> repenting all the time. People who repent
> and discover the joy of the Holy Spirit in
> repentance are very realistic. They are the
> *most* realistic of people. They understand
> human nature. They are not bound by sin,
> but freed from the constraints of sin. Know-
> ing human nature they also know that there
> is always a way out of the despair which sin
> induces. So they know hope[106].

The immediate fruits of penitence, therefore, are freedom,
hope, and a profound realism about the world and the
people in it. This is not depressing since it is founded on
the knowledge of God. Penitence itself is a grace, a gift

105. Private conversation, 1998.
106. Private conversation, 1998

from God. And, Metropolitan Daniel continues, without this grace of penitence a person

> cannot understand the true joy coming
> from weeping. The spiritual fathers often
> speak and write about the importance of
> tears. We think of tears only as weeping for
> what is wrong or what hurts. But penitence
> is also a source of joy. 'Blessed are those
> who weep, for they shall laugh.'[107]

That beatitude promises that weeping will be followed by joy. That is not difficult to understand or to accept. Yet in the literature of ascetics one reads often of the gift of tears, of ascetics who weep continuously for years. For them this gift is not always an entirely sorrowful experience. It is really a source of joy. Fr Cleopa recognises that tears have diverse causes and result from various emotions. They are an important aspect of the process of conversion, and deepen the penitential response to God while in fact being a gift from him.

> Tears come from a realisation of the sin
> done against God.
> Tears are a second baptism, greater than
> baptism itself, since it washes away sins done
> since baptism.
> Tears come from the crushing of the heart
> and humility, from fear of death and the
> terrors of hell.
> Tears are prayer and as such are a gift from
> God.[108]

The realisation of sin committed against God is, far from being a negative self-indulgence, an extremely positive state

107. Private conversation, 1998.
108. *Ne Vorbeşte Părintele Cleopa*, 5:69.

of mind. It is an awareness born of love, a realisation of how much God loves us and therefore of how much sin is a rejection of this love. The knowledge that one has rejected the love offered by such a God evokes tears of sorrow and a contrition born of the desire to put right what is wrong, to make up for the rejection and to assure this loving God of our own responsive love. Fr Cleopa's second kind of tears is surprising, if he really means that this gift is greater than the baptism on which all Christian life is founded. However, Fr Cleopa regularly exaggerated for pedagogic purposes[109] and as he had a great sense of the destructive nature of sin, he wished to focus people's attention on the need to repent of current sin. When Fr Cleopa refers to tears as a 'crushing of the heart', he repeats a phrase which is often used by Romanian spiritual fathers. By it they mean the acceptance of sorrow, grief, pain, insults or anything else which leads to humility. In a later description of this gift, [110] Fr Cleopa describes the tears which come from fear of God as the tears of a servant. Clearly we are servants, and servant attitudes and emotions are often appropriate. Yet in the same place he contrasts these tears with those 'that come from love of God, when a man sees the beauty of God's creation, . . . in the weeping of a son.' In this passage he distinguishes four other kinds of tears. Two of them are good: 'The tears of mercy and love for one's neighbour, for the sick, the suffering, widows. These are holy tears . . . tears born of the fear of death and hell. These, too, are good tears bringing repentance.' But, he adds, there are also 'tears of vainglory which are very dangerous, and tears of spoiled children which come from frustrated greed'. And finally there are the natural human tears brought on by sickness and pain, which are morally neutral.

From these descriptions it can be seen that tears fall basi-

---

109. An opinion confirmed in conversation in 1998 by Metropolitan Daniel, whose spiritual father Fr Cleopa was.
110. *Ne Vorbeşte Părintele Cleopa*, 5:70.

cally into two categories: those that are self-centred and destructive; and those which come either from grief at having sinned against a God who loves us or as a natural emotional response of gratitude to God's goodness and love. In every description of ascetical practices or phenomena we must remember that the primary motive for them is love; or if the motive itself is not love, then the goal must be the acquisition of true love. Fr Cleopa is well aware that not all good deeds spring from love. There is indeed a kind of hierarchy of motives for good deeds which Saint Basil outlined and which Fr Cleopa reiterates in his own words:

> The one who does good deeds out of fear, that is, fear of the works of hell, of punishment: he is in the position of a slave. Someone who does good for reward, that is, to make himself a heaven here on earth: he is in the place of a servant who serves his master for payment, that is, for money. But the one who does good out of love for God, not from fear or for payment: he is in the place of a son of God.[111]

Such is the attraction of the ascetical life. It leads us to the experience of being loved as a child of God. And the process that leads to this experience of God's love is not in the end a process against the natural tendency of the human spirit. It does not do violence to the human spirit since, as Eastern Christianity is particularly aware, 'by virtue of the image of God with which he or she was born, it is natural for every person to grow towards union with God. There

111. *Ne Vorbeşte Părintele Cleopa*, 5:57. Saint Bernard of Clairvaux, in what one can only suspect may be a derivative passage, says much the same in his seventh sermon on the Song of Songs: 'Fear motivates a slave's attitude to his master, gain that of a wage earner to his employer, the learner is attentive to his teacher, the son is respectful to his father. But the one who asks for a kiss, she is a lover.' SC 7.2; *Bernard of Clairvaux: Sermons on the Song of Songs*, 1, translated by Kilian Walsh, ocso (Kalamazoo: Cistercian Publications, 1979).

he is most himself, unless such growth be blocked by obstacles and sin'.[112] And the fruits of ascetical labour are such
that the true ascetic is in no way a repulsive creature, a
peculiar figure, or a kind of religious freak. True ascetics
are filled with God's love and it is this love and the sense of
the presence of God in them which attracts people to them.
People do not come only to grow in love and knowledge of
God, it must be admitted. Some perceive the presence of
God in a holy man as power and come to the spiritual father in the hope of gaining special favours from God. Particularly in a society where people live close to the edge of
poverty, without much social security or health care, people
long for an immediate contact with God to protect them
and their family from disaster, and to heal those who are
sick. People constantly ask priests and monks for their
prayers for safety, security and health. At least part of the
attraction of holy men and women over the centuries has
been the hope that their closeness to God can give others
security in an uncertain and dangerous world.

> Ever since his appearance in Syria in the
> fourth century the lone Christian ascetic has
> been a figure endowed with power. People
> flocked to him for healing and counsel be-
> cause his ascetic feats were evidence that he
> had the ear of God. He was an intercessor,
> a healer of the sick and a protector of the
> weak. He was also an arbiter of Church dis-
> cipline whose ability to communicate God's
> forgiveness of sins did much to lighten the
> burden of the church's rigorous rules. He
> was a living icon of God's power and love.[113]

There is an undeniable ambiguity about this perception of
power in the ascetic. Many have been the ascetics who have

112. Allen, *The Inner Way*, p. 26.
113. Giakalis, p. 4

been corrupted by the aura of power which surrounds them. Many of those who have flocked to the ascetics to make use of their power, for good ends—against illness, oppression or their own sense of weakness—or for bad ends— the pursuit of political power or the desire to take heaven by force. Yet when power and love are united in a single person we find the authentic spirit of the beatitudes, and it is that spirit which a modern Romanian ascetic describes in his introduction to the teachings of Romanian spiritual fathers:

> In the presence of a spiritual father you always feel happy, calm, at peace with yourself, with the world, with eternity. In his cell rises a constant atmosphere of peace and holiness never before met with, an unusual smell of incense, of candles which never go out....Around him you discover another world; you find an abundance of grace, of peace and of blessing. From his heart springs a spiritual joy not found in other hearts. From his eyes fall drops of tears purer than the tears of a child. From his mouth come words of wisdom more precious than that of many rituals.[114]

A prayer by Ephraim of Syria, now prayed throughout Lent in the Byzantine rite, neatly sums up the aims of the ascetical life. In it we recognise the need to work against the laziness of the flesh, to receive the gift of love, to have the grace of seeing sin for what it really is, and to gain the charity which sees only good in other people:

> Lord and master of my life: take from me the spirit of laziness, discouragement, domination, and idle talk; grant to me, thy servant, a spirit of chastity, humility, patience,

114. Bălan, *Convorbire Dohovnicești*, 1:256.

and love; yea, my Lord and King, grant me
to see my sins and not to judge my
neighbour, for thou art blessed for ever and
ever. Amen.[115]

For all their ascetic feats, and the stories about them which
often strike modern men and women as bizarre, those who
practise asceticism in their pursuit of the love of God are
revealed as sane, well-balanced Christians, loving God and
their neighbour with an unselfish love. In coming to know
them one discovers how truly attractive a human nature
redeemed by God can be.

115. *The Lenten Triodion*, translated by Mother Mary and Kallistos Ware
(London: Faber and Faber, 1978) 68.

CHAPTER 8

Portraits of Romanian
Spiritual Fathers

THE ATTRACTIVENESS OF THE TRUE SPIRITUAL FATHER stems from a quality which links spiritual fathers down the ages. To speak about their austerities, their sufferings, the radical nature of their commitment to God, is often to tell a tale which seems frightening and somehow inhuman. But when a disciple actually meets a living, breathing spiritual father—in the desert, in an eighth-century byzantine monastery, in the forests of Russia, or in modern-day Romania—a different picture appears. It is one of gentleness, calm, love; of largeness of heart, wideness of vision, compassion, understanding; and an awareness of the presence of God which is more life-changing to the disciple than any words the father may say. We may test the truth of this assertion by looking at some of the other contemporary Romanian spiritual fathers and comparing them and their teaching with the venerable spiritual fathers whose teaching has inspired their modern-day successors.[1]

FR SOFIAN BOGHIU

One of the half dozen best known fathers in Romania is

1. Much of this chapter depends on Bălan's *Convorbiri Duhovnicești*, a somewhat hagiographical account of spiritual fathers, which has the merit of being recent and based on personal interviews.

Fr Sofian Boghiu of the Antim monastery in Bucharest. This monastery, right in the centre of Bucharest next door to the buildings of the Holy Synod, has an obvious importance in the life of the Romanian Church because of its position at the heart of the Church's administration. Its role has been to maintain a strong life of prayer in the capital city, even in the worst of the communist years. Serafim Joantă, now Metropolitan of the Romanian Church in Central Europe, says that the Antim monastery played a special role in the revival of hesychastic prayer in the Romanian Church between the World Wars.[2] This prepared the ground for Professor Stăniloae's new translation of the *Philokalia*, which had a powerful influence on the Romanian Church after the Second World War. The two patriarchal assistants, Bishop Vincentiu and Bishop Teofan, reside at Antim and have a leadership role in the monastery, but Bishop Vincentiu himself says that Father Sofian is the real father for the monastery.

His distinguishing character, says Bishop Vincentiu is love. 'He has much love. His love gives power to the brothers to keep the Lord's words.'[3] In this Bishop Vincentiu contrasted him with Fr Cleopa, whose spirit is different. Bishop Vincentiu went on to point out what we have already observed in other spiritual fathers: 'He has a very gentle face. It is a joy for brothers to confess to Fr Sofian. They know he will understand even their sins and will help them.'

In the Antim monastery the young monks are encouraged to confess to Fr Sofian every day. This practice is part of the process of teaching the young monks to open their minds completely to their spiritual father. Fr Cleopa also spoke of monks confessing very day. To us this may seem excessive, but it was a regular practice of the ascetical life in the Optina monastery in Russia, and in the other monasteries which derived their spiritual tradition from Paisius Velichkovsky.[4] We can see that in this case confession is

2. Joantă, pp. 201ff.
3. Interview at Mirfield, June 1998.

not linked with receiving communion, but is an ascetical exercise in its own right. Such frequent confession is only for those who are seriously engaged in the ascetical life. The young monk learns through this process to see for himself what kind of thoughts should be encouraged and which ones suppressed. It is part of the process of 'keeping watch' over the mind to ensure that every snare, every temptation, every movement of an evil spirit (as Ignatius of Loyola might have termed it[5]) is identified and destroyed. Yet it has also the purpose of building an attitude of openness and trust between the disciple and his spiritual father. Young monks learn to love their spiritual fathers, and on that love is built the relationship of love with God which will make the spiritual life a life of constant joy.

We may see Fr Sofian more clearly in the description Fr Ioanichie Balan gives of him:

> For more than four decades Archimandrite Sofian Boghiu has maintained the spiritual life in Antim Monastery in the capital, as abbot, as spiritual father, and as a servant of this holy place. A remarkable spiritual personality, well known, who gives honour to the Church of Christ and to Romanian monasticism, having served at its very heart for nearly sixty years.
>
> His Reverence is known and appreciated particularly for three qualities, or three gifts with which God has endowed him: he is a consecrated church painter; a spiritual father and skilled counsellor of the spirit; and a singer by vocation. He was chosen for the Church from birth to witness to the gospel truth through word and colour,

4. See Kavelin, p. 54 n., for a collection of exhortations from Dorotheus, Climacus, and others on the need for this kind of close supervision of one's thoughts.
5. *The Spiritual Exercises*, §313ff.

through spiritual sons and through icons. This is the vocation and purpose of Archimandrite Sofian Boghiu on earth: to beautify and to renew souls and churches, icons and men; to complete what is holy, to teach men, to sing to the glory of God in church; to comfort, to soothe, to sacrifice Christ on the Holy Altar and to sacrifice himself for the salvation of others; to bring hope, order and beauty, to where there is sadness, disorder and hatred; to be always in conversation with God and with men through words and colour, through the warmth of a heart which gives life to the word and through the warmth of colour which gives divine transparency and depth to the icons.

As a painter of icons and churches, Fr Sofian works in the byzantine tradition which encourages meditation and prayer. As a priest and spiritual father, he fosters the growth of good spiritual sons—healing, soothing, skillfully encouraging numerous spirits who are thirsting after eternity. As a renowned *protopsalt* (singer of psaltic music), he gives life and spiritual awareness to worshippers, softening their hearts, drawing out their tears, uniting their thoughts, and raising up their spirits towards God, making the Antim Monastary a living altar, a warm hearth in the heart of the capital.[6]

It may surprise us that Fr Sofian's gifts as an icon painter and a singer are as highly regarded as his gift as a spiritual father. In the Romanian tradition all three gifts, coming from the same hand of God, are equally highly regarded. For a Westerner to appreciate this is difficult. We tend to see icons as

6. *Convorbiri Duhovnicești*, pp. 407-408.

works of art, perhaps beautiful, interesting or moving, depending on their quality. To the Orthodox, however, icons
are a gift from God. Through them Christians are brought
directly into touch with the divine or with the saint through
whom God has revealed himself. A person who is able to
paint an icon that makes this relationship with God possible is
as greatly appreciated as a priest who directs a soul towards
God in prayer. Likewise, for Orthodox people the liturgy has
about it a sacredness and an immediacy in presenting God to
the people. This gives to the various liturgical roles of singer
and celebrant an importance beyond that known by most
western Christians. This understanding of the sacramental
quality of icons and liturgy has been considerably strengthened through the Communist decades, when it was difficult
for priests to teach the people directly and when people found
it sometimes dangerous to consult their priests. Attendance at
the liturgy in a church well endowed with icons became the
main means of teaching prayer and the spiritual life. Communism allowed the cultic aspect of Christianity to continue,
believing it would wither into irrelevance. In fact, worship
was the power and vitality which preserved the faith and kept
the people close to God.

Fr Sofian himself, when asked in what good deeds he
found 'the most peace, joy and spiritual comfort', replied:

> I have found all these things present in my
> heart while celebrating the Holy Liturgy
> which most raises me up spiritually; then
> during and after prayer made attentively and
> with humility; when I have given material
> or moral help to those who ask me for help;
> when I have succeeded, by the gift of God,
> to deliver a soul from sin and when I have
> found myself without blemish in action or
> in word before my own conscience, when I
> know I meet with God.[7]

7. Bălan, *Convorbiri Duhovnicești*, p. 411.

Those few sentences sum up the ideal monastic life: finding joy in the liturgy, personal prayer, works of mercy, and sacramental service. They are ideals, however, not only of the monastic life, but of all serious Orthodox Christians, though we recognise that the opportunity to fulfil them lies chiefly with the monks. The final description of himself as being occasionally 'without blemish' may surprise those of us who are reluctant (perhaps with good cause) to think that we ever do escape from sin, and, of course, it stands in sharp contrast with Fr Cleopa's frequent description of himself as 'rotten one'. Yet it is a vital part of the spiritual father's understanding of Christian life that perfection is possible, even occasionally, in this life and that experiencing some suffering and hardship is worthwhile for the sake of the joy that comes from such freedom from sin.

In the few pages which Balan gives to his interview with Fr. Sofian, little is said about the spiritual life itself. The focus is on sanctification as it is achieved through participation in the liturgy, the icons and the humble monastic life. One paragraph is worth quoting at length, however, because it demonstrates how important to Fr Sofian was his own formation as a monk in the abbey of Cernica, where the great Father Gheorghe (a disciple of Paisius) and Bishop Calinic laid the foundations of the spiritual life more than a century earlier. Speaking of his time there from 1932 till 1940, he says:

> At first I was amazed at the harsh ascetical life of Father Gelasie, the spiritual father of Cernica monastery. When I was near him I felt the presence of divine grace and the odour of sanctity from the manner in which he lived and how he spoke to us about the way of salvation. Also in Cernica I knew the Protosinghel Fotie Petrescu, who attracted me with his love and goodness, whose gentle face gave light and whose spiritual advice seemed to take wing. Almost all of

us pupils of the seminary used to confess to
him. Two other spiritual fathers I knew
somewhat later: the venerable Father
Gheorghe Rosca, who was immensely
knowledgeable in Holy Scripture and a very
good spiritual counsellor, and also Father
Ioan Culighin, spiritual father and renowned teacher of the Prayer of Jesus.[8]

Here, as so often with the great spiritual fathers, one senses
the love and gratitude they feel towards those who taught
them and inspired them in the spiritual life. There is a sense
of handing on the tradition, a tradition which is not just a
body of knowledge, but much more a living way of life.

Fr Constantine Galeriu

Sanctity, however, is not limited to the monks and nor are
they the only great spiritual fathers. Fr Constantine Galeriu
is a married priest in Bucharest who became famous in the
latter days of Communism as one of the few who continued to preach a Gospel which was larger than that which
the communists allowed. In the 1950s he spent years on
the dreaded Danube Canal. Now, at the age of eighty, he
continues to run a city church, to teach homiletics at the
Bucharest Theological Faculty, and to be a spiritual guide.
He is a short man with long, flowing hair and beard and
that special quality of energetic love which seems to
characterise those who are completely taken up in God's
service. The twenty-five pages Bălan devotes to an interview with him[9] focus on questions of a theological nature
concerning Scripture, the doctrine of creation, the nature
of the soul, heaven and the devil, suffering, and the work

8. Bălan, *Convorbiri Duhovniceşti*, p. 410.
9. *Convorbiri Duhovniceşti*, pp. 206-231.

of Christ. Fr Galeriu answers these questions with many ap-
posite quotations from Scripture which support a sound dogmatic theology. One can see how it is that he has developed a
ministry particularly to intellectuals, who flock to his church
to hear academically sound christian teaching given with the
warmth and humility of a true spiritual father.

Fr Ion Negruţiu

A less well known spiritual father can be found in the small
convent of nuns at Timişeni, outside Timişoara. Fr Ion
Negruţiu is about eighty years old. He is a celibate priest,
though not a monk, and spiritual father of Timişeni monastery.

He was an enchanting person to meet. He greeted me very
warmly and insisted on embracing me 'as a brother'. He
would not speak about *duhovnics,* saying he was not a great
duhovnic. He spoke instead about his longing for Christian
unity—and I felt it really was a cause of suffering for him that
Christ's body is disunited. He spoke of the shame and deep
pain he feels because the Church is divided. We are responsible for this, he said. Jesus prays for all to be united[10]. He
said that he understands the crisis in the Church of England[11]
and longs for us all to be one.

> In schism love is replaced by hate. We can't
> claim to be Christian if we hate . For two thou-
> sand years the enemies of Christ and the
> Church have done the same. They have tried
> to divide the Church. We must restore love.
> Hate divides. Hate makes men think they are
> autonomous and can live without the one next

10. John 17:18.
11. This occurred shortly after the ordination of women to the priesthood
in the Church of England, an event which caused much division within the
English church and which greatly hurt those Orthodox who had come to
know the Church of England.

to us. The third millennium will be very
difficult if we don't unite.[12]

It was extraordinary how he revealed different facets of his
personality: playful when we first met, but when he spoke
about the Gospel he did so with a burning love and deep
seriousness. Looking at his eyes and face, I was conscious
of depths of great love. Later he talked about his years in
prison and gave a slightly vainglorious account of his successes after prison. Then he became like an old man, a bit
garrulous. His time in prison was dreadful. He was arrested soon after the War and held in prison for ten years.
Then he was released, told he must behave, and sent to a
resettlement area where thousands of formerly prosper-
ous peasants had been dumped in appalling physical conditions. They had no priest and asked him to be their priest,
so he did. After two years the police returned, told him he
had not behaved himself and imprisoned him for a further
five years. Only after that did he come to Timişoara, where
his highly successful preaching at the cathedral drew the
Securitate's eyes to him once more and he was compelled to
retire to the monastery. He was a gentle, loving, frail man
when I met him, yet when he spoke of the devil I felt and
saw a deep sadness and horror at this evil that can so easily
overcome the world. He knew the reality of evil and was
appalled by it.

He is not without human flaws. Despite a brilliant
academic career, he seems to have held on to his early right-
wing paranoia about Jews and Masons. He is not anti-intellectual. In fact, he is highly intelligent and well read. But
he is at pains to make clear that the way to God is through
love and simplicity, not reason. He is different from the
other spiritual fathers I have met: more relaxed, more
'normal', but very encouraging. He would be a non-judg-
mental confessor, I felt, and one whom it would be easy to

12. Interview in 1997.

love, because he loves. When asked what it is that makes a
priest a good spiritual father, he simply said, 'A priest has
all the grace to give absolution. I don't think about his skills.
It is Christ who absolves, not the priest.' And then he went
on to stress the simplicity of salvation in Christ:

> Even a child can enter the kingdom of
> heaven. Christ is for life. He did not come
> to make theories and theology. A *duhovnic*
> must recognise the importance of every
> single person. He criticizes all theologians
> and bishops because everyone but the intel-
> lectuals recognised Jesus. We must have
> hearts like a child. The greater a theologian
> is, the less he prays. An excess of theology
> kills the sense of prayer. The wisdom of this
> world is madness. Lucian Blaga[13] calls
> knowledge Luciferian. Lucifer is the basis
> of our science.[14]

Such an extreme condemnation of knowledge and science
is not untypical of Romanian spiritual fathers, even though
they themselves are often very well read and knowledgeable. Moreover, Orthodox Christians generally have a very
high regard for learning. The Eastern European respect
for the *intelligentsia* is alive and well and remains in the
Church, and people like to describe their spiritual fathers
as learned men. Some, like Fr Teofil and Fr Arsenie Boca,
are respected as men of culture and theological learning.
Others, like Fr Cleopa, are renowned as men of great wisdom who are 'autodidacts'. No one likes to think of spiritual fathers as being cultural peasants, even though some
like Fr Cleopa are well respected for their ability to speak
effectively to peasants. To some extent, the frequent condemnation of knowledge, erudition, and the ways of the
intellectuals is a necessary assertion that salvation comes

13. Romanian poet (1895-1961).
14. Interview at Timişeni, 1997.

not by learning but by grace. Even so, one feels that quite often the condemnation is unthought-out, and is merely a conventional censure which is not actually lived out—which is fortunate for the Romanian Church. Having said that, one must recognise that Negruțiu's theology, though based on conventional simplicities, is soundly incarnational. To say, as he did, 'God became human in Christ. He was the Son of God', sounds clichéd, but, in fact, it is of fundamental importance, since his confidence that all people can be saved if they turn in simplicity to God is founded on the Church's teaching that God became man. He does hold a pessimistic view of the world and sees disaster impending which threatens to sweep it all away. 'Only Christianity can avoid the cataclysm of the world,' he told me. 'A self-sufficient human being is like an atomic bomb and can destroy the world.' The conjunction of these two statements shows how disastrous he considers the state of the world, founded in individualism and personal sin, to be. It underlines, too, what we have seen in Fr Cleopa's teaching, that individual selfishness, self-centredness, is potentially catastrophic. It cannot just be quietly ignored as something of only marginal significance. The teaching of even the greatest and most subtle spiritual fathers quickly returns to the inherent selfishness which lies at the heart of the human, sinful condition.

Fr Negruțiu understands the problems of the world in terms of sin. Sin in turn can often be best understood in terms of love and faith. A failure to love is a failure to move out of that selfishness which imprisons each person within his own self and causes him to ignore the needs of others. A failure in faith deprives us of an objective understanding of our condition and puts us in a situation of fundamental untruth. When our choices and decisions are based on purely selfish desire, they become destructive. In his words:

> Trouble in the world comes from loss of love
> and loss of faith. One saw that with the
> apostles and the epileptic boy. It is good to

cry, 'Help my unbelief'. The devil can only
be driven out by fasting and prayer. Christ
gives us a model of prayer in the Our
Father.The relationship between Father and
Son is one of love. We can establish our love
by prayer, beginning with this relationship.

Again, this teaching is not original in our modern sense of
that word, but original can also mean 'going back to the origins', and in that sense what he says is highly 'original', as is
very true of most of our spiritual fathers. I often noted how
quickly a spiritual father turns to the New Testament, particularly to the Gospels, to illustrate his teaching. Fr Iustin of Petre
Voda said that the good spiritual father lives very close to Christ
and teaches what he taught. This way of thinking, so close to
the Gospels that one can refer to them appositely and naturally, is one of the attractive features of the *duhovnic.*

Fr Arsenie Papacioc

Spiritual fathers are fascinating as well as attractive people to
meet. Each has his own particular character and though they
preach the same gospel and give the same teaching each does
so with a characteristic spirit that makes him unforgettable.
These marked differences in personality serve to remind us
of the teaching and experience of the Church that God does
not obliterate characters but rather highlights their most attractive features.One of Fr Cleopa's closest friends among the
spiritual fathers of Romania is Fr Arsenie Papacioc. Fr Arsenie
was born in 1914 and after some years as a youngster in the
monasteries of Cozia and Antim, finally made his monastic
profession in Sihăstria in 1949, when Fr Cleopa was abbot
there. Since then he has lived in several monasteries and is
now the spiritual father in the skete of Saint Maria-Tomis
near Constanţa.[15]

15. Bălan, *Convorbiri Duhovniceşti*, p. 452.

By all accounts, and through the witness of his writing, he is a lovely person, laughing and full of enthusiasms and generosity. Despite his friendship with Fr Cleopa, he appears not to share Fr Cleopa's deeply tragic or sorrowful view of life. Together, they seem to be light and darkness. It is not that Fr Arsenie has not suffered. He was in prison for seven years under the communists and admits this was a very difficult experience for him, waiting for the Lord to set him free.

His teaching, as it is recorded in *Vorbeşte ne Părinte Arsenie,* reveals both the strengths and— as they may seem to a Westerner—the weaknesses of a Romanian spiritual father. He is very unjust towards Roman Catholics and chauvinistic in his conviction that only Orthodoxy is true Christianity. He says himself that he will not engage in any discussion with 'sectarians' unless they first admit the truth of Orthodoxy. To some, this may seem narrow-minded and dogmatic, but in him it demonstrates an absolute firmness of faith, a real certainty that comes from living within the life of Christ.

Vorbeşte ne Părinte Arsenie takes the form of conversations with novices at Sihăstria. His advice to them is certainly more relaxed than some teaching we have met. The spirit of love and generosity is paramount. The questions the young monks of Sihăstria ask Fr Arsenie show clearly that they are troubled by scrupulosity—over-eating, fasting, giving, receiving. This is typical of those living under a very demanding regime. Fr Arsenie does not criticise the regime, but he explodes their scrupulosity with common sense and charity. In some ways it is the common sense of his teaching which makes it attractive. One can imagine the serious young novices he is speaking to receiving it with relief. He discourages extravagant fasting or excessive vigils. We are saved by God, he tells them, not by ourselves. We must not do good deeds in the hope of chalking up a good record on the day of judgement. We must do good deeds from love of the people and because Christ himself is in them. There is an ambiguity here, making us ask whether Fr Cleopa and Fr Arsenie are teaching different things. Did Fr Cleopa feel his work with the novices was being undermined by Fr Arsenie's more liberal approach? If asked, they would almost certainly deny a contradiction. Fr Cleopa, or his disciple, Fr Ioanichie Balan, would say that it was their role to teach the novices to take these matters very seriously and not allow themselves to think that the smallest matter relating to fasting, obedience, or sin was in any way trifling. Fr Arsenie's role in the same scheme of things would be to show these young men that the spiritual life is one of freedom, joy, and love. They would not appreciate or be able to receive that gift from God unless they had first earnestly considered the costly nature of their life. It takes great discipline to reach the kind of unselfishness which bears fruit in generosity.

Fr Arsenie is very emphatic on the need to give and receive generously. 'Never refuse an outstretched hand. Receive when something is offered you and give when something is asked of you.'[16] It is this generosity of spirit both in giving and receiving, coupled with the complete absence of anxiety one may expect in a person totally confident of the goodness of God, which characterises all he says.

METROPOLITAN ANTONIE PLĂMĂDEALĂ

In their attractive gentleness, Fr Sofian, Fr Negruţiu, and Fr Arsenie are typical of the Orthodox spiritual father. There is a temptation, however, particularly in the twentieth century West, to contrast the charismatic Christian—the holy man, the prophet—with the institutional, hierarchical churchmen, almost always to the latter's disadvantage. It is true that the strength of Orthodoxy during its centuries of testing under unfriendly regimes and harsh

16. *Vorbeşte ne Părinte Arsenie*, p. 41.

conditions has probably been due at least as much to its charismatic, prophetic figures as to its more institutional leaders. Yet the spiritual fathers themselves do not admit to any fundamental opposition or difference between the two. All are members of the same Church. They need each others' prayers and support. They confess the same faith and hold to the same standards. The bishops themselves hold up the spiritual fathers as signs and guides for the whole Church. It is instructive therefore to turn to one of the best known hierarchs in the Romanian Church, a man whose career has been not untypical yet sometimes ambiguous—Metropolitan Antonie Plămădeală.

Antonie Plămădeală is now the Bishop of Sibiu and Metropolitan of the Ardeal and most of Transylvania. He was born in 1926 in Bassarabia. Having left Bassarabia at the Russian take-over of that country in 1944, he entered the monastery of Slatina, where Fr Cleopa was then abbot. In the 1950s he was imprisoned for five years. In due course and—somewhat surprisingly, considering his imprisonment and subsequent studies abroad—he became an assistant bishop in Bucharest before being elected to the Metropolitanate of the Ardeal in 1986. He is a man of great scholarship who has also served near the centres of power in the rather labyrinthine world of church politics. He is also a good preacher. But, like most Orthodox bishops, his monastic formation is never very far away. Having been a disciple of Fr Cleopa, he is in the great tradition of Romanian, or Paisian, monastic spirituality and speaks with authority.

As a bishop he stands for tradition. One of the key roles of a bishop is to maintain the tradition of the Orthodox Church in the form in which it was entrusted to him, the form in which he believes it came to him from the early fathers. As a monk, too, he is concerned for tradition, for monastic life is always lived in a conscious relationship with the teaching of those who have lived it in the past. As a Romanian he has a passionate love for the culture and tradition of the Romanian people and, loyal Orthodox though he is, he will not hesitate to claim a special place for the Romanian Orthodox Church, because, as he told us once, it combines the intense spiritual life of the Russian Orthodox, which can become anti-intellectual, with the academic life of the Greeks, which can become dry and unspiritual.[17]

He also likes to draw distinctions between the Romanian Orthodox and the West, always to the former's advantage and often with some lack of justice to the West, though he has travelled much there. A common criticism he makes here (and it is one heard quite often amongst Orthodox spiritual fathers) is to contrast the apparent legalism and rigidity of Catholic *monastic life*—his perceptions of which are almost entirely pre-Vatican II—with the freedom which Orthodox spirituality allows. Since the West's perception of Orthodoxy is often that of an obscurantist community hopelessly bound up in the shackles of an unchanging tradition, it is instructive to listen to Metropolitan Antonie's expression of how alive tradition can be.

Western monastic, or religious, life is always based on a rule, or on rules and constitutions which outline the spirit of the life as lived by the monks or nuns in a particular place or Order, and often legislate in great detail for all possible contingencies in the life. This kind of life according to Rule is, according to Metropolitan Antonie, never the pattern for a Romanian monastery. Monastic rules from the past may contain useful information and valuable teaching, but they cannot determine life in the present.[18] A rule is by its nature inflexible. It cannot easily be adapted to an individual; it is the individual who must adapt to the rule. Tradition, however, can be adapted since it is larger, more natural, and presents a way of life which others have already lived. 'In tradition there is more room for freedom.'[19]

17. In a private address in Sibiu in April 1991.
18. *Tradiție și Libertate*, p. 18.
19. *Tradiție și Libertate*, p. 19.

Nor is it difficult to see why there is such freedom. Tradition covers all the centuries since Christ. It is almost always possible to find within this vast corpus of christian life suitable models for a way of life today, or support for a modern development in teaching. That may appear a somewhat cynical view, but on reflection it enshrines the positive truth that tradition is the experience of people. It is monks and theologians, holy men and saints, anonymous Christians who have lived the Christian life, sometimes content just to do that faithfully, sometimes willing to explore new boundaries and deepen human experience of the love of God. To live with tradition is to live with the great company of the Christian faithful, in dialogue with them, often following them closely, but moving on from them into the situation of the present which they did not know. Yet they may still guide us by their experiences. God, after all, is at the centre of tradition and he is unchanging. The experience which the fathers from the past have to share is quite simply their intense experience of God. Orthodoxy has the reputation of never changing its mind. There is less truth in this than most Orthodox themselves would like to believe. What does not change is the experience of God and since it is the spiritual fathers who in their very persons make a loving and intensely attractive God available to others, their teaching about life with God remains almost unchanged down the centuries.

Tradition, then, is never isolated from people, but as Metropolitan Antonie also reminds us, it 'is formed always in a particular culture. As it moves in time and space it must adapt constantly to retain its truth and not to become ossified.'[20] To pretend that such ossification never happens would be foolish, but such ossified tradition quickly dies of itself and is left behind. A living tradition— such as that lived by most Romanian monks—constantly renews itself without being aware that it is doing so.

20. *Tradiţie şi Libertate*, p. 28.

Tradition gives to this great and sometimes amorphous-looking institution of monasticism a real cohesion and common identity in contrast with the western forms of religious life which often emphasise their differences from each other at the cost of a recognition of their likeness. There are, we know, differences among the various Orthodox monasteries, but they are held together by their adherence to tradition. More than anything else, the liturgical life is the vehicle of tradition which unites all monks and nuns—and married priests and lay people too—in the great offering of worship and prayer which the Orthodox see as the primary task of their Church in this world.

How actually is tradition prevented from ossifying? Metropolitan Antonie suggests that it is done primarily in the way it has been by spiritual fathers over the centuries. A monastic spiritual father will often use the phrase 'aşa am apucat de la Părinţi' –'as I received it from the Fathers'. This attests to this sense of a spiritual succession stronger than any rule.[21] But in fact each spiritual father handles the tradition in his own particular way and according to the needs of his disciples. Thus the tradition is constantly filtered through contemporary spiritual fathers and it is this process as much as anything that keeps it from ossification or anachronism.[22] One must never forget that the spiritual father himself believes very strongly that he is following the guidance of the Holy Spirit, and that it is the Holy Spirit whose presence creates tradition and who by it guides the people of God.

PROFESSOR DUMITRU STĂNILOAE

Orthodox theology is very conscious—more conscious perhaps than is western theology—of the action of the Holy

21. *Tradiţie şi Libertate*, p. 32.
22. *Tradiţie şi Libertate*, p. 33.

Spirit. The Orthodox themselves would say that this is because their theology is more clearly based on a doctrine of the Trinity which allows the Holy Spirit greater freedom than does the Western doctrine which sees the Spirit proceeding from the Father and the Son. Perhaps because of this emphasis on the activity of the Spirit, or for historical reasons, or because the liturgy itself has such a central place in Orthodox life, their theology moves easily and naturally into spirituality.

Orthodox spirituality is profoundly theological. Western theology by contrast is often dry and scientific and many believe it can be well done by scholars with no Christian faith. The best Orthodox theologians are clearly men of prayer, and the best spiritual fathers—as we have seen— are well grounded in theology.

So it is that one of the towering theological figures of the Romanian Orthodox Church, indeed of the whole Orthodox theological world in the twentieth century, Professor Dumitru Stăniloae, is regarded also as one of the great teachers of the spiritual life. Born in 1903, he studied first at Cernauţi, then in Bucharest and in other parts of Europe before becoming Rector of the Theological Institute in Sibiu before the Second World War. After the War he was mostly employed at the Bucharest Theological Institute and, like so many of the Romanian church leaders, spent five years in prison between 1958 and 1963. His theological work has acquired a considerable reputation for the creative and subtle manner in which he investigates the nature of the trinitarian relationships and the work of the Holy Spirit in the Church.[23] His greatest contribution to Romanian spiritual life, however, has probably been his translation and com-

23. Little of Stăniloae's work could be published in the West before 1990. The bibliography lists what is now available. Of particular interest is the essay about him by a fellow Romanian, Ion Bria, in *Ecumenical Review*, Vol 33:1 (January 1981) 53-59, and the recent book by Emil Bartos, *Deification in Eastern Orthodox Thought* (1999). Charles Miller's *The Gift of the World* (2000), though brief, is also useful.

mentary on the Romanian *Philokalia*. This project, begun
in the traumatic years of the nineteen forties, and completed only in the nineteen seventies, has arguably done
more than anything else to keep Romanian spirituality
soundly based in the fathers, at the same time interpreting
the fathers in a way that makes sense to modern Romanians. If Father Cleopa has a prime role in the support of
the Orthodox Church through the dark days of Communism and its aftermath, Father Stăniloae's translation of the
Philokalia is a similar *'stâlp'* (supporting tower) for which
educated Romanian Orthodox are particularly grateful.

In his book *Rugaciunea lui Iisus (The Jesus Prayer)* (1995)
Stăniloae gives his own teaching on prayer and it is here
that we see his view of the modern world and its not entirely negative influence on modern Christians:

> In times past the faith of society sustained
> the faith and prayer of the individual. Now
> that society is secularized individuals must
> strengthen their own faith, seeking deeper
> roots. Because they have done it themselves
> their faith will be stronger and they will be
> a source of encouragement and strength to
> others.[24]

This extract deserves comment as it reveals much that is
typical and also untypical of Romanian spiritual fathers. In
common with most Romanian Orthodox, the professor sees
the past as a time when people believed more firmly and
practised more faithfully than they do in the present. There
was in this practice, as generally in society, a stronger
communitarian aspect. People supported each other with a
living consciousness of their christian faith. All this has
changed, first through the onslaught of communism, now
through Romania's involvement with the secular West. Yet,
unlike many contemporary Romanian priests, Father

24. *Rugăciunea lui Iisus*, p. 23.

Stăniloae did not see this as wholly bad. People must put down deeper roots, he thought. They must grow stronger in the faith, and simply because it is a faith they have had to work at, it will be stronger. Having said that, he avoids the danger of individualism by seeing this immediately in terms of encouraging and strengthening others. An Orthodox can never see his faith in terms purely of personal salvation. He is always part of a Christian communion. The seeking of deeper roots will come partly through reading Scripture and studying the *Philokalia*. But it must be sought also in prayer. Indeed, in his opinion, prayer is the natural movement of the Christian spirit:

> Christians today may feel the need to pray more than in the past, simply to save themselves from isolation. In prayer they are in dialogue with God himself.[25]

It is in his understanding of this 'dialogue with God himself' that Stăniloae shows himself to be in the classic Orthodox tradition so typical of the spiritual fathers in Romania. Whether they are accounted academic theologians in the sense in which Stăniloae is so considered, or whether they are simple monk-priests steeped in the *Philokalia* and the daily monastic life, their thinking is truly theological because it is entirely centred on God. God is the reality that underlies the universe. He alone can make sense of it, he alone provides the reference point by which we can understand it. We may see this in the simple teaching on prayer which Stăniloae gives in *Rugaciunea lui Iisus*:

> Through meditation and Scripture God is revealed to us in the world. God and the world are indissolubly bound together.[26]

In this short quotation, we see several important principles which it is important to state even though they are in a

25. *Rugăciunea lui Iisus*, p. 33.
26. *Rugăciunea lui Iisus*, p. 25.

sense taken for granted. The first is the importance given to Scripture. The monks read Scripture continuously. It is true they tend to concentrate on the psalms, the Gospels, and the letters of Saint Paul, though Genesis gets a lot of attention and it is sometimes surprising how much of the Old Testament appears in sermons and writings. The monks pass on their enthusiasm for Scripture to the rest of the Church. Sometimes this is done through the confessional, as penances given. More often one finds that as people begin to take their faith seriously they automatically begin to read Scripture, and the more educated willingly apply their intelligence to its interpretation. In the Holy Liturgy the book of the Gospels is carried into the sanctuary with great solemnity. This is no mere ritual. The reading of Scripture has an important place in the liturgy and people are taught to expect to hear in this the words of God.

Secondly the use of meditation[27] is founded on the conviction that the human mind, flawed and ill-instructed as it may be, is able to think usefully and truthfully about the things of God. This can only be because God has endowed human beings with the gift of reason, and because the Holy Spirit is continually present in the Christian mind. (Saint Serafim of Sarov insists that the Spirit is present in all the world, and even in the minds of those who know nothing of Christ, though to a lesser extent).[28] In meditation, then, the Holy Spirit engages the human mind and enables it to discern much that it could not otherwise see while giving the Holy Spirit also the opportunity to purify the mind and lead it further on the way to God.

Thirdly, all Orthodox spiritual life is founded on the myth of Creation and Fall as given in Genesis 1–3. Despite all the evidences of human sin and corruption and the very great falling away from life with God as God intended it to be,

27. By 'meditation' here is meant the thoughtful consideration of Scripture or theological truths in order to understand more deeply the teaching God has given us.
28. *Saint Serafim de Sarov, Scopul Vieţii Creştine*, p. 38.

even so the world is God's world. He has never abandoned it.[29] Monastic life may be world-denying to the extent that it needs to distance itself from some of society's concerns in order to attend directly to God. But monks and nuns do not leave the world and are constantly concerned for the world. So too the spirituality which flows from monastic life into the lives of married priests and Orthodox lay people never suggests the world should be abandoned for God. Even before the Incarnation God and the world were bound together. Since God became man the world has become part of the process of redemption. 'For the creation waits with eager longing for the revealing of the sons of God.'[30] Monastic spirituality in the East takes very seriously the assertion of Saint Paul that 'God was in Christ, reconciling the world to himself'.[31] In this 'the world' means not simply humankind, but is the whole of creation, marred by human disobedience and restored by Christ's sacramental presence in the world today. The sacraments *themselves,* though part of the close covenantal relationship between God and his people, are also the means by which the world *itself* is taken into the nature of God. [32]

The understanding gained through such meditation may not always be comfortable. Truth is often painful and the beauty of God reveals the ugliness of sin. Clear sight into the things of God makes us aware of the extent to which sin has poisoned God's world. So we find with Stăniloae that, 'Meditation takes us deeper into understanding the love of God and the significance of earthly things till we are led to tears'.[33] Tears are a mark of the spiritual life and are greatly to be desired. They arise from the vision of God, a vision so beautiful that it provokes in us the kind of tears which often come to us when we see real beauty. They

---

29. *Saint Seratim de Sarov, Scopul Vieţii Creştine*, p. 37.
30. Romans 8:19.
31. 2 Cor 5:19.
32. Cp. Fr Moldovan in Chapter 7, p. 211.
33. Stăniloae, *Rugaciunea lui Iisus*, p. 26.

come, too, in response to our perception of the sheer scale
of the disaster which sin has brought upon the world. The
man or woman who has entered into the experience of
prayer in the Spirit will weep for his or her own sin, but
will weep even more for the sins of the people who live
round about. And the suffering which the truly godly men
and women of prayer know when they see the nature of
the world's corruption in the face of all God intended for it
can only be known by them. These tears are not only an
emotional response. The spiritual fathers believe they wash
away the sin and the corruption which keeps us from fully
experiencing God. That is why the spiritual fathers encourage us to pray for the gift of tears.

The grace of understanding has consequences too in the
way that we live. Stăniloae tells us: 'Understanding the true
meaning of things leads us to healthy self control concerning them. God has given us these things in love and for
our growth.'[34] Things do not exist of themselves, nor do
they belong to us. They exist because God created them.
They belong to him and are given to us for our use. This
attitude to the world around us leads us to treat it with care
and respect, and teaches us also to expect to find our way to
God through the people and events of daily life.
Humankind's temptation is always to want to possess (as
Eve sought to possess the knowledge of good and evil).
Much of spiritual discipline must be directed towards free-
ing us from this passion for possession.

> Looking at things and people possessively
> compels us to an unsatisfied pursuit of plea-
> sure. So the Fathers advise us to be freed
> from things and even from people so that
> we may acquire a pure vision and may see
> them as God created them.[35]

34. *Rugăciunea lui Iisus*, p. 27.
35. *Rugăciunea lui Iisus*, p. 26.

One needs constantly to underline that the importance given to freedom from passion is not a negative rejection of God's world or God's people, but rather an attempt to see them truly as they are so that we can give them the honour due and find through them our way to God. It is because Stăniloae has a strong theology of the personal nature of God's relationship with us that he insists that we cannot experience God except through, or at least with, our neighbour.

> Love of God comes to us through our relationship with others because God cannot limit himself to a single person.[36] . . . We must offer also our relationships with each other and that means purifying and improving them.[37] . . . Through our words we are linked to God and to our neighbour. We must respond always to our neighbour's call because in this way we mediate God to them.[38]

In these reflections we see that our relationship with our neighbour is not based on a sentimental idea of how nice good neighbourly relationships can be. Concern for our neighbour is rooted in the belief that all people are made by God. God is universal and cannot be limited to one person or one group of people. If we are going to deal with God at all we have to deal with him as a God who has just as much concern for each of the other people who live around us as he has with us. He doesn't pick and choose. Nor can we. This knowledge compels us then to look at our relationships and to ask ourselves how they appear to God. In offering them to God, we become aware of their very unsatisfactory nature and so we are compelled to do

36. *Rugăciunea lui Iisus*, p. 28.
37. *Rugăciunea lui Iisus*, p. 31.
38. *Rugăciunea lui Iisus*, p. 34.

something about them. As a background to this strong conviction in Romanian spirituality we may see the characteristic village life which Patriarch Teoctist described,[39] a way
of life in which people deliberately seek each other out before the great feasts to beg forgiveness. Such customs are
more difficult to sustain today, but are just as necessary,
particularly in view of the atomised and fragmented nature
of *modern urban life*. Stăniloae recognizes that, whatever
our circumstances, we have a responsibility for our
neighbours. We receive the word of God from them. We
must also give the word of God to them.

One of the ways of making it possible for the word of
God to come to people is forgiveness. Stăniloae develops
this in a way which extends our responsibility for our
neighbour. It is not enough that we simply ask God for
forgiveness. Because most of our sins are committed against
others we must ask forgiveness of them as well as of God.
The confessional alone does not dispose of our sin. Our
relationship with other people still needs to be restored.
And when other people ask us for forgiveness, we must
give it, since their forgiveness is dependent on this.[40] 'To
receive the forgiveness of God we need that of others and
they need our forgiveness in order to receive that of God.'[41]
And Stăniloae gives this an ecclesial dimension, telling us
that in asking for forgiveness a person is not apart from
the Church but inside the Christian body. The Church consists of sinful people seeking to be purified and healed
through each other's prayers. Our prayer for forgiveness
is also a prayer for forgiveness of all other Christians as
theirs is for us.[42]

Prayer, then is never self-centred. It may seem to be self-
centred when I pray for the forgiveness of *my* sin, but 'in
this I am really praying also for all those who have been

39. Above pp. 177f.
40. *Rugăciunea lui Iisus*, p. 76.
41. *Rugăciunea lui Iisus*, p. 77.
42. *Rugăciunea lui Iisus*, p. 81.

affected by my sin'[43]. Indeed, prayer needs to go beyond this.

> Prayer should be made for another in such a way as to feel his pain as much as your own. This kind of praying for each other expresses the universal priesthood of the laity.[44]

The teaching that we should feel our neighbour's pain as much as our own is part of a long tradition in Christianity, but amongst those who are most given to prayer it has a special place. It is part of the generous and unselfish nature of prayer to see more and more of the pain and catastrophe of the whole world and to find one's prayer directed more and more towards this. Fr Silouan of Mount Athos expresses well what many others have said:

> He who has the Holy Spirit in him, to however slight a degree, sorrows day and night for all mankind. His heart is filled with pity for all God's creatures, more especially for those who do not know God, or who resist him and are therefore bound for the fire of torment. For them more than for himself, he prays day and night, that all may repent and know the Lord."[45]

This understanding and experience of prayer, of which Fr Stăniloae is so fully a part, has consequences which may surprise those whose knowledge of prayer is slight, or not formed in the christian tradition. First of all, prayer is never an escape from the world. The person who prays seriously,

43. *Rugăciunea lui Iisus*, p. 38.
44. *Rugăciunea lui Iisus*, p. 37.
45. Fr Sophrony, *St Silouan the Athonite* (Tolleshunt Knights by Maldon, Essex, 1991) 352–cited by Archbishop Kallistos Ware in 'Salvation according to St Silouan', *Sobornost* 19:1 (1997) 35.

by that very fact becomes more intensely related to the world. He never escapes from it, but his freedom gives him an ability to perceive the truth and meet the world's needs at their most critical point. Stăniloae expresses this paradox in a way which makes clear that prayer happens through our incorporation into Christ, and his into us:

> The saint has triumphed over time because he is firmly anchored in time. Through it he achieves the greatest likeness to Christ who, although in heaven, is in this time with us. The saint carries Christ within himself with an unconquerable power of love for the salvation of men.[46]

Secondly, those who see prayer as primarily an intellectual activity, with the mind reaching out to God, or as an emotional expression of feelings towards God, are reminded that prayer must actually unite both mind and heart:

> A prayer which is made only with the mind is a cold prayer. A prayer which is made simply with the heart is purely sentimental prayer which ignores all that God has given us, what he is giving us and what he will give us in Christ[47] . . . The mind must be warmed by the heart, and brings an intelligent content to the heart's warm feelings of the infinitude of God.[48]

This teaching on prayer may put into perspective the condemnation of intellectual life which we noticed above. All spiritual fathers have seen and see the necessity for the whole person being fully engaged in that conversation with God which we call prayer.

Not all Romanian spiritual fathers are national figures.

46. *Rugăciunea lui Iisus,* p. 51.
47. *Rugăciunea lui Iisus,* p. 53.
48. *Rugăciunea lui Iisus,* p. 54.

We have seen already that many people are more than happy with their own parish priests and do not seek out monks or well known theologians to give them guidance and to hear their confessions. A brief look at some of the others I met or heard about in the course of this research may help to fill out the picture.

OTHER SPIRITUAL GUIDES

Fr Serafim Man of Rohia monastery near Baia Mare can only be described as an enchanting person. Born in 1928, he has lived his monastic life at Rohia, being abbot for about ten years. He is now spiritual father to the monastery and is much used by local clergy and communities of nuns. He is a very unsolemn person. When we met he was not wearing a habit (most unusual for a monk in Romania) and abandoned his meal to sweep me off to his room, where he talked excitedly about the spiritual life. It is tempting to think that his influence has been responsible for giving the monastery of Rohia an open, happy spirit unlike the rather gloomy and self-conscious appearance of many other monasteries.

Fr Paisie Olaru, about whom a little book has been edited by Fr Bălan,[49] was born in Moldavia in 1897, and after service in the First World War began his monastic life at Cozancea in 1921. In 1925 he visited Sihăstria and was so drawn by the silence and prayer that he wished to transfer but was not permitted. A man of little formal education, he remained a lay monk until 1943, and was only ordained priest in 1947, after he had been appointed leader of the Cozancea community. This was not a happy appointment and after six months he resigned and moved to Sihăstria, where he became spiritual father. Fr Cleopa took him to Slatina when he went to revive that monastery and Fr Paisie

49. *Părintele Paisie Duhovnicul*, on which this paragraph largely depends.

returned to Sihăstria in 1954. There he remained as a cherished spiritual father until, at the age of 90, he withdrew to the nearby skete of Sihla. There he continued to be visited by his disciples and by nuns from nearby Agapia monastery (who told me how happy they were to struggle up the mountain even through the snow for the privilege of spending time with Fr Paisie.) He died in 1990.

Fr Ion Chilan

Fr Ion Chilan is a parish priest in Ploieşti. Born around 1945 he served first in a country parish, then in Ploieşti itself where his forthright preaching attracted a great deal of attention from the communist Securitate. As soon as communism collapsed he set himself to build a new church in an unchurched area of the town. Conceived on a grand scale, it is still unfinished, largely because of the rampant inflation in Romania. Yet he has a huge congregation. Unusually in a parish church he celebrates the midnight office twice a week and some hundred people attend it. On Sundays the liturgy, which takes place in the cold and bleak crypt, is packed with several hundred worshippers. At Easter the full ceremonies begin at midnight and when they finish around dawn there are several thousand people gathered round the church, unable to squeeze inside. What is the secret of this devotion? Fr Chilan is a huge man who seems to have a love and a range of feelings to match his physique. He works immensely hard, visiting his people and celebrating the daily liturgies (along with his son Fr Ioanin and a retired priest). Hearing confessions is a large part of his parish duty and many university students one meets in his church proudly tell you he is their spiritual father. Fr Chilan is a man whose commitment to God is total and uncompromising. He sees things in strong colours, in terms of this devotion. When I suggested once that communism had at least made the Romanian Church commit itself to God he said firmly, 'I don't need the devil to teach me to love God.'

See him in church and you see two aspects of his love. He celebrates the liturgy with a concentration and fervour that brings tears to his own eyes and keeps the congregation's attention firmly fixed on what is happening behind the iconostasis. After the service the people crowd round him asking for blessings, for advice, for help. Towering above them he seems very much to be a father with his children. He is an uncomfortable father, often very dogmatic, sometimes explosive in his anger, yet the majority of people seem not to be offended by this since the tenderness of his devotion to God is clear in his preaching and in everything he says. Indeed, part of the tension he radiates seems to come from holding in great feelings of love for God, for the Church he has served, for the people of his own congregation, and even for the English priests who visit him. He is outspoken, often offensively, about the failings of the West (which range from the ordination of women, the tolerance of homosexuals, and the encouragement of sects to the failure of western Christians to defend Romania against Russia), and yet he welcomes us with a crushing hug, with tears in his eyes, with a determination that nothing will prevent us from being united with him through our common faith and sacraments.

LAY SPIRITUAL GUIDES

The experience of spiritual fatherhood is not wholly limited to priests. It shades off into others, lay monks, nuns and in exceptional cases lay people. Since only priests can give absolution or permission to receive communion, the relationship with other spiritual guides tends to be informal and people were sometimes confused or embarrassed when we tried to attach the title 'spiritual father' to an unexpected person.

One lay monk who seems to have acquired the stature of a spiritual father is Fr Nicolas Steinhardt. He was a Romanian Jewish intellectual who was imprisoned by the communists between 1959 and 1964. His prison journal[50] is full of joy, love, and the warmth of his feeling towards his fellow prisoners. While in prison he was converted and was baptised in his cell by an Orthodox monk with fellow prisoners, including a Roman Catholic and a Reformed minister, as witnesses. When he was released he made his way to Rohia monastery where he became a monk but out of humility (so the present monks say) refused to be made a priest. He died there in April 1989. His influence has been chiefly through his writings and through his story, which thrills modern Romanians. He writes with great subtlety and in a very literary style of Romanian. Part of his attraction for modern Romanians is that he had been so much a part of the Romanian intellectual world, yet became a humble monk.

Another great Romanian intellectual[51] who was also imprisoned in very harsh conditions was Petre Ţuţea, an economist and a member of the pre-War government before being imprisoned for fourteen years. His courage and wisdom so inspired his fellow prisoners that they recognised him as a kind of living saint. When finally released from prison he lived a very retired life in a flat in Bucharest, watched constantly by the security police and attended by devoted disciples.[52] He died in May 1991.

As a third example of lay spiritual fatherhood we may

50. *Jurnalul Fericirii* (Cluj-Napoca, 1991).
51. For Romanians to be called an intellectual is an honour, and intellectuals are regarded as belonging to a highly respected class of Romanian society. Before the War, as we have seen, there were a number of philosophers, writers, economists and researchers of great ability but right wing opinions. Most of them left the country or were imprisoned. There is a strong feeling today in the Romanian Church that most intellectuals after the War sold out to communism and betrayed the Church, so those who did not are particularly respected.
52. Among these was a young medical student, Dr. Alex Popescu, who is now researching a doctorate on Ţuţea at Oxford University.

look to Professor Virgil Cândea. He is an historian, particularly of art, and also a theologian. He lives in Bucharest and is a member of the congregation attending Fr Galeriu's church. He has published widely, most recently a retranslation of one of Paisius Velichkovsky's works. He is now vice-president of the Romanian Academy. He has a very warm personality and students have found him immensely supportive in their studies and in their personal lives. He matches western standards of critical scholarship while remaining devoted to the monastery of Sihăstria. He considers the tragic events of Romania's recent history a definite action by God to draw Romanians back into his service. This view of history—espoused by Israel's prophets and perhaps by Jesus, too[53]—is not uncommon in Romania, but in Professor Cândea it is united with an unusual degree of culture and scholarship.

And finally one may ask, what about the mothers? It proved very difficult to talk with Romanian nuns about the spiritual life. The conventions do not allow for easy conversation between nuns and monks. Much of what one can say must be gleaned from externals. Romanian monasteries for women are filled with nuns, many very young indeed. This gives an obvious fervour and the nuns work extremely hard while maintaining a high standard of worship and liturgical observation. Unfortunately very few of them are able to study much, either because they come into monastic life young, before having studied, or because they are too busy, or because the tradition of religious life for women has not allowed for much study.

Some there are who have a previous background of education. Mother Filoteia Cosma and Mother Maria Bălan of Agapia are well educated women who have travelled widely. Some nuns at the painted monasteries in Moldavia have a particular expertise in the area of art and iconography, and most women's monasteries have at least one nun who paints

53. See N. T. Wright, *Jesus and the Victory of God* (London: SPCK, 1996) *passim*.

icons and must therefore know something about the theology underlying them. Several are superb administrators, running their large monastic enterprises with astonishing success. Inevitably the largest responsibility falls on the abbess who must both be an administrator and carry the responsibility of the Sisters' formation and spiritual life. One example may stand for them all: Mother Teodora Popoaia of Durau.

Durau was refounded in 1991 after decades in communist hands. Mother Teodora came there from Văratec monastery with seven young sisters. Today there are thirty-five. She has the support of the Metropolitan and has had one or two good young priests to assist, but her sisters are very young. She must coax them out of adolescence and support them through their early trials in the monastic life as well as oversee a large building operation and the establishment of a new monastic life. She looks tired, as she must be in her late sixties, yet has a lovely smile. She resisted talking about herself, sending me off instead to talk with Fr Iustin at Petre Voda. She is clearly a motherly person and sisters relate naturally to her as daughters. She maintains a healthy and happy monastery through her goodness and common sense. It has to be said though that Romanian nuns need a great deal more support and opportunity for study if they are to develop the resources they need to grow in the monastic life.

CHOOSING A SPIRITUAL FATHER

People choose their spiritual fathers for different reasons. As an example of this we may hear what two students for the priesthood said about their spiritual fathers, noting the contrasts in what they were looking for. Adrian Magda spoke of Fr Ioan Ciungu, a priest and teacher in Alba Iulia, his home town. He describes him as the ideal spiritual father because he is a man of humility, a man who, for love of learning, taught the students free of charge, who was a good psychologist and had the gift of discernment which enabled him to see clearly the diseases of the soul and offer the right advice. Adrian saw it as important that Fr Ioan was a man of culture, able to meet the challenges of the modern world unafraid. He is a peacemaker between students and staff and is immensely generous with his time, yet still clearly a man of prayer. He is not a monk but a celibate priest.

Christian Urda, a fellow student in Alba Iulia, comes from Bârsana in Maramures, where his father is the priest. His spiritual father is Fr Vasile Hotico, the priest in the neighbouring village of Vadu Ize. Before coming to Vadu Ize he was the priest in a very poor parish and learned there the patience and love which makes people want to confess to him. He has a special gift for understanding young people. His concern is that people should grow healthy through confession and so he helps people understand their sin and long for its eradication. 'He treats you like a person who has the face of God', said Christian,'and he is very good at choosing exactly the right penance which helps you to understand your sin without making you discouraged.' Both students wanted a priest who was gentle, prayerful, understanding, and focussed on the need to seek real conversion of heart and growth in the spirit through confession. But the first student clearly valued the more cultured, dedicated, celibate priest, while the second chose a country priest who he felt would understand his own circumstances best.

Of first importance in choosing a spiritual father is the sheer attractiveness of the person. This cannot be measured, but is a quality to which all who speak of him give witness. He may sometimes be demanding, he may challenge our standards and our behaviour, but he is filled with love and immensely attractive. It is these qualities of attractiveness and love which make their demanding and sometimes costly teaching palatable and even appreciated. This is as true of

Fr Cleopa with his deeply tragic view of life as it is of Fr
Sofian with his more gentle and hopeful spirit. Such attractiveness is of more than human significance. God is loving. God is attractive. God, despite all the exacting and challenging demands he seems to makes on us, is infinitely
loving. The authentic spiritual father must express these
characteristics, not because he tries to but because, if he is
a true spiritual father, God lives in him. He has been transformed into a person who reveals the nature of God and
he will direct people to God through the love, gentleness
and understanding which are the true marks of the presence of God.

A second important feature is the deep familiarity these
spiritual fathers have with the tradition of the Church. Although all spiritual fathers put the simplicity of Christian
living at the forefront of their lives and make clear their
relative contempt for human learning, yet many are extremely intelligent men, well steeped in the teachings and
spiritual writings of the Church. All have a clear grasp on
the major themes of theology—creation, sin, and redemption through Christ. Reason, they show us, is not opposed
to God but is part of the fullness of human life which can
only come to full fruitfulness when submitted ruthlessly
yet generously to God. Love is the first characteristic of the
spiritual father's teaching, but reason articulates love and
allows us to explain how much of life is unloving and destructive.

A third feature—which may or may not be coinciden-
tal—is the suffering which many of our spiritual fathers
have endured. Fr Teofil has borne a lifetime of blindness.
Most of the others had spells in prison under very unpleasant conditions. Even those, like Fr Sofian, who are not
known to have suffered physically, show quickly a compassion and gentleness which demonstrates a loving understanding of the human condition. Living with such sensitivity to human frailty has always been costly under the
harsh economic and political conditions of Romanian life,

both in recent decades and, if the truth be told, throughout the whole history of the country. The gentleness and hopefulness shown by Romanian spiritual fathers is the fruit of centuries of great suffering by Romanian people.

Finally, I was impressed by the integration of the spiritual fathers into the life of the Church. In the past there have been spiritual fathers who were persecuted by the Church—John Chrysostom, Maximus the Confessor, Symeon the New Theologian and even Saint Serafim of Sarov. They provide outstanding examples of the unfortunate conflict between the charismatic and the institutional life of the Church. In Romania there appear to have been few cases of such ecclesiastical persecution except insofar as the Church was compelled, or allowed itself, to cooperate with communist persecution. The spiritual fathers we met— Fr Cleopa, Metropolitan Antonie, Fr Galeriu, and Fr Stăniloae — show that humble ascetic monks, bishops, married priests, and academics can all be equally highly regarded as masters of the spiritual life. The living experience of God in Christ is central to any healthy understanding of the Church's nature and in present day Romania one is encouraged to find that the Church recognises those who are closest to God as being also at the heart of the Church.

CHAPTER 9

Spiritual Fathers in the World Today

"What do you seek?" (John 1:38)

A S WE TRY TO UNDERSTAND spiritual fatherhood by examining the role of spiritual fathers in Romania, we need to look at four areas highlighted in the material we have considered. In the first place, we need to know what it is people are looking for when they seek out spiritual fathers. Then we must look at what the spiritual fathers themselves are trying to do. Thirdly, we must see them in the context of the local Church, in this case, the Romanian Orthodox Church. And finally, we need to see what they may have to say to the rest of the Christian world.

THE SEEKERS

What brings them? Sometimes a personal crisis, a grave sin that needs the special treatment only a spiritual father can give; a life choice—marriage or the monastic life— which the person feels must be made with more perceptive advice than he can receive at home. Sometimes the person is aware simply of a spiritual hunger, a longing, a restlessness that will not be assuaged. To fill it, they come to Sihăstria, or to Sâmbăta de Sus, or a number of other monasteries, and find there peace, calm, a sense of purpose or a vision of what life could be.

What, then, do they seek? In a word, they seek God.
They may say they seek a meaning to their life; they seek
personal authenticity. They find it in the spiritual father.
They seek out a spiritual father because he knows God.
Where he is, God can be found, God's words can be heard.[1]
The spiritual fathers are points in this world where God
reveals himself; they are people through whom the presence of Christ is made real for others; they are living proofs
of the love and presence of God in this sinful world.

Greek history had a long tradition of young men seeking a greater meaning to their life and finding it with the
great philosophers. What made the difference in the
christian dispensation was that, ideally at least, the seekers
were seeking no longer a knowledge nor even a way of
life. Or if they were seeking such knowledge, they found
that with the Christian holy man they discovered God. In
Anthony, in John Chrysostom, in Benedict, in Fr Cleopa or
Fr Teofil men and women discovered a totally new experience, one they had never known before and one which
they found immensely attractive. Holiness cannot easily be
defined and can never be quantitatively measured. Ultimately, holiness is Christ himself present in a person who
has grown particularly open to Christ and can, by his own
openness, reveal Christ to those in the world also open
enough to perceive Him. Holiness is not a quality anyone
possesses. It is something a person becomes. It is completely
unself-conscious and its unselfish character is one of the
aspects which makes it so rare and so attractive.

Since holiness does not belong to any person, we seri-
ously miss the truth of the spiritual fathers of the Christian
Church if we see them as great individuals apart from the
Body whose life they share and at whose heart they dwell.
To appreciate the spiritual fathers of Egypt long ago or of

---

1. Cp. Timothy Fry OSB, ed., *RB1980. The Rule of St Benedict in Latin and
English with Notes* (Collegeville, MN: Liturgical Press, 1981) Appendix 2:
'The Abbot', p. 333.

Romania today we need to see them within the context of the Church. Here we have looked at Romanian spiritual fathers within the context of their Church, holding the Church in its trial, drawing on the great tradition of the Church through the ages, humanising the institutional Church, acting as shepherds to a shattered and frightened people. Holiness is God. People who do not believe in God can be attracted by holiness, but will not know that it is God's beauty and love that attracts them. The Church is the Body of Christ and Christ's life, passing through the bloodstream of the Church, fills the people of God. Holiness is found in all parts of the Church—not equally, but in some measure everywhere, and in greater measure in certain places, in its sacraments, its monasteries; in the love and compassion its priests and people often show; in the joy and the laughter of Christian people; in the hope which sustains Christians against a frequently dark and often catastrophic world. To understand the place of spiritual fathers in Romania one needs to see them against the historical background of a society which has suffered the traumas of war, foreign exploitation, rape, betrayal, not just over the last five decades, but over six centuries.

In the fieldwork which forms the basis of this study one of the surprising experiences was to find that the most moving and exciting moments often came in interviews with young Orthodox men and women trying to find their way in a new world stripped of many of the old, albeit unhappy, landmarks, a world promising much which, they already perceive, it cannot fulfil. Touching and loving moments were found, too, in conversations with parish priests who have seen the Church through the decades of communism and who, in an unspectacular way, have lived out the challenges given them by spiritual fathers.

Holiness does not reside only in the great. It is to be found in those who seek it with a real longing for God, and as they recognize its character they become transformed by it. There is a simplicity in the process which is deceptive and its central character can easily be missed. Saint Benedict begins his Rule:

> Obsculta, o fili, praecepta magistri, et inclina aurem cordis tui, et admonitionem pii patris libenter excipe et efficaciter comple.

> Listen carefully, my son, to the master's instructions, and attend to them with the ear of your heart. This is advice from a father who loves you; welcome it, and faithfully put it into practice.[2]

Benedict's words encapsulate two of the essential qualities we have seen in the relationship between spiritual father and disciple. 'Listen' and 'love'. Listening requires humility. Listening acknowledges that we have something to learn. Listening admits a willingness to hear and to profit from hearing. Listening in a modern, western, post-cartesian world is often no more than a prelude to argument. Listening for us may admit a hypothesis only with the expectation that it will be debated and probably destroyed. The spirit of the disciple coming to his spiritual father needs to be very different from that. His listening will be the first step in obedience, that word derived from *obaudire,* another Latin word for hearing. The disciple expects to hear and to profit from, to learn from and to obey his spiritual father. This is not a tyranny, though in the West it has sometimes been seen as a tyranny. It is an act of love. 'Incline the ear of your heart and receive the advice of a father who loves you.' The love of a father for the man or woman who has come seeking his guidance is primary to the relationship. It is a love which is compassionate and seeks the good of the person beloved. It evokes in the other a responsive love, a love which is filled with respect.

1. *Rule of St Benedict.* Prologue 1; RB1980 156/157.

LOVE IN A SPIRITUAL FATHER

Love is a quality which must grow or it becomes self-centred or manipulative, and it dies. The aim of the spiritual father is to enable that love to grow by encouraging the occurrence of the right conditions in the person's life. Passions—not feelings, but passions, which are self-centred movements away form God—obliterate love. Passions are selfish, violent, noisy. They destroy peace and calm. Anger drives out peace. Even righteous anger easily becomes self-righteous. Western Christians, insofar as they are socially aware, tend to be angry and cite the example of Jesus driving the money changers out of the temple as a paradigm for their angry engagement with social injustice. Eastern Christians seem often to be unconcerned about social injustice, or fatalistic in their acceptance of it. Is it the example of the spiritual father seeking interior peace above all things that has led to this apparent lack of concern? Can humility and the search for *apatheia* become a supine passivity in the face of evil? Of course it can. But one should avoid an easy identification of the two. True humility is unselfish, unself-centred and taken up with others. Dispassion opens the self up to truly perceiving the purposes and desires of God. These virtues make the Christian more intensely aware of the needs of the world. The spiritual father's concern, however, is not to change this world, but to direct people towards the next. This is a very unfashionable aim in western opinion. It is immediately labelled escapism. It is thought to ignore the responsibility we have towards the world that God has created. It is thought to be a pious quest for an unreal world rather than a confrontation with the reality of the world we live in. Christians may sometimes be escapist or hide in unreality, but they need to do so. The Gospels themselves are sufficient witness of that. 'Seek ye first the kingdom of God,'[3] the Gospel tells us. 'In my father's house are

3. Mt 6:33.
4. John 14:2.

many mansions.'⁴ 'Store up for yourselves treasures in heaven.'⁵ There is no lack of evidence that the first-century Christians, and Jesus himself, were primarily concerned with the life that is to come, though this did not prevent them changing the world by the manner in which they embraced the hope of the life to come. For the spiritual father the next world is the world where God lives and where we, if we are received by him, shall live with him forever.

Most of the *duhovnics* I met in Romania are filled with joy. They may often have hard things to say and a tragic tale to tell, but the love which characterises them is matched by their joy, their enthusiasm for a life spent close to God, and the energy with which they speak of it. Life with God is not for them a gloomy prospect. Romanian Orthodox fear God in a way entirely appropriate to those who follow the God who revealed himself on Mount Sinai, in the teachings of the prophets, or in the horrendous struggle on Calvary. They love God and know they are loved by him, but love is an awesome responsiblity. Fire is warmth and drives out the cold, pushing aside the dark and protecting us from evil. Yet fire destroys what it burns and is not to be played with. God is not to be taken lightly. It is safer to come to God through one of his own. Awe and fear do not necessarily make for a fearful religion. Joy breaks through. In Romania this joy is obvious, especially at festival times, but it is joy seasoned with awe, it is the dawn breaking through after a long night. It is not the superficial happiness that often caricatures joy amongst Christians in the West.

Romanian spiritual fathers embody an ancient tradition within Christianity which has proved surprisingly resilient in very difficult circumstances. At its heart is obedience—to tradition, to the Church, to a spiritual father, and ultimately to God. Obedience is no longer considered a virtue in the West, except in politically conservative segments of society, whose very conservatism makes suspect their motives for

5. Mt 6:20.

demanding obedience. Yet obedience is a christian virtue. Christ obeyed the Father in submitting himself even to death on a cross[6], and through that obedience, making up for the disobedience of Adam and Eve, humankind was restored to God. Modern western theology may change the language and alter the mythology, but the theology remains the same. Men and women are out of kilter with themselves if they live in disobedience to God, and find their true self only in obedience to the deep longings that direct them toward the One who made them. Pagan philosophers hardly ever discussed obedience as a virtue, since their gods made few demands on them. Only Christianity has found in obedience the key to that freedom which all persons desire and only a few gifted souls seem really to achieve. Obedience is an essential part of the relationship between God and humankind, and between the spiritual father and the one who seeks his guidance. Yet it is part of the paradox of Christian life that 'The art of the spiritual father is to give birth to a free man, prostrate before the face of God'.[7]

How can Christians think that obedience gives birth to freedom when it seems to secular man to lead only to slavish dependence?

Freedom for some means captivity for others. The First World War was fought for freedom and a million men died in the trenches in the service of an empty cause. The desire for freedom has caused countless revolutions which, like the Russian Revolution in 1917, have led only to greater, more ruthless and more oppressive dictatorships than the ones they replaced. Political philosophies and personal relationships have offered glorious freedom, a freedom which has rapidly disintegrated into drab ordinariness no different from any other.

Christians point to these dreams and hopes of freedoms as proofs of the sinful, fallen nature of man. Yet Christian-

6. Philippians 2:8.
7. Paul Evdokimov, 'Eschatological Transcendence, Orthodox Life and Freedom', in Philippou (1973) p. 42.

290 Bearers of the Spirit

ity has not done a great deal better in achieving what it has promised than have the secular offerings of freedom. For all the fine sermons, the inspiring literature, the wonderful examples of the saints, the average christian congregation seems distressingly full of the very failings and unfreedoms that afflict the rest of humankind. And no christian person who takes seriously the long business of becoming free has any illusions about the precarious state of his freedom and the ease with which he can slip back into one constraint or another. So it is right that freedom be seen as one of the great goals of the christian life, and right that those who are thought to be guides in the christian life should themselves be free. Fr Alexander Elchaninov tells us:

> You cannot cure the souls of others or help
> people without having changed yourself.
> You cannot put in order the spiritual
> economy of others, so long as therre is chaos
> in your own soul. You cannot bring peace
> to others if you do not have it yourself.[8]

The spiritual father must himself be free. Freedom from sin is one obvious freedom, yet no spiritual father will claim to be always free from sin. The more important freedom is that of being so focussed on God, so given to his service, that nothing other than God constrains him to do anything. To outsiders this may seem to be exchanging one slavery for another, but those who seek to serve God usually experience obedience as freedom. Theologically this is not surprising. 'You have made us for yourself, and our heart is

8. Aleksandr V. El'chaninov, *The Diary of a Russian Priest* (London: Faber– Crestwood, New York: Saint Vladimir's Seminary Press, 1967) – cited by Allen, p. 98.
9. *Confessions* 1.1; translated by Henry Chadwick, *Saint Augustine: Confessions* (Oxford: Oxford University Press, 1991) p. 3.

restless until it rests in you,' said Saint Augustine to God.[9] We are created by God in the image of God and we do not discover who we are until we live in proper relation with God. It is his total givenness to God that makes the spiritual father a sure guide for others who wish to discover freedom.

The disciple comes to the *duhovnic* of his own free will. From the earliest christian centuries the need for a guide has been recognised. Saint Basil describes this need as well as anyone:

> Set about finding a man skilled in guiding those who are making their way toward God who will be an unerring director of your life. He should be adorned with virtues, bearing witness by his own works to his love for God, conversant with the Holy Scripture, recollected, free from avarice, a good, quiet man, tranquil, pleasing to God, a lover of the poor, mild, forgiving, labouring hard for the spiritual advancement of his clients, without vainglory or arrogance, impervious to flattery, not given to vacillation, and preferring God to all things else. If you should find him such a one, surrender yourself to him, completely renouncing and casting aside your own will, that you be found a clean vessel, preserving unto your praise and glory the good qualities deposited in you.[10]

Basil gives us here a fairly exhaustive list of christian virtues, from humility through to generosity to the poor, for whom Basil himself always cared greatly. Yet it is interesting that already in the fourth century he is concerned that the corrupting passions which so easily destroy the good

10. *De renuntiatione saeculi;* PG31:632BC; *On Renunciation of the World,* translated by Sister M. Monica Wagner in *Ascetical Works* (Washington D.C.: Catholic University of America Press, 1962) p. 19.

movements in our souls should be thoroughly expelled. From the fourth-century Basil to the twentieth-century Romanian fathers the concerns of spiritual fathers remain the same. The sinful passions must be utterly driven away. As long as there remains one small sinful passion in the heart it will turn the good thoughts of the heart to evil. It corrupts with selfishness, self-centredness, anger or power.

Selfishness and self-centredness can be found in the concern most of us have to place ourselves ahead of everything else, to be—and to be recognised to be—first in all things, to be comfortable and ensure that life goes on in a way that will bring us the greatest advantage. That may seem an unkind assertion, but few could honestly say that they desire the opposite—to be last rather than first, to be unknown rather than well known, to live life uncomfortably, yet contentedly, if that is to others' advantage. More subtle, too, are the temptations to power and anger. Anger can easily be disguised as righteous anger. We noted above how western Christians often point to Christ as someone who got angry, rightly and justly. That truly righteous anger may be possible, if one is as free of selfishness as Christ was. But it is not difficult to single out many noble causes of the past few decades which have been fatally flawed and ultimately unproductive of anything lasting or good becaused they were conceived and born in anger.

A truly christian life of the spirit is concerned that the goodness of God should be established in the world. The world is created by God and is a part of his dwelling place. The devil may also inhabit it but he has no rights to it, and the story of the incarnation of the Son of God shows that God has by no means abandoned his creation to the devil. The true christian spirit longs to see all things returned to the Father's hands. God still loves the world even though it has become the home of so much evil. God's love for the world is revealed in the suffering of Christ on the Cross and in the battle which was fought and won on Calvary. Love, therefore, is at the heart of the christian life and the

more a person is taken up with the life of God the more he
or she will love those who are called neighbours. Love cannot bear to see the beloved being hurt. Love cannot bear to
see the beloved hurting himself. Love cannot bear to see
one who is loved sliding into the destruction of sin. The
loving christian spirit may be helpless to do anything, but
he will never stop caring, and in that care lies the source of
prayer.

The general christian love of creation may at times have
been masked by a mistaken understanding of what monasticism was intended to be. This misperception is due in
part to the fact that those who are called to be spiritual fathers over the ages, particularly the really well known spiritual fathers, have generally been monks, engaged in forms
of monasticism that can look very much like flight from a
wicked world in order to cultivate the virtues which lead
the monk to God. In fact, as Paul Varghese points out:

> World weariness cannot be the source of
> authentic monasticism. The roots of true
> monasticism lie less in the 'hatred of the
> world' which the New Testament appears to
> enjoin, than in the dominical command, 'Be
> ye perfect as your heavenly Father is per-
> fect.'[11]

We have seen already that in order to understand spiritual
fatherhood we have had to understand something of monasticism. We have observed that, at least in Romania, there
is a close bond between the monastic life and the lives of
Christians in the world which, if not completely free of
tensions, is remarkably all of a piece. Whatever the expectation may be that an extremely ascetic, dedicated monk
will be a harsh and unsympathetic guide for someone im-
mersed in the world, the reality turns out to be different.

11. Paul Varghese, 'The Role of Monasticism in Quickening the Churches
of Our Time', in Philippou (1972), p. 74, citing Mt 5:8; cp. Rm 12:1-2.

Only a few people interviewed found monks harsh and unrealistic. The majority found them, as they found other spiritual fathers, to be loving men in whom the care of fatherhood dominated all else. Fr Ioanichie Bălan, though not in this matter an unbiased witness, may yet speak for most when he says:

> Speaking with a monk you feel that you are speaking with a father, with a spiritual mother, with a friend of Christ, with an intercessor for the whole world. His word gives you courage, his advice drives away violent thoughts, the serenity of his face gives you hope of salvation and his prayer warms your heart which has been hardened by every kind of sin.[12]

We see a similar spirit in the person of Isaac of Nineveh more than a thousand years earlier. He exhorts spiritual companions:

> Be a companion to those who are sad at heart with passionate prayer and heartfelt signs [and] support the weak and distressed with a word as far as you are able so that the right hand upholding the universe may sustain you.[13]

THE ROMANIAN CONTEXT

In Romania today there is another factor which has bound the monks and the people together, and that is the part the monastic life has played in nourishing and defending the people's identity and providing them with refuge in times of danger. Much of Romania's history has been bound up

12. *Convorbiri Duhovniceşti*, p. 256.
13. Isaac of Nineveh, *On the Ascetical Life* 2.17; translated by Mary Hansbury (Crestwood, New York: Saint Vladimir's Seminary Press, 1990).

with the monasteries. Both in earlier centuries when the country was threatened by Turkish or Hapsburg rule and more recently when facing communism, the monks provided a bulwark both for the Church and the Romanian people. And for this Romanians are deeply grateful. Monks may have their eyes firmly fixed on God, but they still love their land. Valeriu Anania, in the introduction to his book on the monasteries of Oltenia, writes:

> The land of our country is sacred through the bones of our ancestors, through the blood and the tombs, known and unknown, of heroes, through the sweat of peasant workers, through the whole burden of our feelings and in the end through itself. Yet this is a quasi-religious sacredness as is that, for example, of a mother, of bread, of a national flag: when an injury is spoken about then, in some way or other, our spirit tends to react violently, in defence. But a place of worship is much more than sacred. It is holy.[14]

Romania's identity is rooted in its past, both secular and Christian. The past defines the people and much of their strength and their charm is derived from their history. Yet it poses problems for the present. How should Romanians live in relation to the world that has forced itself upon them since the collapse of communism in 1989? More particularly, what place do the spiritual fathers of the country have in helping the people to adapt to this new situation?

The problems are vast. Free market economy has not solved the huge economic problems under which the country has laboured for decades. The few have benefitted greatly from it. The majority are, or feel (which is much the same thing) as poor as they ever were. At the same time

14. V. Anania, *Cerurile Oltului*, p. 9.

the opening to the West has brought many opportunities for travel, for buying western goods, for discovering new ways of education, care of children, social assistance. Some of this has been welcomed by Romanians, anxious to improve the lot of the weakest and poorest members of their society. But some are naturally embarrassed that their country has been found so wanting in areas of social care and would rather close their eyes to the problems. The Church has also found that the freedom gained with the fall of communism has brought a host of new difficulties. Religious freedom has led to the re-emergence of the Catholic 'Uniate' Churches. It has brought large numbers of dollar-rich pentecostals into the country. Along with them, and seemingly as part of the same invasion, have come the vices of financial profiteers, of sexual freedom and of other western ideas that overturn the traditional values of Romanian society. Romanians have discovered that being anti-Jewish and anti-Gypsy is simply not acceptable in modern Europe. The temptation in the face of all this is to throw up the barriers, to withdraw into a safe Romanian Orthodox world, to allow free rein to a latent xenophobic nationalism, and to refuse to let change enter a world which has long been regarded as perfect and immutable.

There is no doubt that many of the monks and priests in Romania succumb to this temptation. Yet Romania cannot insulate itself from the Western world and nor do the leaders of the Romanian Orthodox Church wish to do so. Critical as they may be of the West, they recognise that the West has experience in dealing with secularism which, if not always to be imitated—and one can easily argue that most of the western attempts to christianise secularism have failed—must certainly be learned from. Also they recognise that they have a tradition which has been largely lost in the West and which they believe the West needs to discover.

In recent years Orthodoxy has become increasingly familiar to Western Christians. Icons, a liturgy performed in a foreign language amidst clouds of incense and magnificent vestments, a consciousness of tradition which takes Christians back behind the confusions of the modern world—all these can seduce a westerner starved of religious symbolism in an increasingly functional and frightening age. The attraction can sometimes be the sheer otherworldliness of this form of Christianity. Its intransigent refusal to change can give people security in a fast-changing world. Coupled with this is the perennial attraction of the Fathers of the Church, of a patristic age when, it seems, faith was purer and stronger and the vision of God less tarnished than it has become. There is a great deal of fantasy involved in this attraction to Orthodoxy but in the attraction there may well be a perception of truths which the Western churches have forgotten, or at least greatly diminished. Christianity has always insisted that 'by their fruits you will know them'[15] In the tradition of spiritual fatherhood in Romania we may see the fruits and test out the authenticity of what the Orthodox Church claims to have preserved whole and alive from the earliest christian past.

The *duhovnics* we have met—Fr Cleopa, Fr Arsenie, Fr Serafim, Fr Negruţiu, Fr Teofil—have shown themselves to be men of wisdom, compassion, understanding, and love. The tradition they embody is found also—in differing measures—among the ordinary parish clergy, but it is still authentically the same. The men and women we have spoken with in all parts of Romania—young and old, well educated and little educated—have shown a like regard for their spiritual fathers and a moving gratitude for the compassion and understanding they receive. They see them both as fathers who support them in their weakness and as guides who direct them on their way as they journey through life in the hope of reaching the promised kingdom of God when at last they die.

15. Mt 7:16.

LIFE AFTER DEATH

It is their perspective on life after death that makes the
Romanian Orthodox point of view so different from that of
most Western Christians. For all the token nods that are
given in the direction of life in heaven, western Christianity
in the last fifty years at least has become increasingly
centred on life in this world. Today many western Christians
are influenced by the secular non-christian view that
death is a catastrophic end to be delayed as long as possible
and to be resented as a destruction of the one thing that
really matters to us, that is, physical life. Even amongst
Christians of a fairly devout kind, talk of death is often
avoided as morbid and talk of heaven criticised as escapist.
For some the aim of Christian life is to build up the Church
and spread it throughout the world; for others social justice, for making God's kingdom come on earth as it is in
heaven; for others the desire to experience joy, happiness,
confidence, and love now instead of waiting for the future.
While these are all very good goals on which to focus our
Christian life, they need to be complemented by a recognition that there is life after death if they are to have real
coherence for Christians. Then it will be seen that life in
this world is integrally related to life in the next. Indeed,
the Gospel of John and Paul's epistles assume that heavenly life has already begun on earth, at least for those who
have entered into the experience of Christ.

This loss of perspective of eternity amongst western Christians is tragic. The christian hope of resurrection and life
everlasting provides the assurance that, as Julian of Nor-
wich put it, all things shall be well; in the end all manner of
things shall be well.[16] Christian hope is bound up with resurrection but this can only be known imperfectly before
death. The full experience of the risen Christ, of the love of

16. *The Revelations of Divine Love,* ch. 27; translated by Clifton Wolters in
Penguin Classics (Middlesex, 1966).

God, of the fellowship of the Holy Spirit can only be encountered in the presence of God, and that is found beyond the grave. Everything good we experience on earth is a preparation for the far greater good that God has waiting for us when we die[17]. All things material are by nature transitory, even the very best of things, and it is simply because the best of things presage a far greater and more wonderful heavenly reality that they are so valuable and exciting to us now. Without the hope that a confidence of life with God after death gives us, life becomes bleak and despairing, a heroic endurance, a striving after good which we shall never see realised. Yet with this hope life is transformed.

The great saints have always been great lovers of God, and lovers too of men. Their love stretches them out and draws them onwards to the fulfilment that awaits them after death. Saint Paul knew this longing:

For to me to live is Christ and to die is gain. If it is to be life in the flesh, that means fruitful labour for me. Yet which I shall choose I cannot tell. I am hard pressed between the two. My desire is to depart and be with Christ, for that is far better.[18]

The life of the spirit has as its aim the fullness of life in Christ, the fullness of the love of God. At no point do spiritual fathers suggest that life amongst one's fellow men and women is of anything less than the highest importance, but they keep our focus on God. That is one of their main functions, to keep the people of God truly directed towards God and never to allow either the cares or the joys of human life to distract our attention from this main goal.

The ways they keep this focus on God are comparatively few, though developed with great subtlety and perception

17. 1 Cor 2:9.
18. Philippians 1:21-23.

of human psychology. Perhaps the first is the simple instruction to 'keep watch'. We have seen above how great a
concern this has always been to the monks—as we saw it
in the young monk whose first nervous steps in the monastic life were informed by this instruction constantly to
keep watch[19]. In the classic mythology of the spiritual life
we keep watch for the devils, the myriads of servants of the
great Evil One who constantly seek entrance into our lives
in order to turn them away from God. We may now choose
not to believe in devils, but the reality they represent is as
real as it ever was. Anyone who has tried to live the Christian life knows how one falls away, how quickly one is distracted, how a small distraction quickly leads to a larger
distraction, how a small weakness quickly becomes a great
sin. At the same time modern psychology with its Freudian
and Jungian origins, shows us the great festering depths of
the unconscious, exposing to us hints and glimpses of a
swirling world of desires that makes the most extravagant
medieval picture of hell look tame. Every Christian who is
trying seriously to live the life of Christ will be subject to
these uncontrolled desires. Each attempt we make to set
aside things which distract us from God will quickly make
us aware of how much we desire things, comfort, food,
and wealth in either a material, or more dangerously, a
spiritual form. This is particularly true for those who enter
a form of life which asks a commitment to celibacy and
obedience. They quickly discover, if they did not know it
before, what a larger place sexuality has in their identity,
and how the prospect of never fulfilling their sexual potential threatens that identity and seems to deprive them of
one of the major joys of human life. And for all the New
Testament assurances that obedience is the way to freedom,
it will often feel like slavery. Obedience cuts at the will and
is painful. Obedience bruises us as we bump up against it.
Obedience seems to prevent us from growing into the kind

19. Chapter 3, above pp 54ff.

of people we know ourselves to be. Christianity makes hard demands and asks for hard choices to be made, not just by monks, but by everyone who lives it seriously. The tradition we have been looking at shows us that it is all worthwhile.

In any group of people, small resentments grow into bitterness. Small whims become magnified into great hunger. When Christian life gets tough it is easy to lose heart. Is this course really leading nowhere? Has joy gone from life? The only person who can assure this serious Christian that all is well is the very one who is holding him or her to this course of deprivation. The spiritual father will give assurance, not by arguments but by love. The disciple must find in his or her spiritual father the love, the joy, the hope which are the fruits of the Christian life. Then he will know that it is worth going on, not just for the hope of the glory that will come after death, which may still be a long way away, but for the joy he sees in the life of his spiritual father. That is the most convincing of all proofs that this life is leading to God.

In the same way the overriding concern of the monk, to keep watch, will be a major part of all christian endeavour. However, for Christians outside the monastery it will not so much be a watching over the movements of the mind, as watching over the desires of the heart. Lay people must live in a busy world, a world where they are continually meeting people, where they may have very little time for the kind of earnest and even anxious reflection of the young monk. It is in the very contacts they have with others that their salvation is worked out. Their keeping watch must often focus on this, to see that they are always charitable, patient, that anger, resentment, envy, ambition or lust do not enter into their relationships. Just as the monk continually opens his thoughts to his spiritual father, keeping nothing back so the lay Christian should confess every fault of love, every surging of the passions. This, no less than opening the thoughts, can be a hard thing to do. We are ashamed, and rightly ashamed, of what we do. We will not easily admit shame to another. Once again it will be the loving character of the spiritual father that makes such confession possible. A confession that begins in penitence, sorrow, shame and fear is transformed into an experience of love, joy and renewed hope, of human friendship at its best and of divine freedom. Hope is restored and with hope comes a new determination to live.

As the Christian seeker discovers the sins lurking within the heart he quickly realises that their roots must be found and torn out. The teaching of generations of spiritual fathers is that the roots of all sin reach down into the passions. Saint Paul, at the very beginning of Christianity, provided enduring advice on this subject:

> Put to death what is earthly in you: immorality, impurity, passion, evil desire and covetousness , . . . put them all away: anger, wrath, malice, slander and foul talk from your mouth . . . . Let the peace of Christ rule in your hearts, to which indeed you were called.[20]

What Paul makes explicit the spiritual fathers often leave implicit. The point of expelling the evil passions is to allow room for Christ to take up his abode. The aim of this dispassionate life is not, as it may first seem, to escape from real living, but actually to live fully. The early fathers saw the spiritual life as working also in the body. Saint Hippolytus tells us:

> When you have learned to know the true God, you will have a body immortal and incorruptible, like your soul; you will gain the kingdom of heaven, you who have lived on earth and knew the king of heaven; freed from passion, suffering and disease, you will

20. Col 3:5,8,15.

be a companion of God and a co-heir with
Christ, for you have become a god.[21]

The implications of a body immortal and incorruptible are
somewhat problematical for us. No doubt Hippolytus here
is referring to the resurrected body, in which we share in
the resurrection of Christ. Yet a number of other points
can be usefully drawn from this passage, since they reflect
the general teaching of the Greek fathers on whom the
modern Romanian spiritual fathers based their lives. The
first is the obvious point that through freedom from passions come all the good things, both earthly and heavenly,
that we desire. So dispassion is not an escape from life into
a kind of death, but rather a fulfilment of life taking all the
best things of earthly life into life with God. Secondly, the
suggestion that knowing God will lead to incorruptible
bodies may surprise us. Clearly knowing here is far more
than cognitive knowledge. Knowing here must describe
entering into the nature of God so fully that we begin to
partake of its life and incorruptibility. Yet knowing obviously implies the use of the mind as well as the heart. True
spiritual fathers never despise the mind but teach that all
parts of the human person, body, mind and heart, must be
brought into the task of knowing God. That brings us to
our third important point, that if the mind and the will are
involved in this striving after perfection, it is clear that we
ourselves have a large part to play in the work of salvation,
a work which leads us not only to become companions of
God and co-heirs with Christ, but even to become God.

That leads us to two areas of our discussion which can
easily be misunderstood in the West but which have great
importance in the East and may be significant in suggest-
ing ways in which the spiritual fathers of Romania can give
western Christians guidance. These two areas are synergy
and divinisation.

21. Saint Hippolytus. *The Refutation of all Heresies*, 10.30; Ante Nicene
Fathers Library (rpt. 1995), Volume 5:134.

Most of the interviews on which this work was based took place during two successive Lents (or times of the Great Fast) before Easter. During this time serious Orthodox were all preparing for their Easter communions, which for many would be their only communion of the year. Fasting for most meant no meat, perhaps also no dairy products, and as they went into Holy Week, perhaps no food at all. At the same time, people went more to Church, sometimes even to a midnight service. Discussions of the spiritual life and the engagement with spiritual fathers centred on confession, on the nature of sin and the need to eradicate sin through careful searching of the mind and the heart, and through the sacramental grace of confession. We have seen above how much detail Fr Cleopa and other spiritual fathers went into in their searching out the nature of sin, and how much they emphasise the need for a total onslaught on sin, making no compromises, allowing no quarter, treating no sin as small, unimportant or insignificant. One's reaction to all this unceasing war on sin could be mixed. On the one hand it was very impressive and often deeply moving to be allowed to share in the struggle and to see the lengths of honesty and endeavour to which some would go. On the other hand one could feel exhausted. Was this really the freedom that Christ offers us? Where was the joy? Where was the spirit of little children that the Gospel commends? Of course one needed to wait for Easter Day for that. The time of fasting is a time of warfare and battle, soldiers need to be hard and determined, to keep fighting constantly until victory is won; and it is true that on Easter Day a joy breaks through which is far deeper and more widespread than one generally meets in a western Christian society.

Yet behind that there is another nagging concern. Are these good Christian people trying to earn their salvation. It is true that Saint Paul told us to 'work out your own salvation with fear and trembling';[22] and James spends part

22. Philippians 2:12

of his epistle exalting works against mere faith. But Luther did not much like James, and his suspicion of anything that may lead people to think they can earn salvation has remained with the Protestant churches of the West. He is right. Salvation is by God alone. Nothing we can do can ever earn salvation since salvation is and must always be a free gift from God. Salvation comes to us out of God's love and if it were possible for us to earn it for ourselves it would become a thing bought, a thing paid for, a thing we own. We would have a right to it and would be justly proud of our success in earning it. It would no longer be a sign, or indeed a reality, of God's love. God's own status would be reduced from that of the generous giver to that of the mere supplier. Like a shopkeeper he would provide the salvation we want when we managed to gather together a sufficiently large sum of good works. We are back into the Pelagian controversy of the fifth century. Are Eastern Christians Pelagian as they have often been accused? This is no mere academic dispute. Augustine rightly recognised that the Pelagian heresy cut at the roots of God's love which had to give salvation freely if it was to be love at all. At the same time salvation could not ever be earned for the simple reason that mankind was too corrupt, too weakened by sin ever to achieve salvation in the way Pelagius thought he could. What seemed to be a statement of confidence in the human condition turned out to be recipe of despair, as a western society in this century, embracing a secular form of Pelagianism, has discovered only too clearly and often in the disasters and increasing despair of modern life. Are Eastern Christians embarked on a hopeless task, an endless striving after a virtue they cannot attain?

The question is a largely rhetorical one, since any extended experience of Romanian Christian life shows that the answer is 'no'. Christian people do not despair, because they find virtue is accessible, and they experience the joy that comes from a life well examined, repented of, and restored. Christian people have before them the example of their spiritual fathers, both the great monk spiritual fathers and the more accessible parish priests who are living examples of a truly grace-filled Christian life. Such a grace-filled Christian life is not, one hastens to add, ever entirely free from anxiety and fear that failure may be round the corner, that sin may yet get the upper hand. That is, perhaps, as it should be. Experience tells us that no one is ever safe from that catastrophic fall that brings destruction. The Orthodox are always conscious, too, as we westerners are not, of the glory and the majesty of God which co-exists with his love. God can never be taken for granted. One may approach him freely with love, but trembling also with awe. He may be the most loving and compassionate of fathers, but he is not a sentimentalised Father Christmas. Love and glory, compassion and judgment, fear and joy are all part of the human experience of the presence of God. If there is an element of paradox in that then one must not be surprised to find that the salvation which comes to us only out of the free and unbounded generosity of God, must yet be worked for and striven for and never simply assumed.

This is synergy, working together with God for the salvation of our souls and also of course for the redemption of the world.[23] What the devout Orthodox Christian never quite gets over is the privilege of participation in the life of God. We have seen, from this description that participation in God means becoming not just like God, but becoming God ourselves. We find this impossible to describe, since God is God and we cannot claim to be him. Perhaps the closest we can get in language is to say that we partake in the divine nature. The image of God within us has been so completely restored that our nature has become one with the nature of the Christ who dwells in us. The implications are startling. For one thing the process can begin here, and

23. A theological description of synergy is to be found as an Appendix, below, page 329.

the extraordinary sense of holiness which seems to surround the great spiritual fathers is witness to the possibility that divinisation has taken place, to a large degree, in these people. Their large-spiritedness, their ability to say just the words that are needed, or to clothe ordinary words with a significance they would have from no other, the quality they have which makes us take stock of our own lives and see them in a completely new perspective in relation to God, all suggest a change in them which cannot be easily accounted for as mere growth in human personality.

A second result of this is that, once the process of divinisation begins in us, we shall long more and more for its completion. The witness of St Paul and of countless other saints supports this. The focus of life moves beyond the grave. The standards by which we make our judgements of what matters in life become those of God. This does not devalue human life. Indeed the contrary is usually true, that it enhances the value of human life since it becomes increasingly clear just how much this is a gift from God. People gain in significance as people created by God, each uniquely loved by God, each with his or her own calling to God which the spiritual father perhaps must recognise as he helps them along the way.

THE WEST

So we come to the West, so much maligned, so much criticised both by the East and by many westerners themselves. After all this description of Romanian spiritual fathers we find ourselves asking, are there such men or women in our own countries, today? Good priests there are; holy nuns there are; enchanting old people there are. Each of these have about them something of the quality that makes a great Romanian spiritual father so utterly extraordinary. It may seem to be a matter of degree. In the West we speak of sanctification as being the ultimate aim of

Christian life in this world. Sanctification means is to become holy, but it is only a stage towards divinisation.

A further problem may simply be that society and the Church itself simply have no place for the spiritual father comparable to that which he occupies in Romania. In Western churches confession is no longer generally a preparation for receiving communion. So the ordinary parish priest does not play the same kind of mediating role in a christian person's sacramental life as he does in the East. In a larger sphere, the spiritual father has never really had an exact counterpart in the Western Christian world. Confessors had a great influence at certain times and amongst certain people. The spiritual director now has an increasing though often confused significance in Church life. Bishops now often urge their priests to have spiritual directors. Priests often encourage the more devout of their people to find spiritual directors. Yet the role is not clear. Only in a minority of cases does direction involve sacramental confession, though the kind of things discussed may come close to confession on occasion. The model is often that of secular counselling or psychotherapy, even to the extent of basing one's work on that of an atheist, Carl Rodgers! Such relationships may well have their role, even in spiritual direction, but compared with the richness of the eastern tradition as we have seen it they appear very narrow, and considerably limited. Even the advice often given to spiritual directors to keep a distance, not to be emotionally involved, not to take responsibility from the other, can easily deprive the relationship of the fatherly love, the passionate concern, the constant prayer which informs the Romanian father's relationship with those who come to him.

There is, of course, the danger of romanticising the Orthodox spiritual father. We see him only at a distance or in special and carefully controlled circumstances. We do not know what it is to live with him. Our images are affected by Father Zosima in *The Brothers Karamazov*, by an admiration for eastern and patristic spirituality, or by the charm which is characteristic of Romania and which casts its grace upon so many of the people one meets there. Foreign things can often seem much more attractive than the familiar. Hours of attendance in an Orthodox liturgy can be remembered only for the swirling music and the glorious mystery, not for the aching limbs and the hours of boredom. Orthodox biblical criticism and dogmatic theology is quite different from that with which we are all familiar in the West. We find ourselves asking, can I really trust the spiritual insights of a person who believes in Adam and Eve as historical figures? Or does that really not matter? Is not holiness apart from critical theories of academic theology? Does academic theology itself have a legitimate place in this life of holiness? We may find ourselves thinking that an academic theology which believes it is possible to study the beliefs people have about God, and the books of Scripture recording the revelation of God, yet without belief in God must lack all coherence. There may be no doubt in our minds that a simple but holy peasant monk like the late Father Paisie Olaru of Sihla may be a better guide to us in our life with God than the best acdemic theologian. Yet still there are questions about the meeting of East and West which cannot always be answered to the East's advantage.

The modern world is still God's world and the developments within it take place under the hand of God even if they are not always used to his advantage or in the ways he would approve. As Romania struggles to catch up economically, technologically, culturally (in such matters as issues of human rights) with the nations of western Europe she finds herself entering a complex and ambiguous world. It is clear that in terms of sheer material prosperity westerners are far better off than those in the East. It is clear that such material prosperity has not brought the happiness that may have been expected. In literature, art, social studies, statistics of crime, psychological research, or almost any area one can name it can be shown that the flashy exterior which the West presents hides a desperate unhappiness, a deep conviction of the meaningless of life, a constant seeking for experience that will blot out the pointless character of a life stretching away for ever. When Romania first escaped from the communist stranglehold she thought that engagement with the West would bring all manner of good things. Quickly she found that it brought, too, all manner of bad things. Likewise the Romanian Church, having endured and survived four decades of varying degrees and kinds of persecution finds itself stronger than the western churches who have had no such obvious persecution but have had the heart eaten out of them by the insidious secular values and achievements of modern technological man. Yet Romania cannot hide from this unpleasant world. She must find her own way of engaging with the secular agenda and may even learn from the more obvious of the West's mistakes. Her Christian people have a very complicated path ahead.

To their credit it seems to be a challenge they are quite well equipped to meet. Their scholarship may be out of date in western terms, but there is a strong tradition of scholarship and a great desire for academic excellence. As the more stultifying aspects of communist ideology recede into the past people become increasingly free in their thinking and learn the habits of criticism impossible in the past. At the same time, the Orthodox know they have a great strength in their spiritual fathers and the Christian life which has been maintained by the spiritual fathers remains at the heart of Church life. Nor does a passionate devotion exist only in the villages and in the beautiful mountains and valleys where one so often meets large congregations of picturesque people worshipping in exquisite, colourful churches. The Church engages seriously with the modern world. In Iași one can meet the abbot of Golia monastery in the centre of the city, a good and godly priest, who runs a church radio station, is surrounded by computers and directs a modern communications programme that would amaze any western cleric. One can meet Metropolitan Daniel Ciuobotea, whose own spiritual father was Father Cleopa, yet who is on equal terms with any western academic and who seems to combine in himself qualities of spiritual life, learning, administration and monastic simplicity which defy the imagination. In Caransebeş, Bishop Streza, a former liturgy professor, widowed with five children, demonstrates how hard work and a desire to teach can restore a greatly neglected diocese to health. In Timişoara the Metropolitan Nicolae, whose own past compromises with the communists are sadly on record, shows an unusual willingness to admit publicly to the faults of the Church and encourages an opennness to Western values which many in his own country find unacceptable. Also in Timişoara Fr Eugen Jurca exercises a highly effective ministry in a dreary housing estate in a church which is only half built. Angrily critical of his own Church he shows his desire to serve his people in a selfless ministry of spiritual counsel that keeps him hearing confessions till all hours of the night in an icy church. Not all the bishops and priests come up to these high standards. Not all the young people, even amongst those who attend the liturgy regularly, have the intelligent, sensitive commitment to their faith that we have met in Timişoara, Sibiu, Poieşti and Bucharest. Yet many people like these priests have been encountered in these pages and the desire of the young to hold tightly to their Romanian and Orthodox heritage while launching out into a world of computers, modern scholarship and exciting ideas is surprising and moving in its intensity and rescues a westerner from his tired sense of *déjà vu*.

It is tempting at the end of this study of Romanian Orthodoxy to draw comparisons between the situtations in the Romanian and Russian churches. The comparison, if undertaken, must be done with caution. The persecution of the Russian Church took place over a much longer period and was far more virulent, particularly in the 1930s when the Church was driven more or less completely

underground. Theological study in the Russian church was
far less well maintained[24] than in Romania. Inevitably the
compromise which the remnants of the Church made with
the communist government was much greater than in Romania and is taking much longer to recover from. Recent
writings[25] on the state of Christianity, particularly Orthodoxy in the Russian territories, shows a very confused pattern in which people discover faith without discovering
organised religion; or cling to the Church and its traditional beliefs about society for much the same conservative
reasons as they cling also to communism and its remembered security. On the whole the Orthodox Church in Russia seems to have less in the way of resources, spiritual and
intellectual, to cope with the huge change their country is
going through. As in the Romanian Church there is a strong
instinct towards a nationalist understanding of the Church's
role in society and it is alarming to see the Church take up
exclusivist positions against Roman Catholics[26], foreigners
and any other group that threatens their hegemony over
the Russian people.

   Yet if the Russian Orthodox Church life reflects to a
greater degree some of the problems Romanians still face
in the wake of communism, so too are there similar achievements. Jane Ellis tells us:

> There has been no shortage of novices in
> the newly opened monastic communities.
> Many young and educated people have been

24. See A. Johansen, *Theological Study in the Russian and Bulgarian Orthodox Church under Communist Rule* (London: Faith Press 1963).
25. A small number of books on this subject are included in the bibliography.
26. As in Romania the relationship between the Orthodox and Rome is
bedevilled by a history in which Catholic nations conquered parts of Orthodox lands. The establishment and post communist revival of the Eastern
Rite churches further compounds the confusion. By way of contrast, the
Apostolic Letter of John Paul II, *Orientale Lumen*, shows a warm understanding of the Orthodox Church's love for tradition, spiritual fatherhood,
and monastic life.

coming forward to dedicate their lives to monasticism. Some speak of it as the most positive way they can envisage to save their country from the evils of the past and build a better future. A life dedicated to prayer seems to them the surest way of bringing this about.[27]

Other comparisons can be drawn. Jonathan Sutton[28] draws our attention to a poem by Fyodor Tyutchev, *These Poor Villages*, in which poverty takes on the form of Christ. This is part of a literary tradition in which the suffering of Russia takes on a redemptive role for the world. Romanians, contemplating their suffering over many centuries, often endured in protecting a largely unappreciative West from Turkish or Russian advance, often see themselves in the same Christlike role.

The attitudes of Romanians towards their Church after communism are to some extent reflected in these pages, but can usefully be summarised here. Amongst the young there is already considerable ignorance of what life was under communism. In 1990 they were young children and did not know what was happening. This ignorance of what life was like under communism is compounded by the fact that only now is it becoming possible to gather together the information and sources on which the story will eventually be based. Teams of young students are going round the country interviewing people to gather their memories. They meet much enthusiasm and are often deeply moved by what they hear[29]. They also meet much resistance from those

27. Ellis, *The Russian Orthodox Church*, p. 69.
28. *The Way We Are: The Russian Soul*, an unpublished public lecture delivered in Cambridge on 9 November 2000, in the University of Cambridge's public lecture series 'All the Russias: Discourses of National Identity in Russian Culture'. Jonathan Sutton lectures in Russian at Leeds University.
29. I am indebted to Florina Jinga for telling me of this activity in which she is involved.

who do not want the past revealed[30].

Not surprisingly, attitudes towards the Church are very mixed. Some, usually the more nationalist, or patriotic, are thrilled to see the Church able once again to go into schools and universities, into the army and to acquire a seeming influence in the affairs of state. Their hope is that the Church will recover its former pre-War glory and influence. Others accuse the Church of the Philetist heresy in which church and state have become too closely linked.

There are, as we have seen, some magnificent clergy, parish priests who work immensely hard and are using their new freedom to great effect. Some of these have surprisingly modern and western attitudes toward society and show a real understanding of the young. Sadly there are also a great number of clergy who do not know how to respond to the new challenges and who still exercise a largely cultic priesthood. This is not helped by the fact that theological study in Romania has always been somewhat uncritical; students learn to reproduce information rather than think for themselves. There is, it is true, a great interest in study, but it tends to be backward looking with a great emphasis on patristic study and not much on theology outside their own traditon.[31]

As in Russia there is some considerable dissatisfaction with the apparent ease with which the vast majority of church leaders retained their posts after 1990, despite their varying degrees of cooperation with the Communist governments. This is an acutely sensitive issue. Many believe that the Church, broadly speaking, did the right thing, keeping the churches open, the liturgy being celebrated, the sacraments available even at the cost of subservience to the

30. This resistance, in the church as much as in society generally, was partly confirmed through a questionnaire I sent out in November 200 and circulated amongst students in Timişoara and some friends in Sibiu and Bucharest.
31. A happy exception to this is a young dogmatic theologian, Călin Sămărghiţan, who has recently successfully completed a doctoral thesis on Anglican Pneumatology at Cluj University.

communist authorities, and that the rightness of this policy is demonstrated in the Church's current health and strength. Others point out the degree to which the Church remains riddled with nepotism and unfair influence[32] and a reluctance to face and repent of the past.[33] This too is compounded by the despair which many feel when they become convinced that the country is still run by communists with the same priorities as before.

Inevitably there is a considerable gap between older and younger people. The younger people (at least the students) have discovered the internet, are turned towards the West, open to new ideas, to technology and if they are devout want to see their church responding to the intellectual and social challenges which they see western churches trying to meet. Older people, monks especially, tend to withdraw from this alien new world and want to keep foreign influences out. There is a strong desire to return to the safe, old ways.

All this tends to underline the crucial role which the spiritual fathers of the Church will play in the future of Romania, since they are both the custodians of the spiritual life of the Church as they have received it down the ages, and also the wise leaders who must help the young Romanian Orthodox to integrate their new ideas and their generous desires in a christian life which authentically embraces the old while absorbing the new. Our experience has been that on the whole the spiritual fathers of Romania are well equipped to do this.

This brings us to a final point of comparison with the Russian church, that church's tradition of spiritual fatherhood. Despite the political tension that has always existed

32. It is difficult for priests to get jobs unless they know people of influence. There is an unhappy degree of paranoia amongst clergy and church employees who feel continually under threat from those above them.
33. One has to say that Nielson's rather critical account of the Romanian Orthodox Church in his *Revolutions in Eastern Europe* is made from a very western point of view and signally fails to appreciate the nuances and legitimate priorities of the Romanian Orthodox leaders.

between Romania and Russia, ecclesiastically the links have been very strong. We have already seen the ease with which Basil of Poiana Mărului and Paisius Velichkovsky made their homes in Romania and the considerable influence they had on the development of the hesychastic and, later, the philocalic tradition in the Church. We must remember too that until the middle of the nineteenth century most Orthodox worship in Romania was conducted in Church Slavonic. It is clear that over the centuries the borders between the Ukraine and Moldavia particularly were far from impervious to a constant exchange of religious life. So the tradition represented in Romania by the spiritual fathers we have met was strong also in that strand of monastic life developed at Optina, and by the great *startsy* — Sergius of Radonezh in the Middle Ages, and Ambrosy and Seraphim of Sarov in the nineteenth century. Perhaps the most interesting comparison, however, is to be made with Dostoevsky's Father Zosima in *The Brothers Karamazov*. Here Dostoevsky gives a classic descripton of the Elder's role. 'An elder is one who takes your soul, your will into his soul and into his will'.[34] Dostoevsky regarded Zosima as crucial to the refutation of Ivan Karamazov's atheistic arguments,[35] not through a parallel set of 'theistic' arguments but through the sheer quality of his life, the evident holiness which touched everyone who came into his cell, even the buffoon, the elder Karamazov. Indeed it is a curious fact, as Sven Linnér points out[36] that Zosima says very little about God. His holiness seems to come to him almost independently of God, through his own humility and his living of the monastic life. This may simply be because, in Dostoevsky's own view, God cannot be talked about or rationally 'proved', but can only be seen in his creatures. Dostoevsky likewise

34. In Book 1, Chapter 5. Translation by R. Pevear and Larissa Volokhonsky (London: Everyman, 1997) 27.
35. See Sutherland, *Atheism and the Rejection of God*, pp. 101ff, for an interesting discussion of this.
36. Linner, *Starets Zosima in The Brothers Karamazov*.

regarded the monastic life as crucial to the future of Russia[37] and spiritual elders as the real life blood of this monastic life. We have seen already how central Romanians think their spiritual fathers have been to the Church both during the communist time and after it. The intriguing, superficially unprepossessing, but universally attractive figure of Father Zosima stands against the rationalism which tries to dispose of God and calls into question all the arguments for power and influence that have so often seduced the leaders of Christian Churches. In Romania today we find he is not simply a literary figure but a type, one of a scattering of real people whose contribution to their Churches—Russian and Romanian Orthodox, Catholic, Anglican, and Protestant—can never be assessed but will always be greater than we can imagine.

---

37. See *The Brothers Karamazov*, Book 6: 'The Russian Monk'.

Epilogue

*Seeing the crowds, he went up on the moun-
tain, and when he sat down his disciples came
to him. And he opened his mouth and taught
them, saying: 'Blessed are the poor in spirit, for
theirs is the kingdom of heaven'.*[1]

S o BEGINS one of the best known and most loved pieces
of christian writing. Devout Christians, vaguely attached
Christians, even professed atheists and adherents of other
religions proclaim their love for the Beatitudes, often add-
ing that if only Christians taught and lived the Beatitudes
their churches would be full. They may well be right, yet it
is strange that they should so much exalt these words when
their spirit is so far from that by which modern western
society—and perhaps most other societies—lives. Most of
the Christian Church's greatest teachers would agree that
the Beatitudes sum up the teaching and example of Christ.
Benedict cites them in his Rule for Monks.[2] A thousand
years later Saint Ignatius of Loyola, in the key meditation
of his *Spiritual Exercises*, the 'Two Standards', clearly refers
to the Beatitudes when he urges his followers to pray to be
brought 'to the highest spiritual poverty and—if His Divine Majesty would be served and would want to choose
them—no less to actual poverty; to be of contumely and
contempt, because from these two things humility follows'.[3]

1. Mt 5:1-2.
2. Rule 4.33 and 64.10.
3. *The Spiritual Exercises*, 146.

319

Nothing describes the spiritual fathers of Romania and their teaching better than Christ's teaching on the mountain.

'Blessed are the poor in spirit, for theirs is the kingdom of God.' To be poor, or at least free from as much concern for material possessions as is possible, is one of the foundations of a monk's life. To be poor in spirit is to know that we have nothing of our own and that everything we have is given by God. This is the source of great joy since knowing that everything has come to us as a gift from a loving God makes the whole world a place of gifts. It acknowledges the truth of our relationship with God, that since he created the world, it all belongs to him and nothing can truly be called our own. Yet this is not a cause of diminishment, for God sets us free to roam through all his created glory and to look forward with anticipation to having also the glory of heaven as our place of freedom.

'Blessed are those who mourn.' The spiritual father weeps for the world. He weeps for his own sins, for his own alienation from God, slight as that may appear to an observer. He weeps for the insults done to God and the tragedies endured by man. And he weeps for joy; he weeps for gratitude that God has not turned away his face but has himself come into this fallen world and brought salvation to all who accept it. The spiritual father's weeping is sorrow and joy mixed and his tears are considered to be a precious gift from God and one that brings redemption to him and to all for whom he prays. A failure to weep indicates a failure to understand the magnitude of the disaster which is the human condition. It is a failure to see the catastrophic and utterly repulsive nature of sin. It is a failure to feel the terrible nature of humankind's pain, anaesthetised to it as we are by long familiarity. A failure to weep is a failure to love and a failure to see the compassionate love of God, who enters into the pain in order to bring his children out. A failure to weep in the end becomes a failure to rejoice since true, deep joy only comes to us through tears.

'Blessed are the meek.' The Romanian words *smerit*

(meek, humble) and *smerenie* (meekness, humility) are among those most frequently used in relation to the spiritual fathers. For all their stature and their authority they must always show meekness. From the very start of his life in religion, the monk must learn, by obedience absolute and unquestioning, the virtue of meekness. It is not a virtue greatly valued today in the West and to Westerners seems pathetic, spineless, and likely to pander to tyranny. Perhaps it has always seemed so. Nevertheless it is the virtue Christ showed as he went to the cross and the virtue, therefore, by which the world was redeemed. In learning to be meek we imitate Christ. Beside that example, it is difficult for any Christian to spurn the meek. To desire it, though, is itself a gift of grace, for it runs absolutely counter to the assertiveness and independence in which western society nurtures its children.

'Blessed are those who hunger and thirst for righteousness.' Not unnaturally, in recent decades as we have become more and more aware of the injustice of life on earth and the offence this must be to God, we have identified this beatitude with the search and the longing for justice and peace. While there can be no question that the righteousness of God desires justice on earth, righteousness is God's and when we hunger and thirst for righteousness we hunger for God; we long for him to be truly acknowledged as God; we long for the day when his glory will no longer be insulted by the arrogance of man. That is what the spiritual father does as he embarks on his monastic and priestly life. He is setting aside all things but the righteousness of God. He seeks to place God absolutely first in his life and to call others to do the same. As he finds himself called to direct other people's lives in Christ, he will find that this involves setting them on a way to God, helping them to see when they are being lured aside by worldly standards which insult the glory of God. He will teach them to hunger and thirst after the righteousness of God so that they will be scandalised and offended when they find God impugned in the world.

'Blessed are the merciful.' We have seen how the best of the spiritual fathers, those to whom our Romanian Christians turned for advice and absolution from their sins, were above all merciful. They may have been demanding in what they asked. They set high standards and allowed few compromises, but they did not punish, they did not rebuke, they did not mock or grow angry in the face of their penitents' sin. They themselves had known their need for mercy and had found it in God. God is the source and the reason for the mercy they show to others, such mercy as keeps people coming to them with sins which would be shocking or revolting if they were not covered by penitence and sorrow.

'Blessed are the pure in heart.' The late bishop of Oxford, Kenneth Kirk, begins his great masterpiece *The Vision of God*[4] with this Beatitude. The emigré Russian theologian Vladimir Lossky likewise, in a book of the same title, deals at length with the aim of early greek monastic life 'to see God'. Saint Gregory of Nyssa devotes his sixth homily on the Beatitudes to this beatitude and John Keble paraphrased it in one of his best known (if to this writer's ears somewhat insipidly Victorian) hymns, 'Blest are the pure in heart'. It is the promise that 'they will see God' which makes this beatitude central to the lives of those who have left everything else to seek God. Purity of heart is an ideal not commonly sought after in modern western Christianity because it is largely misunderstood. Ordinarily it is seen in sexual terms or in moral terms, but while no one can deny that physical activities have their part in the dirtying of the heart, the main emphasis of the Beatitude is really on the single-minded intention to serve God and no one or nothing else. It is purity of heart that Fr Cleopa is teaching his disciples when he urges them constantly to 'keep watch' over their minds and ensure that any thought, any suggestion of evil, any temptation, no matter how small, that

4. London: Longmans, 1931.

enters there is immediately spotted and expelled. Saint Benedict gives exactly the same advice that we have heard from Orthodox spiritual fathers: 'As soon as wrongful thoughts come into your heart, dash them against Christ and disclose them to your spiritual father'.[5] Purity of heart is one of the main goals of the monastic spiritual life.

'Blessed are the peace-makers.' Peace begins in the heart; or more profoundly it begins in the realm where 'Michael and his angels fought against the dragon and his angels'.[6] Humankind is perceived by christian theology as being in fundamental conflict with God, and therefore, because conflict divides, with each other. Even within most men and women conflict exists and sometimes, as modern psychology has shown, the internal conflicts rage to a disabling and destructive degree. Reconciling this conflict is one of the works of the spiritual father. On one level in his prayer he will be meeting demons in constant combat, defeating them on their own ground and so preserving the Christian people from attack. He will be a man whose own inner conflict has been resolved and who dwells, literally, in the peace of God, so that those who come to him experience the peace that he has won. Then through his advice to them concerning their sins— which will almost always involve conflict or potential conflict with other people—he will be helping them to make peace. It is perhaps as a peacemaker in all these different theatres of war that the spiritual father's work is concentrated.

'Blessed are those who are persecuted for righteousness sake.' We have noted how many of the best known spiritual fathers in Romania were imprisoned or persecuted by the communists. This may be a facile connection, but it is one commonly made in Romania: the spiritual fathers shared the people's suffering in the dark times, not only under communism but on many other occasions, and were their greatest defence. The spiritual fathers stood up courageously

5. *The Rule of Saint Benedict* 4.50.
6. Rev 12:7.

for God because they were concerned for his righteousness. God alone has the right to rule on earth, they believe, and anyone who attempts to rule differently from God must be resisted. This understanding of righteousness is the foundation of a Christian understanding of justice.

'Blessed are you when men revile you and persecute you and utter all kinds of evil against you falsely on my account.' This reminds us again of the *Spiritual Exercises* of Saint Ignatius, where retreatants are invited to ask for 'insults and contempt',[7] or, much further back in time, of the many desert fathers who deliberately brought contempt, mockery, and even violence on themselves, and rejoiced to be so treated. This kind of desire can all too easily be pathological, but it need not be so. Quietly enduring unjust treatment is one of the classic ways in which humility and meekness are achieved. Jesus himself suffered unjustly on his way to the cross and in this showed that humility and meekness triumph over all kinds of power and evil. If most of us find quiet endurance distasteful and shrink from it, this may explain why most of us find humility an unattractive or impossible virtue.

'Rejoice and be glad.' The astonishing thing is that those who embrace the terrifying beatitudes in their fullness and live them out with generosity are not miserable, wretched, or gloomy people, but almost always filled with joy, with a lightness of heart and an openness of spirit that others find irresistible. The life of the Beatitudes carefully considered may seem to the modern mind—perhaps to the minds of most other societies, too—to be sheer madness or unrelieved gloom. Experience shows otherwise. Love, joy, and freedom are their fruit; and if that is true now in Romania, can it also be true for other christian people in the very different societies of the West?

To live according to the Beatitudes is, in one sense, the monastic vocation, and there is no question that this teaching

7. *The Spiritual Exercises*, 146, ed. Puhl. p. 62.

has been at the heart of most of the monastic or religious life lived, at least where it was rightly and honestly lived, throughout the centuries. It is also the Christian vocation. Monastic life really appears to have grown up when Christianity become popular and easy, after Emperor Constantine had made it legal. Thousands of men and women fled actually or metaphorically into the desert where they could live a challenging form of Christianity in literal obedience to the Beatitudes. In contemporary Eastern Christianity monks and lay persons are not divided into two quite different spiritualities, and the devout lay people show that they too can live the Beatitudes, if not in the same manner as the monks at least with a like generosity. This is not to idealise. The majority of Eastern Christians fall far short of the ideal, as do their sisters and brothers in the West. It may be that one of the roles of the spiritual fathers is to be the link through which the monastic life is democratised and made available to the whole people of God. In the West a different climate prevails. Western Christians speak of various 'spiritualities', setting up an apparent division among them. It was not always so. The spiritual teaching of *The Imitation of Christ,* so popular throughout the modern age, was intended not only for the Brothers of the Common Life, but for all manner of Christian people, by whom it was, in fact, taken up. (The flamboyant Etonian, Julian Grenfell, read it regularly from the age of thirteen.[8]) Likewise the teaching of Francis de Sales' *Introduction to the Devout and Holy Life* in the seventeenth century aimed to make a real and costly spiritual life accessible to lay Christians. Today even accepted spiritual teachers of the western church endorse the goals of self-fulfilment and autonomy and see obedience to anyone outside oneself as demeaning, if not actually unhealthy. Modern men and women relentlessly seek freedom, but

8. See Evelyn Waugh, *Ronald Knox* (London: Chapman and Hall, 1959) p. 69.

what they find is all too often only a spurious freedom, for it is the freedom of those who acknowledge no Other than themselves. It is the freedom which has led to the heroic despair and the tragic suicides of many of its exponents in the literary and philosophical world. And if Western Christianity is conscious of being in a constant decline, Christians must ask seriously whether this is wholly because of the unfriendly secular age and the comforting allurements of materialism, to which, in the cause of mission, it assimilates itself. Or is there a deeper failure to live the Gospel of Christ?

Living that Gospel is the central concern of the Romanian spiritual fathers as it was of the Church Fathers and of holy men and women through the ages.Viewed from a modern western perspective their living of the Gospel can seem exotic, strange or wondrous. Seen from within their own country, their style of life, it becomes clear, is simply deeply and passionately Christian. The Christian life expressed in the Beatitudes is the life they received from their own parents in homes and villages throughout Romania, and the life shared with them by their own spiritual fathers in the monasteries. It is a treasure which has been handed down, a vessel of clear water continually refreshed yet always containing the same life and quality that it had in the beginning. They are simply deeply and passionately Christian. Nowhere does one feel oneself so clearly to be receiving the same life of the Spirit which the first Christians knew in the first few centuries after Christ lived on earth. Yet the spiritual fathers are more than messengers, except perhaps in the sense that angels partake of the glory of the God whose message they bear. They become what they teach. Their own transformation into people whose lives manifest the living presence and fiery love of the God they worship is what makes them so attractive to the christian people they live among. And it is because these same people have been schooled in the same values, and desire the same end, a life subsumed in God that so many people recognise their attractiveness and are prepared to accept their teaching as a means to their common end. The end is Christ. We can only live the Beatitudes if we let Christ live in us. The astonishing claim of Christianity is that the person who is God yet became a man will make his life in each one of us and change us into the kind of being that he is, able not only to live the Beatitudes but to share in the life of God.

Synergy

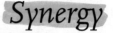

The following account of synergy is by a young Orthodox theo-logian, Călin Sămărghiţan:

The work of the Holy Spirit as a Person, inside us, ontologically claims the free working of our will to grow up into our life in Christ. That means we have to appropriate the work of salvation of our Lord Jesus Christ, through our will, in our doings. From its creation human nature is ontologically opened to the grace of God. Freedom [liberty] is the most characteristic note of the Spirit, 'Where the Spirit of the Lord is, there is freedom'.[1] In Jesus Christ we are released from slavery to sin. Through the grace of the Holy Spirit we are helped not to fall again into the yoke of slavery, but to reach the freedom of the glory of God, to become entirely available to serve and love. The Spirit of Christ is the Spirit of freedom, of the spiritual life. This Spirit is calling us to freedom and he is our strength to increase in it. (Rom 8:2)

As long as our relation with God is strong and healthy, grace is working in us and the person is working together with God. When sin interferes in our relation with God, this sin brings disorder, sickness and slavery, and spoils the natural order of cooperation between grace and freewill. Normally, the grace of God and human freewill work

2 Cor 3:17

together if the image of God is not altered in the human soul. Thus, there exists here a concordance and genuine relation between a person and God. This is *theomorphē*, the divine aspect of a human person, which the Greek fathers speak about.

A person's freewill is created so that it can receive freely the energy of divine grace. Sin spoils this ability of freewill to receive grace. In the original state [of Adam and Eve before corruption] sin does not exist to distort this order. The opposition between nature and grace, between grace and freewill, did not exist because all of them came from God. After corruption set in, when sin came into the world, this order became a problem. In Jesus Christ human nature is restored, the permeability to grace is recovered, real freedom is gained. Now human nature continuously grows up, helped by the grace of the Holy Spirit, to new life in Christ. Both of the graces – of the human's restored image of God, and of human freedom – combine themselves into the deep 'original ego', the authentic one.

God gives everything absolutely free. 'God is the beginning, the middle and the end of every goodness.'[2] We must appropriate everything in a personal free way. God does not force us to accept him. God cannot do anything in us, without us. We must give our consent to the beginning of grace working in us 'as workers together with him';[3] 'we are God's fellow-workers.[4] This is synergy. Grace is a spiritual and personal energy that must be accepted freely as love is.

Grace is necessary for human nature but is distinct from it. Grace comes to a person from outside, from God, as a gift, but it is not foreign to him. A person is saved by the grace of God. This grace confers on that person the image of Christ. The divine energies imbue themselves in our

2. Mark the Austere, *About the Spiritual Life;* in the Romanian *Philokalia* (Sibiu, 1946) 1:232.
3. 2 Cor 6:1.
4. 1 Cor 3:9.

will, causing first the spiritual will. Then, the spiritual will works together with the person helping it to grow up in the life of Christ. This opening to grace and gradual penetration by grace are the normal state of human nature. A dialectical relation exists between nature and grace, between grace and freedom. They differ from each other and form an organic unity. They are tightly joined into the person's deified life.

What is God's place in this synergy? God gives and shares with everyone his blessings. He sanctifies our wishes and renews our human nature. Every person receives God's blessing, without any merit. God makes all good things for us without our will; he almost forces us in his great love.[5]

And which part is ours? It is not in our power either to be born, or to resurrect ourselves after we have died. But the choice of good, the forgiveness of a neighbour's trespasses, good habits, the soul's purity, to keep looking to God—these are in the strength of the human will. All of these will bring absolute happiness to a person. Either the fulfilment or the avoidance of them depends on our strength. No one can force them on us.

The grace of God is conferred by the Holy Sacraments. Both the work of the sacraments and the work of human effort have the same purpose: to make our will the same as God's will, who is really good. After all the blessings he gives us, the Lord demands of us only to wish good things and to think good thoughts. The synergy between the grace of God and human freewill is, in human terms, a matter of participation. Our being is, continuously, a partner of divinity. In this life, our participation in the Godhead moves from one step to another, in a real progress of spiritual life to deification. In this spiritual progress, the grace of God helps the natural powers of the human being to develop themselves beyond the limits of its natural powers, beyond

5. Nicolas Cabasila, *On Life in Christ* (Sibiu, 1946) p. 46; *Nicholas Cabasilas: The Life in Christ*, translated by Carmino J. deCatanzaro (Crestwood: Saint Vladimir's Seminary Press, 1974).

the edges of human nature. There a person is nourished with 'immortal food,'[6] that means with God himself, when the human person becomes God.

Participation in God is conditioned by two aspects of human life: the intellectual aspect (thought without error about the real Being) and the moral aspect (rejection of any passion from the soul—*apatheia*). 'Man is united to God in two ways: one is not to have erroneous ideas about reality such as false notions about God as held by pagans and heretics. Secondly one must have a pure mind which banishes every passion from the soul. . .'[7] for a person truly establishes certitude within himself, that is faith, when he looks steadily at the truth and lives by it after having been cleansed from every defilement of evil.'[8] God created man as a human being who can taste his promised blessings, as a person who can freely answer him. The foretaste is participation, it is working together, but it is longing too, for a kingdom increasingly thoroughgoing.

6. Maximus the Confessor, Century 2.86; *Capitum Theologiae et Oeconomiae* (PG 90:1168A).
7. Gregory of Nyssa, *In Canticum Canticorum*, 13; PG 44:1041D; McCambley, 231.
8. Gregory of Nyssa, *In Canticum Canticorum*, 13; PG 44:1044A; McCambley, 231.

The books cited below in Romanian have not been translated
into English. All quotations from them appearing in this book
are my own translation.

Allen J. J. The Inner Way. Grand Rapids, Michigan: Wm. B.
Eerdmans. 1994.

Anania, V. Cerurile Oltului. Diocese of Râmnicu Vâlcea.
1990.

Andersen, J. Religion, State and Politics in the Soviet Union
and Successor States. Cambridge: Cambridge University
Press. 1994.

Bălan, I. Convorbiri Duhovnicești 1. Diocese of Roman,
Romania.1993.

――――. (ed). Părintele Paisie Duhovnicul. Iași Trinitas.
1993.

――――. Viața Părintelui Cleopa. Iași. Trinitas. 1999.

Băncilă , V. Duhul Sărbătorii. Bucharest. Editura Anastasia.
1996.

Barrois, Georges (trans. and ed.). The Fathers Speak.
Crestwood, New York. St Vladimir's Seminary Press.
1986.

Bartos, E. Deification in Eastern Orthodox Thought. An
Evaluation of the Theology of Dumitru Stăniloae. Carlisle.
Paternoster Press, 1999.

Basil of Caesarea. Saint Basil. Ascetical Works. Translated
by M. Monica.Wagner. Washington, D.C. The Catholic
University of America Press. 1962.

Bejan, D. Oranki-Amintiri din Captivitate. Bucharest. Editura
Tehnica. 1995.

Benedict of Nursia. RB1980. The Rule of St Benedict.
Collegeville. Liturgical Press. 1980.

Benedicta Ward SLG (translator). *The Sayings of the Desert Fathers*. Mowbray. London. Cistercian Publications. Kalamazoo. 1975.

Brown, Peter. *The Rise of Western Christendom*. Oxford. Blackwell. 1996.

Bryer, Anthony and Cunningham, Mary. (edd.). *Mount Athos & Byzantine Monasticism* Aldershot. Ashgate. 1996.

Buga, Ion. *Pastorala*. Bucharest. Internaţional Scorpion. 1992.

Cabasilas, Nicholas. *A Commentary on the Divine Liturgy* Translated by J.M. Hussey and P.A. McNulty London. SPCK. 1960

———. *The Life in Christ*. Translated by C.J. DeCatanzaro. Crestwood, New York. Saint Vladimir's Seminary Press. 1974.

Chadwick, Owen. *The Christian Church in the Cold War*. Harmondsworth. Penguin. 1992

Chitty, D. J. *The Desert a City*. Crestwood, New York. St Vladimir's Seminary Press. 1995.

Clement of Alexandria. *Quis dives salvetur*. J.-P. Migne, Patrologia Latina, 9. Translated by W. Wilson in The Ante-Nicene Fathers series, Volume 2: 591ff. Edinburgh. T & T Clark – Grand Rapids. Eerdmans. 1994. The Greek text and an English translation by G. W. Butterworth are also available in the Loeb Classical Library. Clément, Olivier. *The Roots of Christian Mysticism*. London. New City Press. 1993.

Constantinu. F. *O Historie Sinceră a Poporului Român*. Bucureşti. Univers Enciclopedic. 1998.

Cleopa, Ilie. *Despre Vise şi Vedenii*. Romania. Anastasia.1993.

———. *Valoarea Sufletului*. Bacău. Bunavestire. 1994.

———. *Ne Vorbeşte Părintele Cleopa*. 1 & 2. Diocese of Roman, Romania. 1995.

———. *Ne Vorbeşte Părintele Cleopa*. 5. Diocese of Roman, Romania. 1997.

Cioran, Emil. *Ispita de a Exista*. Bucharest. Humanitas. 1992.

Coman, Ioan G. *Probleme de Filosofie și Literatură Patristică.* Bucharest. Editura Institului Biblic. 1995.

Cross F. L. and E. A. Livingstone, edd. *The Oxford Dictionary of the Christian Church.* Oxford. Oxford University Press. 1997.

Dostoevsky F. *The Brothers Karamazov,* Translated by Richard Pevear and Larissa Volokhonsky. London. Everyman. 1992.

Dunlop, J.B. *Staretz Amvrosy.* London. Mowbrays. 1972.

Ellis, J. *The Russian Orthodox Church: Triumphalism and Defensiveness.* London. Macmillan. 1996.

Evagrius Ponticus. *The Praktikos and Chapters on Prayer.* Translated by John Eudes Bamberger. Kalamazoo. Cistercian Publications. 1981.

Evdokimov P. *The Sacrament of Love.* Translated by Anthony P.Gythiel. Crestwood, New York. Saint Vladimir's Seminary Press. 1986.

Florovsky G. *Bible, Church and Tradition.* Belmont, Massachusetts. Nordland Publishing. 1972.

Galeriu, Father. *Jertfă și Răscumpărare.* Romania. Harisma. 1991.

Gallagher, T. *Romania after Ceaușescu.* Edinburgh. Edinburgh University Press. 1995.

Giakalis, A. *Images of the Divine.* Leiden. Brill.1994.

Gray, P.T.R. *The Defence of Chalcedon in the East.* Leiden. Brill. 1979.

Gregory of Nyssa. *Commentary on the Song of Songs.* Translated by Casimir McCambley ocso. Brookline, Massachusetts. Hellenic College Press. 1987.

Gothóni, René. *Paradise Within Reach. Monasticism and Pilgrimage on Mount Athos.* Helsinki. Helsinki University Press. 1993.

Hackel S., ed. *The Byzantine Saint.* Studies Supplementary to *Sobornost,* 5. London. Sobornost. 1981.

Hall, C. M. ' "Jesus in my Country". The Theology of Nichifor Crainic.' Unpublished thesis, King's College, London. 1986.

Hausherr, Irénée. *Penthos. The Doctrine of Compunction in the Christian East.* Translated by Anselm Hufstader. Kalamazoo. Cistercian Publications. 1982.

————. *Spiritual Direction in the Early Christian East.* Translated by Anthony Gythiel. Kalamazoo. Cistercian Publications. 1990.

Hitchins, K. *Rumania 1866 - 1947.* Oxford. Oxford University Press. 1994.

Hussey, J. M. *The Orthodox Church in the Byzantine Empire.* Oxford. Clarendon Press. 1986.

Ignatius of Loyola. *The Spiritual Exercises.* Translated by Louis J. Puhl. Chicago. Loyola University Press. 1951.

Isaac of Nineveh. *On Ascetical Life.* Translated by Mary Hansbury. Crestwood, New York. St Vladimir's Seminary Press. 1989.

Joanță, S. *Romania. Its Hesychast Tradition and Culture.* Wildwood, California. Saint Xenia Skete. 1992.

John Paul II. *Orientale Lumen.* Rome. 1995.

John Cassian. *The Conferences.* Translated by Colm Luibheid. Classics of Western Spirituality. Mahweh, New Jersey. Paulist Press. 1985.

John Climacus. *The Ladder of Divine Ascent.* Translated by Archimandrite Lazarus Moore.London. Faber and Faber. 1959.

John of Damascus. *On The Divine Images.* Translated by David Anderson. Crestwood, New York. Saint Vladimir's Seminary Press. 1980.

John of Damascus. Writings. Translated by Frederick H. Chase. Fathers of the Church series, Volume 37. Washington D.C.: The Catholic University of America Press, 1958, rpt. 1981.

Kaariainen, K. *Religion in Russia after the Collapse of Communism.* New York. Edwin Mellen Press. 1998.

Kadloubovsky, E. and G. E. H. Palmer. *Early Fathers from the Philokalia.* London. Faber and Faber. 1954.

Kavelin, L. *Elder Macarius of Optina.* Platina, California. Saint Herman of Alaska Brotherhood. 1995.

Kelly, J. N. D. *Goldenmouth. The Story of John Chrysostom.* London. Duckworth.1996.

Kontzevitch, I. M. *The Acquisition of the Holy Spirit.* Volume 1. Platina, California. Saint Herman of Alaska Brotherhood. 1996.

Krivocheine, Basil. *In the Light of Christ. Saint Symeon the New Theologian.* Translated by Anthony P. Gythiel. Crestwood, New York. Saint Vladimir's Seminary Press. 1986.

Lewis D. C. *After Atheism. Religion and Ethnicity in Russia and Central Asia.* London Routledge Curzon. 2000.

Linnér S. *Starets Zosima in The Brothers Karamazov.* Stockholm. Hylea Prints. 1981.

Livingstone, E., ed. *Studia Patristica XXII and XXIII.* Leuven. Peeters Press. 1989.

Lossky, Vladimir. *The Mystical Theology of the Eastern Church.* London. James Clarke. 1957.

———. *The Vision of God.* London. Faith Press. 1963.

———. *In the Image and Likeness of God.* London. Mowbrays. 1975

Louth, Andrew. *Maximus the Confessor.* London. Routledge. 1996.

McGuckin, Paul [John]. *Symeon the New Theologian. Practical and Theological Chapters.* Kalamazoo. Cistercian Publications. 1982.

Meredith, Anthony. *The Cappadocians.* London. Continuum. 1995.

———. *Gregory of Nyssa.* London-New York. Routledge. 1999

Meyendorff, John. *A Study of Gregory of Palamas.* London. Faith Press. 1964.

———. *Gregory of Palamas and the Orthodox Tradition.* Crestwood, New York. Saint Vladimir's Seminary Press. 1974.

———. *Christ in Eastern Christian Thought.* Crestwood, New York. Saint Vladimir's Seminary Press. 1975.

Miller, Charles *The Gift of the World. An Introduction to*

the Theology of Dumitru Stăniloae. Edinburgh. T. & T. Clark. 2000.

Mother Mary and Kallistos Ware, translators. *The Lenten Triodion*. London. Faber and Faber. 1978.

Nellas, P. *Deification in Christ*. Crestwood, New York. Saint Vladimir's Seminary Press. 1987.

Nichols, A. *Light from the East*. London. Sheed and Ward. 1995.

Nicodim Aghioritul. *Carte Foarte Folositoare de Suflet*. Introduction by Nicolae Corneanu. Timişoara. Mitropoliae Banatalui. 1986.

Nielson, N. *Revolutions in Eastern Europe*. Maryknoll, New York. Orbis. 1991.

Origen, *Contra Celsum* 4.63. Translated by Henry Chadwick. Cambridge UK. Cambridge University Press. 1953.

Paladie. *Istoria Lausică*. Translation and introduction by Dumitru Stăniloae. Bucharest. Institutlui Biblic. 1993. [See Palladius, below]

Palamas, Gregory. *The Triads*. Translated Nicholas Gendle. Classics of Western Spirituality. Mahweh, New Jersey. Paulist Press. 1983.

Păcurariu. M. *Istoria Bisericii Ortodoxe Române*. Bucharest. Biblical and Mission Institute. 1994.

Palladius. *The Lausiac History*. [See Paladie, above]. Translated by Robert T. Meyer. New York. Newman Press. 1965. Translated W. K. Lowther Clarke. London: S.P.C.K. – New York: Macmillan. 1918.

Papacioc, Arsenie. *Ne Vorbeşte Părintele Arsenie, 2*. Episcopiei Romanuliu. 1997.

Părăian, Teofil. *Gânduri Bune Pentru Gânduri Bune*. Mitropoliei Banatului. 1997.

———. *Ne Vorbeşte Părintele Teofil, 1*. Episcopiei Romanului. 1997.

The Philokalia. The Complete Text. Translated by G.E.H. Palmer, Philip Sherrard, Kallistos Ware. London-Boston. Faber & Faber. Volume 1. 1979. Volume 2. 1981.

Volume 3. 1984. Volume 4. 1995.

Philippou, A.J., ed. *The Orthodox Ethos*. Oxford. Holywell Press. 1964.

———. *Orthodoxy and Freedom*. Oxford. Studion Publications. 1973.

Plămadeală, A. *Tradiţie şi Libertate în Spiritualitatea Ortodoxă*. Sibiu. 1995.

———, ed. *Romanian Orthodox Church*. Bucharest. Church Publishing House. 1987.

Plato. *The Republic*. Translated by A.D.Lindsay. London. Everyman.1906, 1948.

Puhl Louis J. See Ignatius of Loyola.

Rousseau, Philip. *Basil of Caesarea*. Berkeley. University of California Press. 1994.

Schmemann, Alexander. *Of Water and the Spirit*. London. S.P.C.K. 1976.

———. *Church, World and Mission*. Crestwood, New York. Saint Vladimir's Seminary Press. 1979.

Shalin D.N. *Russian Culture at the Crossroads*. Oxford. Westview Press. 1996.

Smolitsch I. *Moines de la Sainte-Russe*. Paris. Maison Mame. 1967.

Saint Serafim de Sarov. *Scopul Vieţii Creştine*. Iaşi. Editura Pelerinul. 1997.

Seton-Watson, R.W. *A History of the Roumanians*. Cambridge: Cambridge University Press. 1934.

Stăniloae, Dumitru. *Theology and the Church*. Crestwood, New York. Saint Vladimir's Seminary Press. 1980.

———, ed. and trans. *Filokalia*. Bucharest. 1980.

———. *The Experience of God*. Brookline, Massachusetts. Holy Cross Orthodox Press. 1994.

———. *Rugăciunea Lui Iisus şi Experienţa Duhului Sfânt*. Sibiu. Deisis. 1995.

———. *Orthodox Spirituality. A Practical Guide for the Faithful and a Definitive Manual for the Scholar*. Translated by Jerome Newville and Otilia Kloos. South Canaan. Saint Tikhon's Seminary Press. 2002.

————. *The Victory of the Cross*. Oxford. Fairacres Press. 1970.

————. *Prayer and Holiness*. Oxford. Fairacres Press. 1982.

————. *Eternity and Time*. Oxford. Fairacres Press. 2001.

Steinhardt, N. *Jurnalul Fericirii*. Cluj-Napoca. Editura Dacia. 1991.

————. *Dăruind Vei Dobândi*. Baia Mare. Diocese of Maramureş. 1992.

Sutherland S. *Atheism and the Rejection of God*. Oxford. Blackwell. 1977.

Theodore the Studite. *On the Holy Icons*. Trans. Catharine P. Roth. Crestwood, New York. Saint Vladimir's Seminary Press. 1981.

Touraille J. *Le Christ dans le Philocalie*. Paris. Desclée. 1995.

Travis, J. *In Defense of the Faith*. Brookline, Massachusetts. Hellenic College Press. 1984.

Turner, H. J. M. *Saint Symeon the New Theologian and Spiritual Fatherhood*. Leiden. Brill. 1990.

Urzica M. *Biserica şi Viermii Cei Neadormiţi* . Anastasia. Eseu Teologic, 1998.

Velichkovsky, Paisie. *Cuvinte Despre Ascultare*. Bucharest. Anastasia. 1997.

Vintilescu, P. *Spovedania şi Duhovnicia*. Iulia. Diocese of Alba. 1995.

Ware, Kallistos. *The Orthodox Church*. Harmondsworth. Penguin. 1963.

————, ed. *The Art of Prayer*. London. Faber and Faber. 1966.

————. *The Power of the Name*. Oxford. Fairacres Press. 1986.

Wimbush Vincent L. and Richard Valantasis, edd. *Asceticism*. New York. Oxford University Press. 1995.

Zamfirescu, D. *Paisinismul*. Bucharest. Vânturilor. 1996.

Zander, Valentina. *St Seraphim of Sarov*. London. SPCK. 1975. Crestwood, New York: Saint Vladimir's Serminary Press. 1985.

Zernov, Nicholas. *Eastern Christendom*. London. Weidenfeld and Nicholson. 1961.

BOOKLETS

Preot Gheorghe Calciu Dumitreasa. *Cele Şapte Cuvinte Către Tineri*. [Seven Words to the Young. Sermons given in March/April 1978]. n.d. n.p. *Moarte si Înviere la Mânăstirea 'Brâncoveanu' Sâmbăta de Sus*. Sibiu. 1993. *Mirfield Gazette*. Christmas 1936. Christmas 1937. *Ortodoxia. Revista Patriarhiei Romîne*. Anul X, Nr. 2. April-Junie 1958.
Mother Maria. *The Realism of the Orthodox Faith*. Library of Orthodox Thinking. N.p. n.d.
Monastères de Roumanie. Renaissance de Fleury, 162.Abbaye de Fleury. Juin 1992.
Romania: Special Issue. Frontier No.3. Oxford. Keston Institute. 1998.

ARTICLES

'Rânduiala Sfântei Mărturisiri la Români', *Candela* 43. 1932.
Branişte, E. 'Sfaturi şi Îndrumare Pentru Duhovnici.' *Mitropolia Olteniei*, 8. 1956. Pp. 10-12.
Bria, I. 'The Creative Vision of D. Stăniloae'. *Ecumenical Review*, 33:1. January 1981. Pp. 53-59.
Colotelo, M. 'Importanţa Tainei Mărturisirii în Pastoraţie'. *Telegraful Român*. 33-36. 1996
Cândea, V. 'L'Athos et les Roumains'. In Bryer & Cunningham, *Mount Athos and Byzantine Monasticism* [above].
Epstein M. 'Minimal Religion' (1982) in Epstein M., A. Genis and S. Vladiv-Glover. *Russian Post-Modernism*. N.p. 1999.

Heppell, Muriel. 'The Role of the Spiritual Father in Orthodox Monasticism.' in Judith Loades, ed. *Monastic Studies* II. Bangor, Wales. Headstart History. 1991.

Forster C. 'L'Orthodoxie Aujourd'hui, dans les pays de l'Est et chez nous.' Lecture at Nancy. 29 April 1999.

Izvoranu, S. 'Sfături şi Orânduiri Pentru Duhovnici.' *Glasul Bisericii*, 1959,1-2.

Marius, T. 'Mişcarea Isihasta şi Legaturile cu Românii.' *Revista Teologica.* January-March 1995.

Miron, V. 'Importanţa Tainei Sfântei Spovedanii in Activitatea Pastoral-Misionara a Preotului Ortodox'. *Ortodoxia 17:3-4* (July 1995) 29-54.

Myroslav, T. 'Orthodox Ecclesiology and Cultural Pluralism' in *Sobornost* 19:1. 1997. Pp 56-65.

O'Keefe, J. 'Sin, *Apatheia* and Freedom of the Will in Gregory of Nyssa'. *Studia Patristica, 22.* 1989. Pp.52-59.

Plămădeală, A. ' Liberty and Tradition in Orthodox Monasticism', in *The Tradition of Life. Romanian essays in Spirituality and Theology,* Supplement to Sobornost, No.2. Ed. A. M. Allchin. 1971. Pp. 33-47.

Popescu, A. 'Petre Tuţea (1902-1991): The Urban Hermit of Romanian Spirituality.' in *Religion, State and Society,* 23-24. Oxford. Keston Institute. 1995. Pp. 319-341.

Scrima A. 'L'Avènement Philocalique dans l'Orthodoxie Roumaine'. *Istina 3* 1958. Pp. 295-328.

Sutton, J. 'The Way We Are: The Russian Soul' Unpublished lecture. Cambridge [UK]. 2000.

Stăniloae D. *Sobornost*, Series 5, No. 9 (1969):
'Some Characteristics of Orthodoxy'. Pp 627-629.
'Tradition and the Development of Doctrine'. Pp. 652-662.
'The World as Gift and Sacrament of God's Love'. Pp 662-673.
——. 'The Tradition of Life'. Romanian essays in A. M. Allchin, ed. *Spirituality and Theology* Supplement to *Sobornost* No.2 (1971):
'St Callinic of Cernica'. Pp 17-32.

'Christian Responsibility in the World'. Pp. 53-73.
Stoenescu, N. 'Viaţa Creştină dupa Sfântul Isaac Sirul.' *Studie Teologice* 37. November-December 1985. Pp. 673-690.
Ware, Kallistos. 'The Monk and the Married Christian.' *Eastern Churches. Review,* 6:I. Spring 1974. Pp. 72-83.
———. 'Salvation and Theosis in Orthodox Theology', in *Luther et la Réforme Allemande dans une perspective œcuménique.* Cambésy: Éditions du Centre Orthodoxe du Patiarchat Œcuménique, 1983. Pp. 167-184.
———. 'The Understanding of Salvation in the Orthodox Tradition.' In R. Lannoy, ed. *For Us and for our Salvation.* Utrecht-Leiden. 1994. Pp. 107-131.

Cenobitic   monastic life lived in community,
                     with common meals and
                     common worship.

Church Fathers   those theologians and writers of
                     the early centuries of Christianity
                     who wrote in Latin, Greek, and
                     Syriac and who are now recog-
                     nised as providing the theological
                     and spiritual bases for the
                     Christian Church.

Duhovnic   a spiritual father.

Fast seasons   Orthodox Christianity keeps four
                     seasons of fasting: seven weeks
                     before Easter; two weeks before the
                     feast of Saint Peter and Saint Paul
                     (29 June); two weeks before the
                     Dormition of Mary (15 August); and
                     five weeks before Christmas.

Fathers   See Church Fathers.

Iconostasis   The screen, which is covered with
                     icons, placed between the altar and
                     the congregation in an Orthodox
                     church.

Idiorrhythmic — A monastic life style which, unlike cenobitic life, allows a monk or nun to follow his or her own pattern of worship, prayer, fasting, and daily discipline.

Lambeth Conference — A gathering of all bishops of the Anglican Communion which takes place every ten years.

Night office — A service of psalms and readings which has long been associated with monastic life (sometimes called Vigils or Matins), but in fact has a place in Orthodox parish worship as well.

Office — One of the services of psalms and readings which priests and monks or nuns say at various time during the day.

Pravila — The individual rule of devotion which each monk has for himself.

Protosinghel — A title given to senior monk-priests in Romania.

Securitate — The security police under communism.

Skete	A small monastery usually of two or three monks or nuns living a life more given to prayer and contemplation than is possible in a large monastery.
Starets	In Romania the *starets* is simply the abbot of a monastery, whereas in Russia he is a recognised spiritual father.
Staretsa	An abbess.
Synergia, synergy	From the Greek *syn* + *ergon* : 'work with'. The doctrine that we need to work with God in achieving sanctification.
Typikon	The pattern of liturgical life for a monastery.
Utrenie	The office of morning prayer celebrated both in monasteries and in parish churches.
Vecernie	Evening prayer.
Voivode	Feudal barons and landowners who exercised considerable power throughout the Romanian territories until at least the eighteenth century.